The Insider Edge

The Insider Edge

How to Follow the Insiders for
Windfall Profits

GUY COHEN

WILEY

John Wiley & Sons, Inc.

Published by John Wiley & Sons, Inc., Hoboken, New Jersey.
Published simultaneously in Canada.

For general information on our other products and services or for technical support, please contact our Customer Care Department within the United States at (800) 762–2974, outside the United States at (317) 572–3993 or fax (317) 572–4002.

Wiley also publishes its books in a variety of electronic formats. Some content that appears in print may not be available in electronic books. For more information about Wiley products, visit our web site at www.wiley.com.

Library of Congress Cataloging-in-Publication Data:
Cohen, Guy.
  The insider edge : how to follow the insiders for windfall profits / Guy Cohen. – 1st ed.
    p. cm. – (Wiley trading ; 582)
  Includes index.
    ISBN 978-1-118-24528-6 (hardcover); ISBN 978-1-118-28484-1 (ebk);
ISBN 978-1-118-28434-6 (ebk); ISBN 978-1-118-28255-7 (ebk)
  1. Stocks.   2. Profit.   I. Title.
  HG4661.C595   2012
  332.63'22–dc23
                                                                    2012015372

Printed in the United States of America

10 9 8 7 6 5 4 3 2 1

Contents

Preface   vii

Acknowledgments   xiii

Introduction   1

March 8, 2008   3
March 2008   5
March 2009   6
April 26, 2010   7
March 2011   8
Summer 2011   9
September 7, 2011   10
"Informed Trading" and the OVI   11
The Insider's Rationale   12
Trading Breakouts   13

CHAPTER 1   The Most Popular Chart Patterns: Why Chart Patterns Are So Important   15

Price Bars   16
Support and Resistance   20
Trends   30
Flag Patterns and Consolidations   33
Head and Shoulders   43
Indicators   48
Learning Points   51

**CHAPTER 2 The OVI: Guide to the Insiders:
              Introduction to the OVI   53**

What Is the OVI?   59
When to Use the OVI and When Not to Use It   64
The OVI with Stocks   78
Learning Points   105

**CHAPTER 3 Flags and Channel Breakouts in
              Detail: Focusing on the Patterns
              That Work Best with the OVI   109**

Bull Flags   110
Bear Flags   118
Flags with a Strong OVI Signal   127
Channel Breakouts   128
Setting the First Profit Target   134
Learning Points   146

**CHAPTER 4 The Trading Plan: The Complete
              Trading Plan   151**

Order Types   153
The Trading Plan   155
Learning Points   214

CHAPTER 5 Putting It All Together   217

Summary of the OVI Trading Method   219
A Few More Examples   221
Action Steps   226
Summary of Tools for You to Use   239
Take the Next Step Now!   240

About the Author   241

Index   243

Preface

Between January 1, 2008 and February 28, 2008, Bear Stearns (BSC) shares traded in a range between $68.18 and $93.09.

On March 3, 2008, Bear Stearns closed at $77.32 (see Figure P.1). At around this time most commentators (famously including those on CNBC) were suggesting that BSC could be a takeover target and, as such, were bullish on the stock's prospects.

At the same time, an unknown new indicator plummeted to its lowest possible reading for BSC. In itself that wasn't the key factor. It's the fact that for the next two weeks the indicator remained at its most negative reading for all but two days.

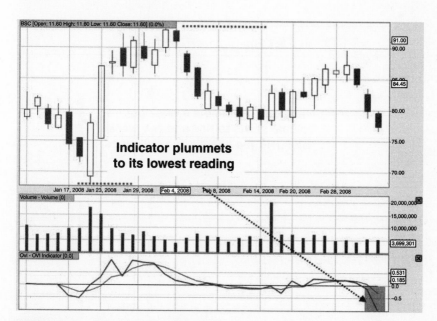

FIGURE P.1   BSC March 3, 2008 Chart
Source: OVI Charts. Courtesy of FlagTrader.com. Go to www.theinsideredge.com for more information.

Exactly two weeks after the unknown indicator plummeted, BSC went into free-fall, reaching a low of $2.84. Bear Stearns was indeed taken over, but at $10 per share, a far cry from the heady heights of $77.32 (see Figure P.2).

This was one of the most dramatic declines in the history of the stock market, and yet not one commentator saw it coming.

And yet, there were people who DID see it coming—and they made a fortune from it, too.

How do we know this? Well, the "unknown indicator" measures options transactions for individual stocks. And in the case of BSC, the indicator went crazy to the downside *two weeks before* BSC collapsed!

Someone, somewhere knew something ...

In this book you're going to learn how to spot another Bear Stearns, or, more positively, how to spot a meteoric rise in a stock before it happens. The unknown indicator is now unveiled.

Whatever your trading experience or proficiency may be, this book is for you, provided you want to make money in the markets.

That's a pretty bold statement, but the reason this book is for you, regardless of your prior experience, is because the method within is effective, simple, and easy to apply.

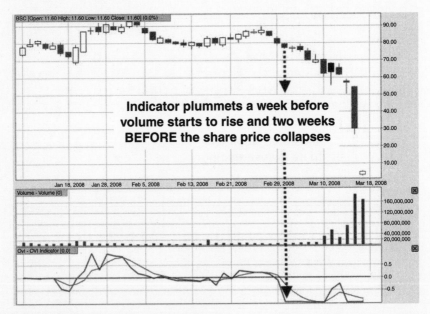

FIGURE P.2   BSC March 17, 2008 Chart
Source: OVI Charts. Courtesy of FlagTrader.com. Go to www.theinsideredge.com for more information.

This is music to the ears of anyone who just wants to make money from the markets. It doesn't matter what your proficiency is; we all want a time-efficient way to make money from the markets, and this book delivers exactly that.

I should also emphasize that this is *not* a book on options! We will refer to options because part of our method relies on following what the savvy options traders are doing, but this is specifically not an options book.

The way we do this is by following a simple indicator that is derived from options transaction data. See the diagram in Figure P.3. If you can identify where this line is positive (above the horizontal line) or negative (below the horizontal line), then you qualify. It's that simple!

The basic premise of this book is as follows:

Chart Pattern + Indicator + Trading Plan = Success

What you'll discover during the book is *what* chart pattern, *what* indicator, and *how to implement* the trading plan.

The uniqueness of this book resides with the special indicator (the OVI), which is derived from options transactions data. We're basically going to follow what the savviest traders in the market are doing. We stick to a simple chart pattern to improve our odds further, and we implement a safe trading plan that enables us to make windfall profits if a trend develops.

So, what exactly is the OVI?

Well, it's an indicator that oscillates between -1 and $+1$. When it's positive (and there's a corresponding chart pattern) then we focus on buying opportunities. When it's negative (and there's a corresponding chart pattern) we focus on shorting opportunities.

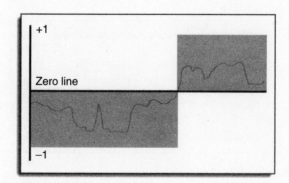

FIGURE P.3   OVI Simple Line

The OVI is derived from options transaction data, but again, this is *not* a book about options! I think that's clear now, isn't it?! The premise is that the savviest traders will congregate in the options markets, and the OVI is effectively spying on them.

Later on we'll go into the reasons why the smart money trades options, but for now it's worth considering that the smart money likes to accumulate positions quickly and quietly. Options are a vehicle for doing just this, and the OVI's job is to help us observe what's happening.

Imagine having a bird's-eye view of what the smart money is doing . . . well that's just part of the story.

As you'll read many times in this book, we only ever use the OVI in conjunction with a *tradeable chart pattern*, and we observe the OVI only in the context of a price chart.

In the first example (shown in Figure P.4) you can see how the indicator was positive before Apple Inc. (AAPL) broke out to the upside twice in a month. This led to a profit of over 50 points and 30 points, respectively.

In the next example (shown in Figure P.5), you can see how the OVI was negative preceding BAC's several breakouts to the downside. Within four months of the first obvious breakout, the stock had halved in price.

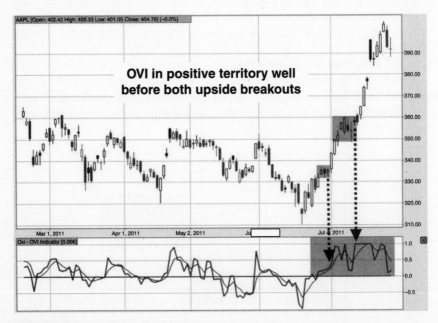

FIGURE P.4   AAPL Breakouts Chart
Source: OVI Charts. Courtesy of FlagTrader.com. Go to www.theinsideredge.com for more information.

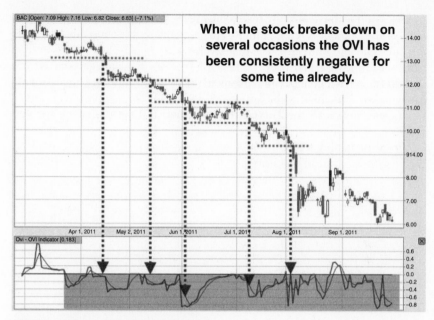

FIGURE P.5 BAC Breakouts Chart
Source: OVI Charts. Courtesy of FlagTrader.com. Go to www.theinsideredge.com for more information.

So now that you've had a teaser of what's to come, here's a summary of what you'll learn in this book.

In **Chapter 1** we're going to review the most popular chart patterns. Not too many, just the most important and relevant ones for our purposes. This will serve as a useful refresher for advanced traders and a good introduction for novices. (In Chapter 3 we'll focus exclusively on a couple of patterns that will become your obsession in the years to come.)

Chapter 2 is all about the OVI and how we can use our guided discretion to legitimately follow the insiders. We combine this indicator with our favored chart pattern in order to make high-probability trades. I'll also explain what the OVI is, why it works, and also why it should be used in combination with our favored chart patterns.

In **Chapter 3** we're going focus in detail on my favorite chart patterns. This sets the scene for creating our trading plans in **Chapter 4**. In **Chapter 5** we wrap up and summarize everything for you to make your practical next steps.

The greatest traders make use of surprisingly simple processes. I accept that the OVI is derived from specialized and complex algorithms, but as you'll discover, to your delight, interpreting it is wonderfully simple.

As you may have already realized by now, we're going straight into the meat of the subject. I hope you like this approach; it means this is a book you can read and understand in quick time.

Plus I'm giving you tools to use for free so you can get started immediately. As such, I believe this will be one of the best investments you'll make.

Please now read the **Introduction,** where I'll set the scene for you in full.

Good luck, and enjoy!

Acknowledgments

First, I want to say a big thank you to my colleagues at the OVI Traders Club and FlagTrader.

And to my inquisitive students: Your challenging questions help me create solutions more than you could imagine. Without you, there would be no OVI, and without the OVI this book could never have been conceived.

The Insider Edge

Introduction

I n the preface I made a bold statement that whatever your trading experience, this book is for you.

Here's another bold statement—or series of statements:

(i) More fortunes have been created from the stock market than any other financial instrument. Sure, there are folks who've made their fortunes from Forex, commodities, futures, options, and other instruments. But *many more* fortunes have been made from stocks. Why? Because they're more accessible and because stocks, like no other instrument, give certain people at certain times an edge that no other instrument can give. And that edge is what I call "privileged" information.

It's a fact that some folks are going to know what's going on with certain companies at certain times. Sometimes this information is intuitive because they have proximity to the business—for example, a supplier or customer to the business has no inside information, per se, but has a general feel for how things are going for that corporation. Sometimes the information is more intimate—for example, information held only by the company's officers and close advisors.

Whatever the case, I'm certainly not advocating illegal insider trading, but whether we like it or not it's always going to happen to some extent. Sometimes it will be legal and sometimes it will be illegal. We'll focus on the legal side of it, because in our method, we're going to follow what looks like informed trading. This "informed" trading may be completely innocent, and all we're going to do is follow it.

You don't need to be an insider or even have any information per se to make use of privileged information. Besides, even those with supposed inside information often get it wrong because the market may have already factored in certain information beforehand.

As such, insider trading doesn't necessarily translate to profitable trading.

Suffice it to say for our purposes, being able to observe *transactions* in the financial markets is far more important than the specific information on which they may be based.

In this book I'm going to show you how to follow the traders who appear to have privileged information, and how to translate that into profitable trading for you.

(ii) There is one type of chart pattern that is responsible for more success than any other pattern or indicator. The pattern is easy to find and, crucially, easy to use in order to create a robust trading plan.

In this book I'm going to focus on the chart pattern (and its close relations) that will massively increase your odds of success.

(iii) Combining (i) and (ii) together to create a robust and simple trading plan will give you a phenomenal edge in the markets.

In this book I'll show you how to combine (i) and (ii) to create a safe trading plan that will also give you the ability to trade for windfall profits.

Remember: Successful trading is all about having an "Edge." By focusing on the easiest market to trade in, the most reliable chart patterns, by following the insiders, and by constructing a solid trading plan, you will have a serious edge.

Trading is a deeply psychological game. Many would-be traders make the mistake of overcomplicating things and taking the more-is-more approach. It may seem counterintuitive at first, but take my word for it that the less-is-more approach is the most productive and profitable way.

By sticking to a simple trading plan we can have certainty as to what we do, and our job then is to ensure our trading plan (no matter how repetitive it may be), which puts the odds of success firmly in our favor.

Sounds simple, doesn't it? Yes. But it's apparently not that easy—especially for those who are looking for the Holy Grail... and be honest, you've thought about that too, haven't you?

Well, if you haven't, I certainly have... but I never found it. The OVI is pretty good compensation, though.

Over the last few years my students have come to rely on some of my rather bold statements regarding the markets. Remember: It's easy to look like a fool in the markets. Fortunately I've been on the money the vast majority of the time, but even if I hadn't been, my students would have come to little or no harm. In this book, you're going to discover how I make my statements and why my students (including you) are protected even if we get things wrong.

This book is all about making money when circumstances allow and about not losing (much or anything) when we get things wrong.

Although I've made a rather nice habit of getting things right, a good trader doesn't have a catastrophe when he or she gets it wrong. In fact, the best traders sometimes don't lose a bean when they get it wrong; how's that for improving your odds? If you can be wrong and yet not lose money, you're already on your way.

This is what this book is all about. It sure does help, though, if you have a way of being right more often than being wrong—then you really do have some good odds of making money.

We have a way of getting things right and protecting ourselves at the same time, just in case we're wrong. And that's what you're going to learn in this book. The process is quite simple, as are the tools we use to make our decisions. Of course, there is sophistication behind the method, but you'll be relieved to know the sophistication is all behind the scenes, specifically behind the tools we use.

Just to get you revved up, I'm going to name just a handful of simple examples where I communicated with my private traders in advance of something happening in the markets.

MARCH 8, 2008

On March 8, 2008, I emailed and blogged my subscribers of impending volatility to come in the markets....

> *"I think this year will be a bumpy ride. The charts and my con-tacts on Wall Street are extremely bearish... **in particular watch out for late summer / early autumn (you heard it here first!).** All traders are going to have to be very prudent with the selection of trades, and that means you're going to have to be patient, and vigilant..."*

As you can see in Figure I.1, the market duly crashed in late summer of 2008. Yet people on Wall Street were privately predicting it back in February/March of that year, almost with a casual certainty. And my OVI indicator was showing negativity from May 2008, over three months *before* the crash started.

The heaviest stock market crash since 1929 followed that autumn. In this book you're going to learn how you could have anticipated the bearishness well in advance. More importantly, you're going to learn how to anticipate the market in the future, and how you can play the market *safely* each and every time.

Here are a few more keynote examples, just to whet your appetite.

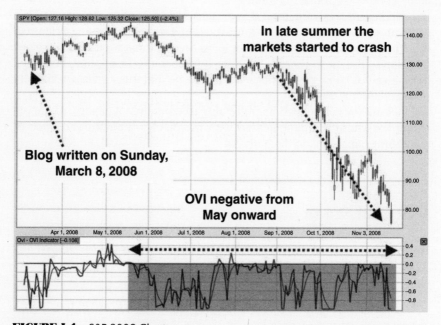

FIGURE I.1 S&P 2008 Chart
Source: OVI Charts. Courtesy of FlagTrader.com. Go to www.theinsideredge.com for more information.

MARCH 2008

As you saw in the preface, at the beginning of March 2008, Bear Sterns (BSC) had been trading in a range between $68.18 and $93.09 for the previous two months (Figure I.2). Nothing extraordinary in that, though there were rumors circulating about Bear and other potentially vulnerable banks.

Despite the innuendos, most commentators, including famously CNBC and Jim Kramer, considered Bear Stearns to be a relatively safe proposition. In this book I will show you what was going on behind the scenes. Instantly you'll see that if they had had access to just one indicator, they would never have been so blasé about Bear Sterns.

FIGURE I.2 BSC March 2008 Chart
Source: OVI Charts. Courtesy of FlagTrader.com. Go to www.theinsideredge.com for more information.

MARCH 2009

On March 8, 2009, I contacted my students (coincidentally an exact year after March 8, 2008) with this missive:

> *"Remember, a change of direction may well follow such a nice trend, but as I wrote some weeks ago, I believed that the post Jan-Feb earnings season would be lucrative and that has proved to be the case..."*

Friday, March 6, 2008, turned out to be the market low from the 2008 crash (see Figure I.3).

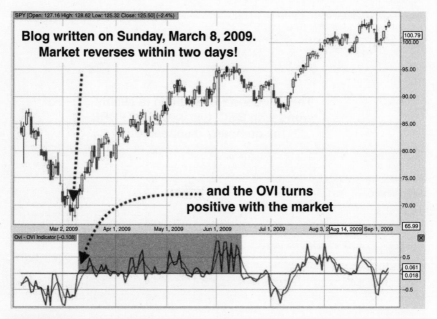

FIGURE I.3   S&P 2009 Chart
Source: OVI Charts. Courtesy of FlagTrader.com. Go to www.theinsideredge.com for more information.

APRIL 26, 2010

On April 26, 2010, the S&P reached a peak of 1219.80. On that day I e-mailed and blogged my students to warn them of impending volatility and the likelihood of a downturn (see Figure I.4). April 26 happened to be the high of the market until November that year.

FIGURE I.4 S&P April 2010 Chart
Source: OVI Charts. Courtesy of FlagTrader.com. Go to www.theinsideredge.com for more information.

MARCH 2011

In March 2011, at a live trading summit, I suggested the prospects for Research in Motion (RIMM) were bleak at the time. In June 2011, RIMM was down over 50 percent. By October 2011 RIMM was down 67 percent from the breakout point in March (see Figure I.5)!

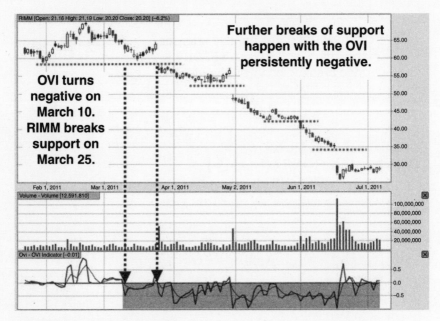

FIGURE I.5　RIMM 2011 Chart
Source: OVI Charts. Courtesy of FlagTrader.com. Go to www.theinsideredge.com for more information.

SUMMER 2011

Through the summer of 2011, I continuously e-mailed and blogged my members of increasing volatility to come and that 2011 was looking increasingly like 2008 all over again. By the fall, all major commentators were making the same statements—that 2011 resembled 2008—yet we were months ahead of them (see Figure I.6).

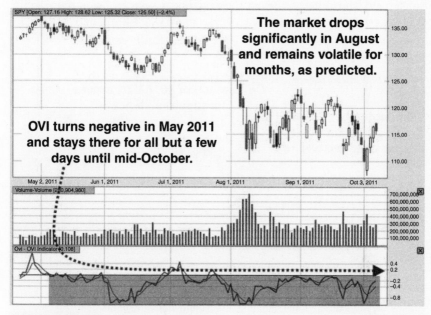

FIGURE I.6 SPY Summer 2011 Chart
Source: OVI Charts. Courtesy of FlagTrader.com. Go to www.theinsideredge.com for more information.

SEPTEMBER 7, 2011

On September 7, 2011, I highlighted Amazon.com, Inc. (AMZN) as a classic breakout opportunity. On September 16 AMZN broke out for 12.52 points and continued the next day (see Figure I.7). I went on to suggest taking profits immediately. In the following days AMZN reversed back down to its breakout point!

On these and many other occasions, my students have increased their accounts significantly, with some actually multiplying their accounts many times over. They have achieved these stellar results by using the specific strategy contained in this book.

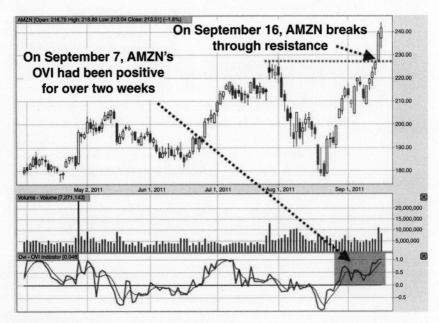

FIGURE I.7   AMZN September 2011 Chart
Source: OVI Charts. Courtesy of FlagTrader.com. Go to www.theinsideredge.com for more information.

"INFORMED TRADING" AND THE OVI

In this book I'm lifting the lid off a method of trading that has, up until now, only been seen by my inner circle of private traders. In terms of breakout trading, much of what we're doing is actually known, but with me there is a special twist.

You see, this book contains something that is not referenced in my other books, nor is referenced anywhere else. It contains the "OVI" (Options Volatility Indicator).

The OVI is a proprietary indicator that is derived from options transaction data. However, please note, this is *not* a book on options. This is a book about stock trading, but the *special twist* is that we are utilizing the OVI to help refine our decision-making.

By revealing this rather special indicator in a book, inevitably eyebrows will be raised by those concerned that this is simply a ruse to promote membership. In order to counter that suggestion from the outset, any reader of this book may go to www.theinsideredge.com and view my top-12 OVI charts for free. Considering the OVI is unique and extremely expensive to put together, I think that's a pretty good deal, don't you?!

So, just by having this book, you have access to the OVI charts for the three main indices: the Dow, the Nasdaq, and the S&P. You'll also have access to my commentaries and blogs.

Once you log onto this book's web site you'll receive video tutorials on how to use the OVI. You'll also receive regular communications from me, and you'll be under no obligation to take things further. The value you'll receive just by observing the OVI for the "OVI Express12" stocks and reading my ongoing commentaries will reward you for this book many times over. I'm confident of that.

I think it's important to mention from the outset that the most important thing about this book is that it helps you make money. It should make your trading life easier, more efficient, more enjoyable, and certainly more profitable, even if you're just using the simple OVI charts for the top-12 stocks and reading my commentaries.

If nothing else, just look again at the S&P OVI chart for the summer and fall of 2011 (shown in Figure I.8). As you can see, the indicator went bearish in May, the market trended downward, and the OVI stayed negative throughout the summer.

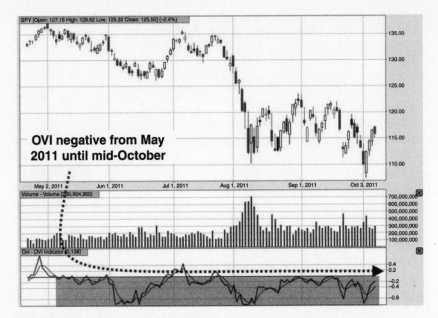

FIGURE I.8 SPY Summer 2011 Chart

Source: OVI Charts. Courtesy of FlagTrader.com. Go to www.theinsideredge.com for more information.

The most powerful application for the OVI is with certain individual stocks (as I'll detail in Chapter 2) and with a breakout chart pattern (as I'll explain in Chapter 3). It's worth noting that, despite the line looking so simple, hundreds of millions of rows of data are being processed every night to create it.

The idea is to create a way of trading that can literally take just minutes of your time to trade on any given day. We achieve this by monitoring a small basket of stocks. If there's an opportunity, we take it; if there's not, we wait to play another day.

THE INSIDER'S RATIONALE

Imagine you are an "informed" trader. You have information on a stock you consider to be valuable, information from which you can make money.

So if you see the stock at a great price you're going to want to:

- Keep your trades **discreet,** so you can ...
- **Accumulate** your position without affecting the share price, and use
- **Leverage** in order to get as much as you can as soon as possible.

Informed traders can achieve all these things in the options market. What the OVI does is spy on their activities, giving us a chance to get in on the action. This is what gives us the Edge.

When it comes to hidden trading activities, there are sometimes references to "dark pools" of volume that don't appear on the Level II screens. This is simply because a dark pool occurs when an institutional buyer and seller match their positions directly. There's not much more to it, and not much we can gain from it.

The OVI is derived from options transaction data. Even on a daily basis this data is massive. When you look at an option chain it can resemble the grids of numbers from the movie *The Matrix*. As such, this data can be overwhelming to the uninitiated.

However, deep within options transaction data resides some very powerful information as to what the smart money is up to. As such I sometimes refer to it as the "hidden money." The OVI translates the "matrix" of numbers into a simple line that gives us a clue as to hidden money activity.

When we align the OVI with a consolidating chart pattern, we can have a remarkable edge, as the indicator will often precede a price breakout.

This is the Insider Edge!

TRADING BREAKOUTS

Even without the OVI, this book contains a powerful and safe trading method that is used by some of the world's greatest traders, including William O'Neill and Dan Zanger.

Breakout trading is a safe method that also allows you to make windfall gains. Windfall gains will increase your batting average over time. It's not enough to simply have a decent ratio of small to medium wins. That's not going to get you very far without excessive leverage.

The biggest trading fortunes have been made from trends. The best way to ride a trend is to catch it on a breakout. When you find yourself on a trend it can be like a rocket ride, and when you're on one of those you certainly don't want to be knocked off it.

The trading plan I teach you allows for a combination of a conservative first profit and then a windfall if the trend continues in your favor. This gives us the best of both worlds.

When the markets are not trending, trading can be more difficult or frustrating, but a good trend is always worth the wait.

When the markets are choppy, we often find that my method isn't finding the opportunities. This is great because the method is protecting us.

Part of being a great trader is knowing when not to trade as well as knowing when to trade.

Remember the premise for this book:

Chart Pattern + Indicator + Trading Plan = Success

Let's now go to Chapter 1, where we'll review the most important chart patterns for our purposes.

CHAPTER 1

The Most Popular Chart Patterns

Why Chart Patterns Are So Important

In this chapter I am showing chart examples without the OVI indicator. This is deliberate. You'll see some of the same charts with the OVI displayed in Chapter 2.

The study of charts is known as technical analysis. This comes in two forms:

1. Chart patterns—seen directly by looking at the charts.
2. Indicators—typically these are mathematical algorithms derived from price and volume.

For the purpose of this book we're going to focus on chart patterns, and as we progress through the chapter I'll explain why. Principally it's because they're the purest interpretation of price action, and as traders we want our main focus to be on price!

Chart patterns are vitally important to traders, and frankly should be just as important to longer-term investors as well. Traditionally long-term investors focus more on the financial reports of a company. The problem with that approach is that a share's stock market performance is not correlated perfectly to the past quarter's results. It's also based on future estimates, the market's view of management, and the quirks of the market itself.

Charts give us a visual representation of how the markets are interpreting a company's financial performance, its management capabilities, and its future prospects.

Over many decades, technical analysis has proved that familiar patterns will form repeatedly and that some patterns may give rise to the increased possibility of a particular future event occurring. So, for example, one pattern may often lead to a stock rising, and another pattern may often lead to a stock falling.

The idea, of course, is that chart patterns increase our odds of success. But that's not the whole story. The real secret is that the most useful chart patterns are the ones around which you can implement a simple and safe trading plan.

Not all chart patterns are conducive to this, so in this chapter I'm only going to focus on the ones that have proven to be the most reliable to recognize.

Understanding chart patterns will not guarantee you success. But align a reliable chart pattern with a robust trading plan *and* the OVI—well, now you have a great chance of achieving great results!

So this chapter is an overview of the patterns I consider the most useful for us moving forward.

PRICE BARS

When I look at charts I typically view them as candlestick charts. It's just a personal preference, and just in case you're not familiar with them, here's a quick summary of how to view price bars in a chart.

Typically we view a price chart from left to right, with time on the horizontal axis and price on the vertical axis. (In Figure 1.1 you'll also see volume bars underneath the price chart. Each bar corresponds with the price bar above it.)

Individual Price Bars

Each price bar shows the price activity over a certain period of time. Price bars can literally be for a "tick," or a minute, or for a 5-minute, 30-minute, 60-minute, daily, weekly, monthly, or yearly period, depending on the length of time you're looking at.

Obviously the shorter time frame you trade, the shorter the time period of the chart you'll want to look at. In this book we're focused on the daily bars, meaning each bar represents one day.

Price bars can be represented in different ways. The simplest way to depict the price range for a particular period of time is by way of a simple vertical bar that displays the high and low points for that bar.

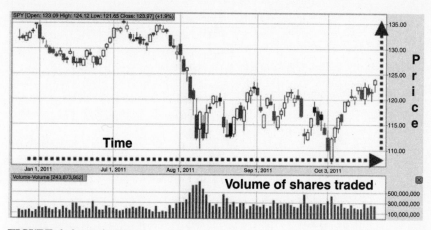

FIGURE 1.1   Basic Chart
Source: OVI Charts. Courtesy of FlagTrader.com. Go to www.theinsideredge.com for more information.

The most common way to view price bars is a simple vertical bar that displays the high and low, and a left horizontal tag for the opening price and a right horizontal tag for the closing price (as shown in Figure 1.2).

As you can see, the extremes of the bar represent the high (h) and the low (l). The left tag represents the price the stock *opened* at for the day (o), and the right tag represents them price the stock *closed* at for the day (c).

So each bar contains the following information for its period of time:

- **OPEN**: the price at which the stock opened on that day.
- **HIGH**: the highest price the stock reached that day.
- **LOW**: the lowest price the stock reached that day.
- **CLOSE**: the price at which the stock closed that day.

In the example in Figure 1.2, the stock closed lower than the open, we can see that quite clearly. You can also see it moved higher than the open at some point during the day. It also moved lower than the final close at some point during the day.

FIGURE 1.2   Simple Price Bar

FIGURE 1.3   Candlestick Up

FIGURE 1.4   Candlestick Up

Now let's look at the same bar but using a Japanese candlestick (see Figures 1.3 and 1.4).

With the candlestick, we still have the low and the high as vertical lines (shadows), but what we have instead of the left and right tags is the top and bottom of the body of the rectangle.

When we have a hollow body as in Figure 1.3, it means that the price closed higher than it opened.

When we have a filled body as in Figure 1.4, it means the price closed lower than it opened.

When you view price charts you'll notice that the bars on the chart will often be in color. Typically, if the close is higher than the previous day's close, then the bar will be green. If the close is lower than the previous day's close, then the bar will be red.

You can get a scenario where the stock close is higher than the open on the specific day, but the close is still lower than the close of the previous day. In such a case the bar will be *hollow* and *red*. Table 1.1 is a summary.

TABLE 1.1   Reading Japanese Candlesticks

Close vs. Open	Close vs. Previous Day's Close	Candlestick Appearance
Close > Open	Close > Previous Close	Green + Hollow
Close < Open	Close > Previous Close	Green + Filled
Close > Open	Close < Previous Close	Red + Hollow
Close < Open	Close < Previous Close	Red + Filled

> means "higher than."
< means "lower than."

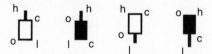

FIGURE 1.5   Extreme Candlesticks

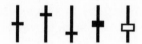

FIGURE 1.6   Doji Bar Candlesticks

Specific Candlesticks   One advantage of using candlesticks is that the individual candlestick bars have their own patterns. I'm not a candlestick guru, but there are a couple that are worth knowing about and that are obvious when they appear.

We already know that the candlestick is comprised of a body and shadows. The body contains the information about open and close prices. The top of the upper shadow is the high of the bar, and the bottom of the shadow is the low of the bar.

If the extreme (high or low) of the day was exactly at the open or the close, then there may not be shadow for a particular candlestick (see Figure 1.5).

Sometimes we'll encounter a price bar where the open and the close are at similar levels within the same bar. These are known as Doji bars (see Figure 1.6).

A Doji is thought to represent uncertainty in the market, which could herald a significant change in market direction. Dojis come in all sorts of shapes and sizes, as outlined above, and can have varying degrees of proximity between the open and the close of the bar, and also the relative position of the open and close.

As my personal rule of thumb, if the distance between the open and the close is within 20 percent of the range of the bar then I'll consider it a Doji. So, if the range of the bar is, say, $2.00, then provided the open and close are within $0.40 of each other I'll view it as a potential Doji. Of course it's more powerful if the open and close are really close together; the nearer they are to each other (particularly in the case of a wide-ranging price bar with long shadows), the greater the perceived uncertainty of the market.

A variant of the Doji and another candlestick bar that often signifies a reversal is a Hammer bar (see Figure 1.7). The Hammer is characterized by the open and close being relatively close together and being positioned at one end of the candlestick. Candlestick theory talks about different types of Hammer bars, a few of which are depicted in Figure 1.7.

FIGURE 1.7   Hammer Bar Candlesticks

In the context of an extreme in price being formed, a Hammer bar can signify a reversal. The same applies to a break of support or resistance. If it occurs with a Hammer bar, the break of support or resistance may turn out to be short-lived.

Let's not get too hung up on individual price bars though.

Price bars tend to make more sense when they're viewed in the context of other price bars. The collection of bars can then start to resemble recognizable chart patterns.

Chart patterns come in two forms: continuation patterns and reversal patterns. Our main focus for trading will be continuation patterns. This is because the fastest way to make money in the markets is by hitching a ride on a trend.

Before we discuss how to define a trend, let's define one of the basic tenets of chart reading: support and resistance.

SUPPORT AND RESISTANCE

Support and resistance are bread-and-butter terms for both novice and seasoned traders.

- Support means a "floor"—typically created by the achievement of a previous high or low. If a price breaches support, this can be interpreted as weakness with further falls likely to follow.
- Resistance means a "ceiling"—typically created by the achievement of a previous high or low. If a price breaches resistance, this can be interpreted as strength with further rises likely to follow.

Where clear lines of support and resistance have already been established, the psychology of these levels comes into play. Around a resistance level some traders may become nervous and sell their existing long positions in case of a bounce down off the resistance level. Other traders may look on a break of the resistance level as a sound reason to buy in the hope that the stock will continue on its upward trend.

Similarly, where a stock drops to a support level, those who are already shorting the stock may look to cover their shorts by buying back the stock in case of a bounce up off support. Other traders may look at a break of the support as an opportunity to go short in the hope that the stock continues its downward trend for some time.

The biggest challenge with trading is that we don't have hindsight. Sounds obvious, doesn't it!? We don't know in advance whether the stock is going to break or bounce off these support and resistance levels, so we must use a trading plan that not only keeps us safe but also enables us to play for windfall profits. More about that later; for now it's crucial to understand two things:

1. Do not fall into the trap of trying to forecast the markets.
2. Do appreciate the role that a well-defined chart pattern plays in forming a well-defined trading plan.

When support and resistance lines are broken, they may form the opposite of what they were before: Former support can become new resistance, and former resistance can become new support.

Here's an example of Apple (AAPL), which formed a resistance level around $320, which subsequently became a support level (see Figure 1.8). The resistance (R) was first hit in November 2010. The stock then bounces off it and becomes a bit sticky around that level in December 2010. Several months later the stock tests the level twice—in April (S) and June (S) —but does not close below the $320 level.

FIGURE 1.8 AAPL Chart: Resistance and Support
Source: OVI Charts. Courtesy of FlagTrader.com. Go to www.theinsideredge.com for more information.

At this point it's tempting to believe that if the stock does close below $320 it will continue to slide. What happens next, then, is quite surprising.

AAPL breaks the $320 support level the very next day, and closes below it too. However, it does so with a gap down[1] and with a Hammer candlestick bar.

In the context of an extreme in price being formed, a Hammer bar can signify a reversal. The same applies to a break of support or resistance. If it occurs with a Hammer bar, the break of support or resistance may turn out to be short-lived (see Figure 1.9).

In this case, AAPL has broken support and formed a new price extreme low but the Hammer bar is making the break ambiguous. We therefore need to ensure that if you were in the trade already, and if the stock does reverse back above $320, you'd be closing it with a very small loss.

As it happens, here the Hammer bar did signify a reversal, and the stock roared back within a day and didn't look back. If you had already gone short, the key would be to close your trade by buying back the stock as soon as it got back into the trading range above $320 (see Figure 1.10).

As you'll discover later, our trading plan involves placing stop-limit orders. These orders prevent us from being "gapped into" a trade. In this

FIGURE 1.9   AAPL Chart: Hammer Bar
Source: OVI Charts. Courtesy of FlagTrader.com. Go to www.theinsideredge.com for more information.

---

[1] Our particular trading plan ensures that we do not trade gaps by placing our trades as stop limit orders.

AAPL [Open: 398.10 High: 399.14 Low: 390.75 Close: 392.87] (−0.6%)

Hammer bar signifies immediate reversal. ·········▶

FIGURE 1.10 AAPL Chart: Hammer Reversal
Source: OVI Charts. Courtesy of FlagTrader.com. Go to www.theinsideredge.com for more information.

case, we might have wanted to short AAPL if the stock had traded through $319.59—meaning the stock price touched that price during trading hours. However, we would not have wanted to have our trade entered at anything below this.

So the order would have been a sell (to open) stop-limit order at $319.59. This means that the broker could not execute our trade at any price lower than $319.59, or any price higher than $319.59. This gives us more control and a more restful night's sleep in the case of gapping stocks!

Most traditional and online brokers will have the facility for stop-limit orders without any problem. Some types of brokers (like spread-betting companies in the UK) do not have this facility yet, in which case you would place your orders during trading hours right after the open.

As a trader you should not be obsessed with trying to nail the high and the low, or the precise turning point of a stock price. In fact, that's a road to ruin. What you want is to jump onto a trend when it's breaking through support or resistance areas.

As you've just seen, support and resistance lines can be very easy to spot when they're formed from previous highs or lows. Note also that they don't need to be horizontal lines. Support can be formed by joining the lows of an up-trending stock. Resistance can be formed by joining the highs of a down-trending stock.

A Brief Rant about Fibonacci, Elliott Wave, and Gann

Support and resistance points can also be formed by other mathematically derived levels, such as pivot points (used primarily in Forex trading) and more exotic techniques like Fibonacci, Elliott Wave, and Gann.

These techniques do have their fan bases, and can have their relative merits. However, having studied Fibonacci, Elliott Wave, and Gann comprehensively over many years, I eventually concluded that *for me* only the most elementary use of Fibonacci was worth considering without going completely insane or running around in circles. We'll cover the simple and effective way of using Fibonacci when we apply our trading plan in Chapter 4.

As a quick summary, the techniques of Fibonacci, Elliott Wave, and Gann rely on the natural order of number sequences and various ratios that are derived from them.

The problem with these techniques is that they presume the markets are preordained by some force of nature or divine energy. If this is the case, no one has yet cracked the code without using hindsight—which means no one's really cracked the code at all!

Don't get me wrong. These theories do have some validity in the markets as the same numbers and ratios do keep cropping up as key support and resistance levels time and time again. The numbers also have validity in terms of counting time periods.

However, it is pretty much impossible to know in advance which numbers will occur at a particular time. And this makes these theories very difficult, and in some cases dangerous, to trade.

The problem is exacerbated by scholarly types who analyze ad nauseam which ratio is going to happen at a particular time—and once in the bluest of blue moons they'll get it right! But as I keep saying, even a broken clock is right twice a day . . . and for the rest of the day it's hopeless.

Elliot Wave analysts can never even agree among themselves which "wave of a wave of a wave" we're in, so what chance do the rest of us have?!

Gann specialists can't agree on what his favorite number was and which paper is his genuine transcript!

And Fibonacci experts can't agree on time, price, ratios, or numbers.

This gets us to the nub of the problem: By getting obsessed with a particular number or ratio for a particular stock to reach before you enter or exit, you're indulging in magical thinking and forgetting what trading is all about.

- Trading *is* about making money from the opportunities that the market brings with wonderful regularity.

- Trading is *not* about being right all the time. That would be a virtually impossible aim.
- Trading *is* about maximizing the reward when you're right.
- And trading *is* about minimizing the damage when you're wrong, and embracing the fact that being wrong is part of the game.
- In this way trading is a probability game of numbers. You have to play in order to be paid.
- In my trading plan, which you'll learn in Chapter 4, you can sometimes be wrong and not even lose a dime! Now that kind of approach starts to put the probabilities in your favor.

So, a quick summary on Fibonacci, Elliott Wave, and Gann.

Fibonacci   In the case of Fibonacci, each number in the sequence is the sum of the two previous numbers. Starting with zero, the sequence runs like this:

0, 1, 1, 2, 3, 5, 8, 13, 21, 34, 55, 89, ...

As the sequence develops, each number will divide into its successor by 1.618 times, and into its predecessor 0.618 times. 0.618 is the reciprocal of 1.618 and is known as the Golden Ratio. From here, new numbers can be discovered by squaring, square-rooting, subtracting from 1 to arrive at 0.382, et cetera.

The permutations and combinations are mind-boggling, and the seriously obsessed can then start to veer into Lucas numbers and even planetary and lunar ratios.

The principle idea behind using Fibonacci in trading is to identify a natural point of support or resistance where a stock may reach. This can be in terms of identifying a retracement point where the stock has been trending, and then retracing to a target price. Or it can be in terms of identifying a target point where the stock may reach during its trend.

Here's the problem in practical terms: Because the method embraces the idea that the markets are divinely operated, Fibonacci enthusiasts become obsessed with being right.

Remember, trading is a deeply psychological game. And your trading plan must take this into account. The psychology is to make money over the medium term. You don't have to be right all the time in order to achieve this.

Let's take an example of how I've seen this played out more times than I care to imagine!

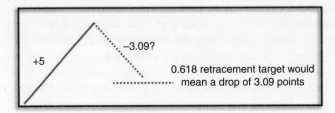

FIGURE 1.11 Fibonacci Retracement

Fibonacci Retracement Example Stock ABC rises by 5 points. Fibonacci analysis says the stock is dead certain to retrace by a ratio of 0.618, meaning the stock should fall by 3.09 points.

The immediate problem here is that the target presupposes that that high has been reached and that the retracement target will be reached before a new high is made (see Figure 1.11).

So, what if the 0.618 target that they were convinced of isn't reached? Well, they start to convince themselves that it will be. They have to be right. And then when they're not right, they make excuses and then wait until they are proved right. And this starts to mess with their trading plan. In fact, there is no plan.

Because instead of trading what they're seeing, they're making decisions based on what they want to see. They're making decisions based on the need to be right. And that is not what trading is all about.

Fibonacci Expansion Example This is the other common use of Fibonacci. Where is the stock price going to reach during its trend? Bearing in mind that many automated trading systems may be set to buy or sell at different Fibonacci target levels, this target-setting strategy does have some merit (see Figure 1.12).

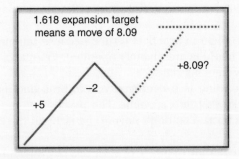

FIGURE 1.12 Fibonacci Expansion

However, the problem occurs when you ask the questions of which level (there are so many of them!) and what happens if the stock doesn't reach that level? Again, for many Fib enthusiasts, the priority is being right, and that priority will deplete their accounts.

In Chapter 4 you'll discover we do have a use for this target-setting strategy. If used correctly, you have a trading plan that is based on sensible principles that will keep you safe when you're wrong and allow you to make a windfall if you get it right.

In terms of using Fib to set our profit targets, I'm not wedded to the precise ratios either. I just want a sensible place at which to take partial profits and a simple method of grabbing a windfall if the market is generous enough to keep trending for me.

Elliott Wave   I'm going to deliberately keep this short!

The Elliott Wave Principle is tied in with Fibonacci numbers and ratios. The theory is that prices undulate in waves. These waves are sequenced in the basic Fibonacci ratios.

The basic structure is that you have a five-wave impulse followed by a three-wave, A-B-C retracement. In a complete Elliott Wave sequence there are 34 waves as follows:

5   3   5   3   5   3   5   5

Add the numbers together to see the corresponding cumulative wave count below (Fib numbers in bold)

5   **8**   **13**   16   **21**   24   29   **34**

Now, here's where it can start to get bewildering. . . .

Within one wave can exist another smaller set of waves, and within that smaller set of waves can exist an even smaller set of waves, and within that even smaller set of waves can exist a yet tinier set of waves. . . .

And to exacerbate the conundrum, Elliott Wave experts rarely agree on whether they're looking at a five-wave impulse or an A-B-C retracement. And this is before we even get to the rules of how to trade the darn thing!

Here's where I sit on all of this: If the so-called experts can't even agree what wave we're in, then the method has to be a dud as far as making money from it is concerned.

Trading is all about keeping it simple. Elliott is so confusing and mind-boggling that if you get into it, you'll be trapped in a never-ending cycle of fascinating confusion—and, more worryingly, you won't make any money from it!

Furthermore, it's worth mentioning that Elliott experts have been predicting the end of the world as we know it for donkey's years, and, as far as I can see, the markets are still here and the world is still here. One day they'll be right, but remember the broken clock! In the meantime, let's keep it simple and learn how to make money from the markets. I wasted three years on all this stuff. It was interesting, but it got me nowhere.

Gann   I'm going to deliberately keep this one short, too!

W. D. Gann was a renowned trader who started his career at the turn of the twentieth century.

Believing that highs and lows were all related by certain ratios, Gann was an early advocate of using Fibonacci numbers to make price target projections. In fact, Gann numbers are either the same or only fractions away from the Fibonacci numbers, and he was among the first proponents of linking price with time.

During my adventures I did have success with Gann, but the successes can cause problems later on. How so? Because once you start to believe in the numbers, it can seriously affect your capacity for objectivity in future trades. These numbers can work once in a while, or even as if by magic during a sequence of trades.

But sooner or later they stop working! At that point you're left like the Wile E. Coyote cartoon character, running off the edge off the cliff and suspended in mid-air until the inevitable drop. "How come it doesn't work anymore? This was perfect. There must be something wrong with the markets!"

For what it's worth, here are the major Gann levels. But that's not where it ends. In fact, it's only the start, because Gann also used percentages and angles, combining price with time. And guess what? They sometimes work like magic! But more often than not they don't, and that leaves you in the trading wilderness.

The Major Gann Levels   Gann calculated four levels that appeared to have significance to stock prices. He also calculated many other levels. In fact, my mischievous side considers that between Gann, Elliott, Fibonacci, and Lucas numbers, just about every number in the universe is covered!

$$G1\ Level \quad \frac{All\ Time\ High\ Price}{2}$$

G1 is the most important Gann level, representing a key support level. If price breaks below G1, then it is likely to drop further to G3. G1 then becomes resistance.

$$G2\ Level\quad \frac{(\text{All Time High Price} + \text{All Time Low Price})}{2}$$

$$G3\ Level\quad \frac{\text{All Time High Price}}{4}\quad or\quad \frac{G1}{2}$$

G3 is the second most important Gann level. G3 acts as support when G1 has been breached. If G3 support is breached, it then becomes resistance.

$$G4\ Level\quad \frac{(\text{All Time High Price} - \text{All Time Low Price})}{4} + \text{All Time Low Price}$$

So, if you feel you want to pursue a scholarly approach, by all means read up on more of this. My own feeling is that it will have you fascinated but ultimately running around in ever-decreasing circles—and then you'll return to the method I teach you in this book!

Whatever you choose to do, keep things simple. You're not here to become a scholar. You're here to make money from the opportunities that the markets conveniently offer you.

To do this effectively you need a trading plan that is simple to understand, is easily repeatable, and keeps you sane.

After years of seriously detailed Gann and Fib analysis, I could see that the techniques weren't for me, other than the very simple "first-profit-target" method I detail in Chapter 4.

Support and Resistance Summary

Support and resistance levels can be formed by a number of methods, ranging from simple horizontal lines extended from previous lows and highs, to complex algorithms based on obscure concepts.

The important thing to remember is that support and resistance are psychologically sensitive areas for traders. Given that trading is a psychological game, it's vital to keep your trading plan as simple as possible. We'll see examples of breakouts from support and resistance in Chapter 3.

The art of trading is not to be right. It's to win over the medium term. Some traders become obsessed about being right and use methods that are unworkable without hindsight. Don't fall into that trap.

In order to win, you do not have to achieve perfection. In fact, striving for perfection in trading is seriously misguided.

When it comes to support and resistance the simplest and most effective support and resistance is formed from previous highs, previous lows, and simple trend lines.

TRENDS

Trading in the direction of the trend will yield you the biggest profits you'll ever make in the markets. The challenge is how to jump on one and ride it for as long as possible.

What Is a Trend?

Prices move up, down, and sideways. There are two types of trends: an uptrend and a downtrend (see Table 1.2).

The easiest way to identify a trend is to eyeball it. Some traders define trends by using moving averages or moving average crossovers. I think this is flawed, because slower-moving averages can allow for massive retracements that can hurt you.

The main things to identify when defining a trend are what timescale you are measuring and what timescale you are trading. For example, a stock that has been trending up in the last two months could have been trending down for the previous six months, and vice versa.

Let's take a look at a few charts of the same stock where you can easily see if there's a trend or not.

Clearly in Figure 1.13 we can see AAPL is trending up from February 2009 until October 2011. Within that longish-term trend, we can see that it made three significant retracements, taking the stock to within touching distance of the rising trend line.

If we zoomed into the chart and took a snapshot during these retracements we might not consider the stock was in an uptrend.

In Figure 1.14 we're taking the same stock, AAPL, during the period from April to August 2010. We know in the longer-term context that AAPL was in an uptrend. But the chart shows it to be going sideways.

TABLE 1.2 Defining a Trend

Uptrend	An uptrend can be described as a sequence of higher lows in conjunction with higher highs.
Downtrend	A downtrend can be described as a sequence of lower highs in conjunction with lower lows.

FIGURE 1.13   Up-trending Chart
Source: OVI Charts. Courtesy of FlagTrader.com. Go to www.theinsideredge.com for more information.

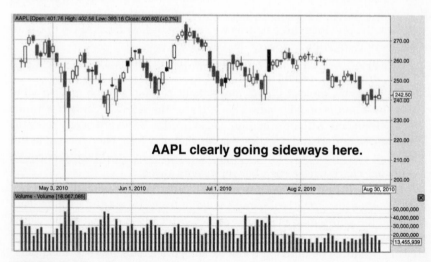

FIGURE 1.14   Sideways Chart
Source: OVI Charts. Courtesy of FlagTrader.com. Go to www.theinsideredge.com for more information.

FIGURE 1.15 Down-trending Chart
Source: OVI Charts. Courtesy of FlagTrader.com. Go to www.theinsideredge.com for more information.

In Figure 1.15 we see the same stock again, from June to September 2010. Although it's not steep or severe, the stock looks like it's trending downward. Again, it's a simple matter of eyeballing the chart.

So in the previous three figures we can see that within AAPL's uptrend, it had periods of going sideways and even down.

The important question is: What time frame should you be observing for the purposes of trading a trend?

Well, when I look at charts, my default setting is to be able to view about nine months of daily bars. This gives me the relevant context without overwhelming me with information. I also need to be aware of any relevant longer-term support and resistance areas that may have been formed in the past. That can be achieved in a couple of seconds by quickly referencing a weekly bar chart, where each bar represents a week.

Figure 1.16 shows AAPL for most of 2011, and the immediate thing I notice is that the stock looks more volatile from August to October. This reflected the entire market's performance, which also exhibited increased volatility in the wider indexes like the S&P 500. You can easily observe increasing volatility by noticing wider-ranging price bars, increased gapping, and an overall sense of a chart becoming "messier."

Trend Lines

Apart from eyeballing the chart, the easiest way to identify a trend is by creating a trend line. Trendlines are far more reliable and simpler to use than moving averages.

I can see clearly that from August onward AAPL is more volatile than it was in the months before.

FIGURE 1.16 Nine-month Chart
Source: OVI Charts. Courtesy of FlagTrader.com. Go to www.theinsideredge.com for more information.

With an uptrend, we draw the trend line below the lows, as per Figure 1.13.

With a downtrend, we draw the trend line above the highs, as in Figure 1.15.

Sometimes a stock will be in a trend, make a retracement without hitting the trend line, or will just touch the trend line. This type of reaction shows the trend line has some significance for other traders.

Sometimes a trend line will be breached before the price suddenly bounces back and resumes its trend. This will shake out the traders who have stops near the trend line. If this happens to you, you may need to consider how to jump back on the trend safely. (I'll get into this during Chapter 4.)

A break of the trend line, particularly with rising volume, may signify the end of that trend.

FLAG PATTERNS AND CONSOLIDATIONS

Flag patterns are among the most powerful chart patterns in the stock-trading world. Not only do they provide a good signal but, more importantly, they give us the ability to construct a simple and effective trading plan. This combination makes them so powerful.

Flags can be further distinguished into pennants, triangles, and wedges. For our purposes let's call them all flags or tight consolidations. The idea is that we trade them only when they break out of their tight consolidation in the direction of the dominant trend.

A flag pattern is made up of two parts:

1. A thrusting surge or step (the flagpole).
2. The flag (the consolidation).

The thrust or step can occur in either an upward (bullish) or downward (bearish) direction. This is the direction of the dominant trend, and that's the direction in which we're going to trade. An analogy would be fighting the tide.

The flag part temporarily interrupts the trend before it resumes. Our job is to jump onto the trend as the flag breaks in the direction of the dominant trend.

The flag part consists of the price pattern rebounding off two short-term lines of support and resistance—sometimes as little as three consolidating bars—before the breakout happens or fails. If the breakout never materializes, our trading plan ensures we don't lose because our entry stop-limit order only executes if the breakout occurs (without a gap).

Bull Flags

A bull flag occurs when the dominant trend is up. We're therefore hoping for the stock to rise and break the flag's short-term resistance. However, our trade is only activated when the stock has traded upward past the resistance level. I'll cover flags with real examples in Chapter 4 but for now I'll give a summary, referencing Figure 1.17.

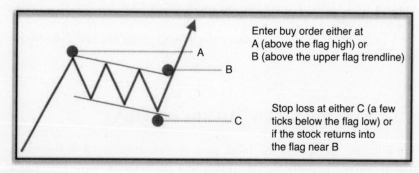

FIGURE 1.17 Bull Flag

The short-term resistance can either be the very top of the pattern or the higher trendline if the bull flag consolidation forms with lower highs.

- You enter your buy order at either point A or B.

    Point A is just above the highest point of the flag. This is the most conservative entry point, because it requires the highest point of the flag to be broken. If this occurs with increasing volume, then so much the better, because increasing volume indicates buying conviction behind the rising price, which makes it more likely to keep going.

    Point B is just above where the price would break out above the higher trend line of the flag pattern. This is more aggressive than Point A and the danger is of a double top[2] forming at the top of the entire pattern at Point A. Again, if volume is increasing as the break happens, then so much the better.
- If the entry is activated then you need a sell stop loss. You can have this set at either Point C, or below Point B, inside the flag, if you want a tighter stop loss.

This is your basic trading plan for a bull flag, within the context of an upward trend.

The short-term resistance can either be the very top of the pattern or the upper trendline if the flag consolidation forms with lower highs (see Figure 1.17).

Notice how I've drawn the bull flag consolidation moving slightly downward against the direction of the main upward trend. It's preferable that the bull flag consolidation moves either sideways or slightly downward against the direction of the dominant trend.

This helps our trading plan with particular reference to entering our buy order when a resistance level is being breached at either Point A or B. If the flag consolidation occurs in the same direction as the main trend, we wouldn't be able to identify a Point A or B, and our trading plan would become muddled.

---

[2]A double top occurs when the price approaches a previous high (which is forming resistance) and then reverses.

FIGURE 1.18   Bull Flag Chart
Source: OVI Charts. Courtesy of FlagTrader.com. Go to www.theinsideredge.com for
more information.

In Figure 1.18 you can see the bull flag forming in the shaded square.

The thing to note in this chart is that the bull flag forms at the end of
a bowl type of pattern. The bowl is in itself a bullish pattern, and therefore
the combination of the bowl and the bull flag is one of the most sought-after
patterns in the markets, because we're combining two bullish patterns into
one. This is known as a cup and handle.

Cup and Handle   Cup and handles vary in terms of the steepness of the
cup and the position of the handle (flag) relative to the first lip of the cup
(see Figure 1.19). Typically we play them as standard flags, but do bear in
mind that the first lip of the cup (on the left side of the diagram) does in
itself form a resistance level.

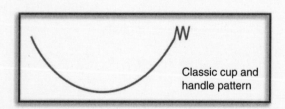

FIGURE 1.19   Cup and Handle

Bear Flags

A bear flag occurs when the dominant trend is down. We're therefore hoping for the stock to decline and break the flag's short-term support. However, our trade is only activated when the stock has traded downward below the support level. We'll go through examples of this in Chapter 4, but here's the summary, referencing Figure 1.20.

The short-term support can either be the very bottom of the pattern or the lower trendline if the bear flag consolidation forms with higher lows.

- You enter your sell short order at either point A or B.

    Point A is just below the lowest point of the flag. This is the most conservative entry point, because an entry requires the lowest point of the flag to be broken. If this occurs with increasing volume then so much the better, because increasing volume indicates selling conviction behind the falling price, which makes it more likely to keep going.

    Point B is just below where the price would break out below the lower trend line of the flag pattern. This is more aggressive than Point A, and the danger is of a double bottom[3] forming at the bottom of the entire pattern at Point A. Again, if volume is increasing as the break happens then so much the better.

- If the entry is activated then you need a buy stop loss to cover your short. You can have this set at either Point C, just above the upper flag trend line, or above Point B, inside the flag, if you want a tighter stop loss.

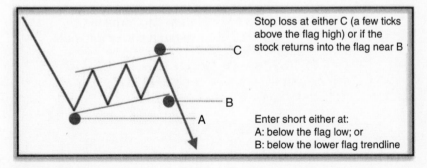

FIGURE 1.20   Bear Flag

---

[3]A double bottom occurs when the price approaches a previous low (which is forming support) and then reverses.

This is your basic trading plan for a bear flag, within the context of a downward trend (see Figure 1.20).

Notice how I've drawn the bear flag consolidation moving slightly upward against the direction of the main downward trend. It's preferable that the bear flag consolidation moves either sideways or slightly upward against the direction of the dominant trend.

This helps our trading plan with particular reference to entering our short order when a support level is being breached at either Point A or B. If the flag consolidation occurs in the same direction as the main trend, we wouldn't be able to identify a Point A or B, and our trading plan would become muddled.

In Figure 1.21 you can see the bear flag forming in the shaded square at the bottom-right of the price chart.

Similar to the bull flag example, in Figure 1.21 the bear flag forms at the end of an upside-down bowl. The upside-down bowl is in itself a bearish pattern, and the combination of the reverse bowl and the bear flag is known as a reverse cup and handle. Again this is highly sought after, as it is the combination of two bearish patterns in one.

Reverse Cup and Handle   As with the standard cup and handle, the reverse equivalent can also vary in terms of the steepness of the upside-down cup and the position of the handle (flag) relative to the first lip of the

FIGURE 1.21   Bear Flag Chart
Source: OVI Charts. Courtesy of FlagTrader.com. Go to www.theinsideredge.com for more information.

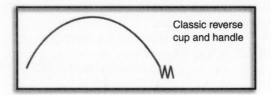

FIGURE 1.22 Reverse Cup and Handle

cup (see Figure 1.22). Typically we play them as standard flags, but do bear in mind that the first lip of the cup (on the left side of the diagram) does in itself form a support level.

Rounded Tops, Rounded Bottoms, and Flag Failures

There are three possible outcomes to a flag pattern formation:

(i) The flag breaks out in the direction of the dominant trend and keeps going. In such a case our trade is triggered by the breakout and we're going to make good profits.

(ii) The flag breaks out in the direction of the dominant trend and reverses. In such a case our trade is triggered by the breakout, and if our first profit target is not reached, the reversal may cause us a potential small loss. If our first profit target is reached then we'll make a small profit despite the reversal. (More about the trading plan in Chapters 3 and 4.)

(iii) The flag doesn't break out at all. In the case of a failed bull flag, this is known as a rounded top. In the case of a failed bear flag this is known as a rounded bottom.

One of the great merits of our trading plan is that if there is no breakout, then our trade is not executed, and therefore we cannot make a loss. Given that trading is all about putting the odds in our favor, how good is it to have a trade "fail" and yet we don't lose a penny?!

FIGURE 1.23 Rounded Top
Source: OVI Charts. Courtesy of FlagTrader.com. Go to www.theinsideredge.com for more information.

Let's look at an example of a rounded top and then a rounded bottom.

In Figure 1.23 we can see a promising bull flag forming. If it breaks upward and above the top of the flag our buy stop limit order would be executed.

However, the breakout never materializes. We were "wrong," but our trading plan ensured we weren't punished for it (see Figure 1.24).

FIGURE 1.24 Rounded Top
Source: OVI Charts. Courtesy of FlagTrader.com. Go to www.theinsideredge.com for more information.

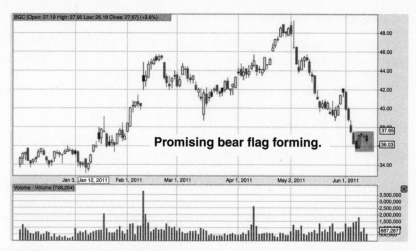

FIGURE 1.25 Rounded Bottom
Source: OVI Charts. Courtesy of FlagTrader.com. Go to www.theinsideredge.com for more information.

Figure 1.25 shows a similar story, except we have a promising bear flag forming. If it breaks downward and below the bottom of the flag, our sell stop-limit order would be executed.

Again, here the breakout never materializes. We were "wrong," but our trading plan ensured we weren't punished for it, as shown in Figure 1.26.

FIGURE 1.26 Rounded Bottom
Source: OVI Charts. Courtesy of FlagTrader.com. Go to www.theinsideredge.com for more information.

The Megaphone Pattern

The megaphone pattern is the anti-flag pattern! It's like the opposite of a consolidation, where instead of the price bars getting tighter as with a flag consolidation, the bars actually get wider.

The pattern exhibits increasing volatility and is often found near the culmination of a rising trend. When you see this occurring it can often spell the end for that uptrend.

In April 2010, I spotted such an example as it was happening and warned my members rather fortuitously on the high of the market on April 26 (see Figure 1.27).

The resulting decline was stupendous and was dubbed the "flash crash" (see Figure 1.28).

Be aware of this pattern, as it's a fantastic precursor to further volatility and often a down move.

Another bearish pattern is the head and shoulders pattern.

FIGURE 1.27 Megaphone Pattern
Source: OVI Charts. Courtesy of FlagTrader.com. Go to www.theinsideredge.com for more information.

FIGURE 1.28   Megaphone Pattern
Source: OVI Charts. Courtesy of FlagTrader.com. Go to www.theinsideredge.com for more information.

HEAD AND SHOULDERS

Head and shoulders patterns can take two forms: standard and reverse.

Standard Head and Shoulders

A head and shoulders pattern occurs when a high is made, followed by a higher high, which in turn is followed by a lower high (see Figure 1.29). Effectively the middle high (the head) is sandwiched between two lower peaks (the two shoulders).

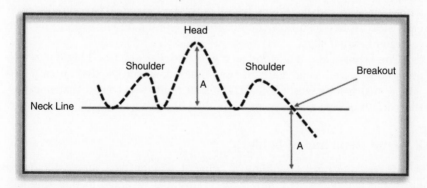

FIGURE 1.29   Head and Shoulders

FIGURE 1.30   GS Head and Shoulders Setup
Source: OVI Charts. Courtesy of FlagTrader.com. Go to www.theinsideredge.com for more information.

The chart is telling us that the price didn't have the strength to rise past the highest high. This can be interpreted as weakness.

The anticipated decline in the price can be estimated as the amount of distance (A) between the neckline and the "head" high.

At any point after the second shoulder we may see bear flag patterns develop as the stock trends downward. In such cases we need to be aware of the wider context of these bear flags being within a bearish head and shoulders pattern, and take advantage of the situation by shorting on the breakdown of the bear flag.

In the chart of Goldman Sachs (GS), we can see a prolonged bear flag forming with support at $150 (see Figure 1.30). This was one of the easiest trades you'll ever spot. The bear flag was forming in the context of a broader head and shoulders, which in this instance had two shoulders on each side. Notice also how the neckline is sloping downward in this case (another bearish sign).

The setup is about as good as it gets and was one that I highlighted to my students well in advance of the breakout, which yielded an easy $15 within two weeks (see Figure 1.31). You really don't need that many of these kinds of easy trades to make trading like this a very enjoyable hobby.

Reverse Head and Shoulders

A reverse head and shoulders is what it sounds like: an upside-down head and shoulders. The implications are also reversed in that this is a bullish setup.

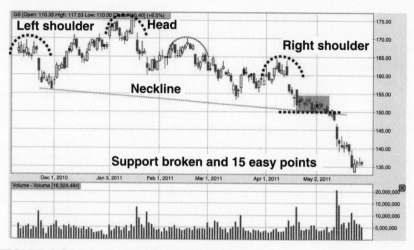

FIGURE 1.31 GS Head and Shoulders Breakout
Source: OVI Charts. Courtesy of FlagTrader.com. Go to www.theinsideredge.com for more information.

A reverse head and shoulders occurs when a low is made, followed by a lower low, which in turn is followed by a higher low. Effectively the middle low (the reverse head) is sandwiched between two higher lows (the two reverse shoulders).

The chart is telling us that the price didn't have enough momentum to fall below the lowest low. This can be interpreted as imminent strength to come.

The anticipated rise in the price can be estimated as the amount of distance (A) between the neckline and the reverse head low, as shown in Figure 1.32.

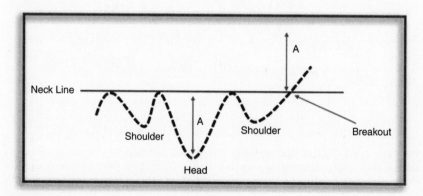

FIGURE 1.32 Reverse Head and Shoulders

At any point after the second shoulder we may see bull flag patterns develop as the stock trends upward. In such cases we need to be aware of the wider context of these bull flags being within a bullish reverse head and shoulders pattern, and take advantage of the situation by buying on the breakout of the bull flag.

In the following charts of Google (GOOG), you'll see how we identified a reverse head and shoulders and two bull flags that were wonderfully tradable and which I alerted my students to in advance.

Figure 1.33 shows the first bull flag forming just below $485 in the context of a reverse head and shoulders. If the flag breaks out to the upside, we'll be in the trade.

As you can see, the setup is obvious. When you see the corresponding OVI in Chapter 2 you'll be even more enthused.

In Figure 1.34 you can see the explosive breakout from this bull flag with the result that the stock rests just below $520 and forms a second bull flag just above the reverse head and shoulders neckline.

So we're now sitting on a $20 profit per share—pretty good for just a few days—and we have a second bull flag setting up, the difference being that this time the new bull flag is forming above the reverse head and shoulders neckline. This, too, was one of the easiest trades you could ever spot (see Figure 1.35).

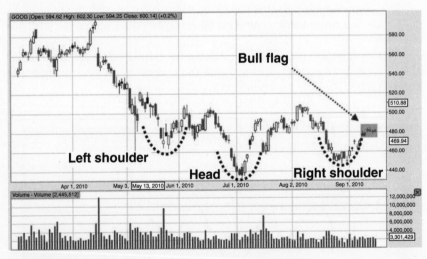

FIGURE 1.33   GOOG Reverse Head and Shoulders Setup 1
Source: OVI Charts. Courtesy of FlagTrader.com. Go to www.theinsideredge.com for more information.

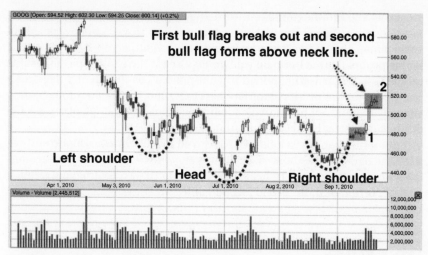

FIGURE 1.34 GOOG Reverse Head and Shoulders Setup 2
Source: OVI Charts. Courtesy of FlagTrader.com. Go to www.theinsideredge.com for more information.

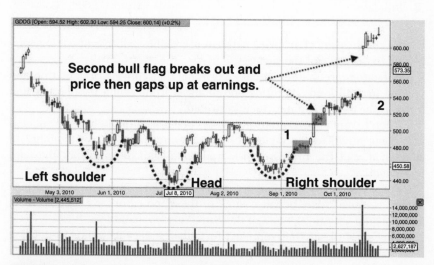

FIGURE 1.35 GOOG Reverse Head and Shoulders Breakout
Source: OVI Charts. Courtesy of FlagTrader.com. Go to www.theinsideredge.com for more information.

From the first flag breakout to earnings was a $60 move up. At earnings Google (GOOG) gapped up a further $60! Now, earnings is a sensitive area, and in reality you would not be sitting on $120 worth of points-profits. This is because you would already have taken partial profits on the first flag breakout, added to your position as the second flag broke out, taken partial profits again pre-earnings, and would therefore be in a virtually bulletproof position as at earnings, having taken plenty of profits off the table.

For a number of reasons GOOG looked like a fantastic opportunity at this time and this was borne out. However, you would not bet on earnings (a) without sitting on very healthy profits and (b) without having taken a decent portion of those profits off the table.

INDICATORS

Technical analysis comes in two forms:

1. Chart patterns
2. Indicators

As you've seen, chart price patterns are visible patterns of what is happening to the price of the security.

Indicators are mathematical algorithms that convert price action and volume into all kinds of ratios and analysis from which it is hoped that future price movement may be interpreted.

I don't want to denigrate indictors, because ultimately your success will come down to the quality of your trading plan and your ability to stick to it. But the problem with traditional indicators is that they are so subjective.

For example, which moving average, MACD or stochastic settings should you use? Also, because most of these indicators are created from averages of past prices, most of them are *lagging* in nature.

That's not to say that you can't formulate a decent trading plan using them, but again, which settings should you use? And, surely one setting won't fit all the stocks that you want to trade.

With my OVI indicator there are no such dilemmas and the indicator is *leading*, not lagging.

So, what about the leading indicators that I ranted about earlier such as Fibonacci, Elliott Wave, and Gann? Well my rant was mainly about the fact that these methods can seriously affect your trading psychology and trading plan because of their propensity to encourage magical thinking on behalf of the trader.

The notion that the markets are preordained isn't necessarily magical thinking in itself, depending on your beliefs. But the notion that you can tap into this force and foretell the markets' precise turning points would most definitely be magical thinking! The fact that fans of these methods can never agree on the numbers, combined with my own misadventures with them, is enough for me to largely discard those methods (just in case you hadn't noticed from my rant earlier!).

Moving Averages, MACD, Stochastics

There is so much information available for these lagging indicators that it would only be worth detailing them here if we were going to construct a trading plan from them, or if I felt the need to make a nuclear-style warning about them!

Instead I'll just summarize what they're all about.

Moving Averages   Moving averages are the most widely recognized and simplest of technical indicators. A moving average is simply a line that depicts the average closing price of a sequence of bars on a price chart. For example, on a daily chart, a 200-period moving average is the average of the last 200 days' closing prices.

The important moving averages are considered to constitute important levels of support and resistance. In this regard the 200-day and 50-day moving averages would be the most important to consider.

In terms of their constitution, as we look at today's chart before the close, today's moving average figure includes what happened yesterday but not today. Similarly, before tomorrow's close, tomorrow's moving average figure will include what happened today but not tomorrow.

Moving averages are considered useful for the way in which they smooth price action and eliminate outlier price bars, more commonly known as "noise."

Another popular use of moving averages is to deploy two different moving average lines on a chart and use their crossovers as trading signals. The idea is that when the shorter (50-day) moving average crosses through the longer (200-day) moving average, this produces a signal. Where the faster line crosses up through the slower line is considered bullish; where the faster (50-day) line crosses down through the slower (200-day) line is considered bearish.

One major weakness with moving averages is that they only really work with prices that are trending up or down. Where a stock is oscillating sideways for months, you'll find arbitrary crossovers that make no sense. Also, where a stock trends in a parabolic fashion, the moving averages cannot get near the stock and could leave you with a dangerously distant stop placement.

I tend to have a 200-day moving average on my charts and that's about it.

MACD   Moving average convergence-divergence (MACD) is a moving average of the difference between two moving averages. As such, it is a measure of momentum in the price movement.[4] As the moving averages move further apart, this is a sign of increasing momentum. Since MACD depicts the relationship of two moving averages, it can be used as either a trend indicator or a measure of whether the price is overbought/oversold.

MACD can be drawn as lines or as a histogram under a price chart, and can be interpreted in several ways.

The conundrum with MACD is which settings to use. However, there are decent trading plans that can include MACD parameters. For our purposes in this book we don't need to go through them, as we don't use MACD in our trading plan.

Stochastics   A stochastic is an oscillator that is used to determine whether a market is overbought or oversold. As with most technical indicators, it works best in conjunction with other indicators and chart patterns.

Stochastics measure the relationship of a sequence of closing prices with their highs and lows. It consists of two lines, %K and %D, and ranges between 0 percent and 100 percent. A reading of 0 percent shows that the close was the lowest price that it has traded during the preceding specified time periods. A reading of 100 percent shows that the close was the highest price that the security has traded during the preceding specified periods.

Aside from determining which settings to use and how to use the lines, the main problem with stochastics is that often an overbought/oversold stochastic reading may have you exiting a trend that still has a long way to run. When stocks trend for a while, the stochastics will have the appearance of being overbought or oversold, depending on the direction of the trend.

Again, for our purposes in this book we don't need to go through stochastics in detail, as we don't use them in our trading plan.

---

[4]Gerald Appel, *The Moving Average Convergence-Divergence Method.* (Signalert, 1979).

Relative Strength Index (RSI)   The relative strength index (RSI)[5] is a measure for overbought/oversold analysis. Using a horizontal 50 percent midline most followers of RSI take a buy signal above the midline and a sell signal below the midline.

The RSI measures the internal strength of a single security and does not compare the relative strength of two securities.[6] It is a price-following oscillator that ranges between 0 and 100. A popular method of analyzing the RSI is to look for a divergence where the security itself is making a new high, but the RSI is failing to exceed its own previous high, and vice versa. A divergence is interpreted as an indication of a likely reversal.

It is thought that the RSI forms chart patterns in itself that may not actually be visible on the price chart. Such patterns would include support, resistance, head and shoulders, and flags.

My main use for RSI has been to determine if a stock is trending over specific time periods.

The weakness with RSI is that, because it has a minimum and maximum, extreme levels imply the imminent end of a trend that may, in fact, have much longer to run. For example, when the RSI reading is 10, the indicator only has only 10 more points to fall, whereas the market may have a lot further to fall in relative terms. The same applies for a strong uptrend where the RSI is in the 90s (suggesting an imminent end of the move) but the uptrend keeps going.

LEARNING POINTS

For me the best indicator for price action is price itself. Therefore I focus predominantly on price patterns and the key support and resistance levels.

Volume is also important, as it demonstrates the appetite of investors for a price breakout. As the price starts to move decisively either up or down, increasing volume suggests conviction from investors being behind the move, and therefore a sustained move is more likely. In the context of breakouts we'll discuss volume in Chapter 3.

---

[5]See J. Welles Wilder Jr., *New Concepts in Technical Trading Systems* (Trend Research 1978).

[6]The comparison analysis tool is called the Comparative Relative Strength (or Comparative Strength), which measures one security's performance against another's. The Comparative Strength is used to compare how a stock is performing compared with its sector, an index, or another security within the same industry or sector. Comparative Strength is calculated by dividing one security's price by another's (the comparison security).

For now you have a good understanding of the patterns that will form our bread and butter, and therefore the ones we're going to focus on:

- Support and resistance
- Flags and consolidations

The idea is that we trade breakouts from these patterns. If there's no breakout, we can't lose money because our trades are only triggered upon the breakout occurring.

In Chapter 2 we're going to add a touch of magic to all this in the form of the OVI. In the context of breakout trading, the OVI can be seen to be a *leading* indicator, as well as an uncanny indicator of potential informed trading activity.

CHAPTER 2

The OVI: Guide to the Insiders

Introduction to the OVI

The OVI is a technical indicator that I created a few years ago. Effectively it was 10 years in the making owing to techniques I was experimenting with. These techniques involved the merging of traditional chart pattern analysis with options transaction data. Do not worry: You do not need to know anything about options trading per se. Just understand that many intelligent and "informed" investors gravitate to the options market for increased discretion and leverage.

T rading just the chart patterns themselves is very powerful. This is why that was covered in Chapter 1. The pattern always comes first. With a properly constructed trading plan (which we'll cover in Chapters 3 and 4), you're very well set whether you choose to make the OVI part of your trading life or not. However, the OVI will undoubtedly give you a significant edge.

In the Introduction you saw several examples of the OVI being uncannily prescient with numerous stocks, including the famous example of Bear Stearns. Used correctly, the OVI is an amazing tool that we add to the already-excellent strategy of trading flags and breakouts. For many traders, the OVI has become almost addictive, as they trade only the most obvious opportunities as and when they present themselves. This is a perfectly acceptable way to trade and tends to result in trades nearly every week. Some people like more action, which is fine, but when you're being less selective your results are likely to be more erratic.

The OVI originated when I was quizzed by a client who was desperate to know how I kept spotting stocks that looked very likely to make a breakout. The technical analysis part was easy to explain, and we covered that in Chapter 1.

The more intriguing part was what I told him about the options element. Basically I was observing options transactions on certain stocks that were either approaching a support or resistance point, or forming a consolidating chart pattern like a flag. By observing increasing activity in the options volume and open interest, and combining it with the chart pattern, I was able to have an almost uncanny ability to pick which stocks were more likely to break out in the direction of the trend.

If they didn't break out, I wouldn't be in the trade anyway, and the observations on options activities had a direct impact on my batting average. What I was looking at was the options chain for a particular stock (see Figure 2.1). If you've ever seen one of these (and you don't have to in order to use the OVI) it looks a bit like something from *The Matrix* movies: lots of numbers in grids, rows, and columns. To the untrained eye, it would look like gobbledygook. To the trained eye, it would have some useful information. To the expert eye, it could contain a treasure chest of information.

Options Symbols Explained

Here's a quick review on options symbols. If you don't trade options you really don't need to know this.

Each option has its own ticker symbol, which contains information pertaining to the stock, the expiration, whether the option is a call or a put, and the strike price.

Looking at Figure 2.1, the calls are on the left half of the screenshot and the puts are on the right. Take the first symbol we can see at the top left of the screenshot.

GS120121C00045000

The constituent parts of the symbol are as follows:

Stock	Expiration Year	Expiration Month	Expiration Day	Call/Put	Strike Price
GS	12	01	21	C	00045000
Goldman Sachs	2012	January	21st	Call	45

So the top-left option is a Goldman Sachs January 2012 call that expires on the third Friday—the 21st of January.

The equivalent put option would be identical except the "C" would be replaced by a "P."

GS120121P00045000

When I tried to explain what I was looking at, my student went blank. Being a visual type, I went on to explain that, in my mind, I would visualize that these grids of numbers were transformed into a single line that goes up and down.

Even as I said those words a thought popped into my head: Why not *create* a line that goes up and down?

And that was the genesis of the OVI.

Effectively, this (Figure 2.1):

The Goldman Sachs Group, Inc. (GS)
On Oct 26: **115.86** ↑0.95 (0.83%)

Options

View By Expiration: Nov 11|Dec 11|**Jan 12**|Apr 12|Jan 13|Jan 14
Options Expiring Friday, January 20, 2012

Calls Symbol	Last	Change	Bid	Ask	Volume	Open Int	Strike Price	Puts Symbol	Last	Change	Bid	Ask	Volume	Open Int
GS120121C00045000	N/A	0.00	69.20	72.70	0	0	45.00	GS120121P00045000	0.19	↓0.02	0.18	0.21	41	667
GS120121C00050000	N/A	0.00	64.35	67.75	0	0	50.00	GS120121P00050000	0.32	↓0.01	0.28	0.33	200	1,846
GS120121C00055000	N/A	0.00	59.35	62.80	0	0	55.00	GS120121P00055000	0.39	↑0.07	0.39	0.42	213	2,019
GS120121C00060000	37.75	0.00	54.40	57.90	0	22	60.00	GS120121P00060000	0.47	0.00	0.44	0.50	1	8,060
GS120121C00065000	39.82	0.00	50.05	53.20	0	22	65.00	GS120121P00065000	0.61	↓0.02	0.55	0.63	64	6,369
GS120121C00070000	33.40	0.00	45.10	48.20	0	94	70.00	GS120121P00070000	0.84	↑0.08	0.69	0.78	4	5,999
GS120121C00075000	42.85	0.00	41.35	42.30	3	147	75.00	GS120121P00075000	0.93	↑0.05	0.85	0.95	26	6,916
GS120121C00080000	36.50	↓1.50	36.40	37.10	6	246	80.00	GS120121P00080000	1.17	↑0.03	1.08	1.20	305	8,405
GS120121C00085000	33.50	↑1.00	31.75	32.90	12	353	85.00	GS120121P00085000	1.52	↑0.02	1.43	1.55	123	12,650
GS120121C00090000	27.40	↑0.20	27.15	28.25	20	805	90.00	GS120121P00090000	1.99	↑0.02	1.92	2.02	111	8,403
GS120121C00095000	23.00	↑0.40	23.05	23.40	4	840	95.00	GS120121P00095000	2.65	↑0.13	2.55	2.67	324	7,806
GS120121C00100000	18.80	↓0.28	18.70	19.55	135	2,529	100.00	GS120121P00100000	3.45	↓0.02	3.35	3.50	222	8,901
GS120121C00105000	15.05	↑0.45	15.10	15.30	102	3,114	105.00	GS120121P00105000	4.70	↑0.05	4.45	4.60	240	3,116
GS120121C00110000	11.60	↑0.25	11.60	11.75	125	4,565	110.00	GS120121P00110000	6.10	↓0.10	5.85	6.10	54	10,317
GS120121C00115000	8.55	↓0.30	8.55	8.75	1,048	3,093	115.00	GS120121P00115000	7.90	↑0.55	7.90	8.10	133	9,116
GS120121C00120000	6.40	↑0.35	6.10	6.25	635	6,891	120.00	GS120121P00120000	10.30	↑0.30	10.45	10.65	85	9,997
GS120121C00125000	4.15	↑0.05	4.15	4.30	242	3,948	125.00	GS120121P00125000	13.80	↑0.20	13.45	13.70	39	6,109
GS120121C00130000	2.83	↓0.07	2.77	2.83	598	6,608	130.00	GS120121P00130000	16.42	↑0.42	16.60	17.30	3	9,411
GS120121C00135000	1.90	↑0.03	1.80	1.90	259	3,848	135.00	GS120121P00135000	21.45	↑0.70	20.45	21.40	18	8,577
GS120121C00140000	1.17	↑0.07	1.15	1.22	445	9,235	140.00	GS120121P00140000	25.75	↑0.05	25.25	25.70	11	9,346
GS120121C00145000	0.66	↓0.09	0.72	0.80	34	5,802	145.00	GS120121P00145000	30.85	0.00	29.45	30.40	56	5,673
GS120121C00150000	0.47	↓0.03	0.44	0.50	574	10,012	150.00	GS120121P00150000	34.00	↓0.10	34.15	35.50	1	6,453
GS120121C00155000	0.29	↑0.05	0.26	0.32	67	14,530	155.00	GS120121P00155000	39.24	↓1.36	39.10	40.00	5	4,972
GS120121C00160000	0.20	↓0.02	0.16	0.27	76	8,600	160.00	GS120121P00160000	57.38	0.00	44.00	44.90	10	3,523
GS120121C00165000	0.13	↓0.03	0.12	0.20	11	5,665	165.00	GS120121P00165000	61.55	0.00	48.80	49.80	1	3,533
GS120121C00170000	0.14	↑0.01	0.05	0.15	55	7,197	170.00	GS120121P00170000	66.80	0.00	52.80	55.10	4	2,464
GS120121C00175000	0.09	↑0.01	0.07	0.14	10	4,761	175.00	GS120121P00175000	58.50	0.00	58.80	60.05	11	1,171
GS120121C00180000	0.05	0.05	0.05	0.13	1	6,658	180.00	GS120121P00180000	64.14	↓15.97	62.65	65.80	2	411
GS120121C00185000	0.06	0.04	0.04	0.16	0	3,299	185.00	GS120121P00185000	69.00	0.00	67.75	70.20	10	309

FIGURE 2.1 Option Chain

Became this (Figure 2.2):

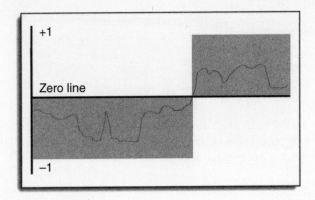

FIGURE 2.2 OVI Simple Line

It's crucial that you appreciate that we only use the OVI together with our favored chart patterns, the flag, consolidations, and channel breakouts through support and resistance. In this way, the OVI effectively becomes a leading indicator.

Inevitably I'm going to have to explain *something* about options at some stage in this book. Before I do, I want to ensure you appreciate how easy the OVI is to use.

Take a look at Figure 2.3. The OVI is the thicker and more jagged of the two lines displayed below the blanked-out SPY (S&P 500 Exchange Traded Fund) price chart. (The smoother line is a moving average of the OVI, which we don't tend to use.)

As you can see, running from left to right, for the first two thirds the OVI is negative, and for the last third of the chart the OVI turns positive.

Without knowing anything about what's inside the OVI, take a guess at the general direction of the S&P (or SPY) just by looking at the OVI:

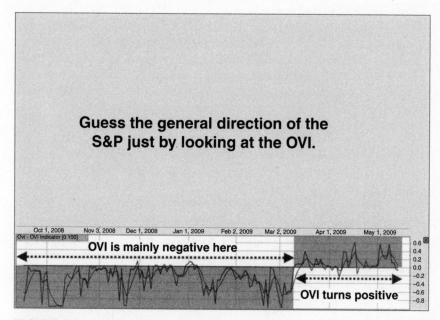

FIGURE 2.3   SPY Blank Chart with OVI
Source: OVI Charts. Courtesy of FlagTrader.com. Go to www.theinsideredge.com for more information.

Logically you might surmise that in the first two thirds of the chart the SPY is likely to be in a downtrend, and in the last third of the chart it's more likely to be in an uptrend. Did you guess that?

Here's the answer in Figure 2.4:

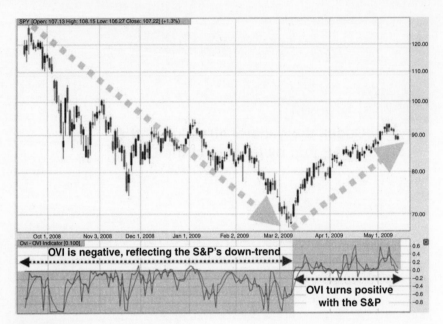

FIGURE 2.4   SPY Chart with OVI
Source: OVI Charts. Courtesy of FlagTrader.com. Go to www.theinsideredge.com for more information.

In the first two thirds of the chart, the OVI is persistently negative, so it's no surprise that the S&P was trending downward during that period of time. When the trend reverses, the OVI reacts instantly and turns positive.

When markets trend like this, they give us opportunities to enter trades on breaks of support and resistance, and they also give us opportunities to take profits.

The idea is to trade in the direction of the dominant trend upon the breakout of support (if the market is trending down) or resistance (if the market is trending up).

Now that you can see how easy it is to interpret the OVI, we must briefly mention *what* it is, along with a quick introduction to options. This will help you appreciate why the OVI is such a useful indicator when it's appropriate to use it.

The extraordinary thing about what you've just seen is that the OVI has nothing to do with the price chart, and yet the correlation between the two is there for all to see.

It means that there is a very definite link between the activities of options traders and the overall direction of the market. Furthermore, that link is almost immediate—it does not lag—and can therefore be very powerful if used in the right context with the right trading plan. As good as it is, the indicator is not good enough just on its own. For me, that has to be the case for any indicator, as price pattern is always paramount.

WHAT IS THE OVI?

As mentioned in the Introduction, the OVI measures options transactions data for any individual stock that is optionable, and then plots it as a line that oscillates between −1 and +1. In the middle of this range is the horizontal zero line.

Essentially the OVI is an algorithm that measures the buying and the selling of share options and simplifies it into that line. Now, when you consider that a stock like Apple (AAPL) has around 1,000 individual options, that's a lot of simplification to make all of those into just one line that oscillates between −1 and +1. Consider that my database contains hundreds of millions of rows of data that are analyzed every night, and at the end of the process is that simple line!

To be fair, not all of the options for one stock are going to be relevant to the sentiment of investors toward the stock in question, so the art is to know which options are relevant for each stock. This is part of the secret sauce.

In order to explain this more, you have to know a few options definitions.

Options 101

An option is defined as the *right, not the obligation, to buy or sell an asset at a certain price before a predetermined date.* This definition gives us a lot of the information we need to understand the very basics of options.

- *The right, not the obligation*

    Buying an option conveys the right, not the obligation, to buy (in the case of calls) or sell (in the case of puts) an underlying asset—in this case, shares. When you buy an option you are not obligated to do anything, and your maximum risk is simply your investment.

    If buying gives you the "right, not the obligation," then logic dictates that selling (naked) may convey an obligation. Selling naked means when you've sold something you don't actually own (i.e., short) and have no other position to cover you from a potentially unlimited loss. Selling naked therefore imposes a potential obligation and unlimited loss if it goes wrong. Done correctly, this will rarely happen, but nevertheless shorting options should be only for experienced traders.

- *To buy or sell an asset*
  Calls:
  - A call is an option that conveys the right to buy. Therefore when we buy a call we're paying a premium that gives us the right to buy stock at a fixed (strike) price before a predetermined (expiration) date.
  - Buying a call is bullish because if the stock rises, so will the intrinsic value of the call.
  - Selling a call (naked) is neutral to bearish, depending on what strike you sell.

  Puts:
  - A put is an option that conveys the right to sell. Therefore when we buy a put, we're paying a premium that gives us the right to sell stock at a fixed (strike) price before a predetermined (expiration) date.
  - Buying a put is bearish because if the stock falls, the intrinsic value of the put will rise.
  - Selling a put (naked) is neutral to bullish, depending on what strike you sell.

  So, as you can see, the buyer and the seller have exact opposite risk profiles, which is completely logical.

- *At a certain price*

  The strike (or exercise) price is the fixed price at which the option can be exercised. The strike price is not the premium you pay (or receive) for the option.
  - If you buy a 40 strike call option, then you have right to buy the stock at $40. In practice, you would only want to exercise that right if the stock is trading at more than $40 in the market.
  - If you buy a 40 strike put option, then you have the right to sell the stock at $40. In practice, you would only want to exercise that right if the stock is trading at less than $40 in the market.

- *Before a predetermined date*

  This is the date before which the option can be exercised.
  - At expiration, the call value is only worth the stock price less the strike price. This is known as the *intrinsic value* of the call.
  - At expiration, the put value is only worth the strike price less the stock price. This is known as the *intrinsic value* of the put.

  Traditionally, U.S. equity options expiration dates fell on the Saturday after the third Friday of every month—effectively after the Friday close.

However, some larger stocks now have weekly options, though these are far less liquid.

So, for our purposes, we're still focused on the options expiring on the third Friday.

Why the OVI Works

In the Introduction I made the case that "informed" investors may actively trade options in order to accumulate large positions quickly and discreetly.

Remember the "insider's rationale":

- Keep your trades **discreet** so you can
- **Accumulate** your position without affecting the share price, and use
- **Leverage** in order to get as much as you can as soon as possible!

Informed stock traders can only achieve all these aims in the options market. The OVI is tracking the options transactions, and when we align that with our favored chart patterns, we give ourselves a distinct edge.

When big players like institutions (or informed investors) take a position in a stock, because of the sheer size of the commitment they want to make, it can take them days or weeks to build up a position (long or short) because they're trading in terms of millions of dollars.

Sometimes they need to accelerate this process, and this can be achieved in the derivatives market by way of buying or selling call and put options.

What Goes into the OVI   In terms of what goes into the OVI, a bit like the Chicago Board Options Exchange's Volatility Index (CBOE VIX), it's been an evolving formula. Essentially there are three components that may indicate whether the big, savvy, smart, or informed investors are bullish or bearish toward a particular stock:

1. Option volume
2. Open interest
3. Implied volatility

I'll explain each one of these briefly and in laymen's terms, but, whatever happens, do not be scared by the word options!

Option Volume   This is defined as the number of option contracts that are traded in a day. U.S. equity options are traded in lots of 100. This means that each contract represents 100 shares. Therefore when you see your broker quote a price of 5.30 for an option, the actual cash price is 5.30 × 100 = $530 per contract.

Open Interest   Not to be confused with volume, open interest depicts the number of options contracts that are not closed or delivered/exercised on a particular day.

To distinguish between volume and open interest, it helps to have an example.

In an option chain, the options are identified by type (call or put), strike, and expiration. So each option has a unique strike/expiration combination. In this example, let's say we're dealing with a company called ACME's January (2013) 50 strike calls. In such an example the option symbol would be:

ACME130119C00050000

All transactions in Table 2.1 are for this particular option. Remember that volume is reset every day, whereas open interest is cumulative both up and down.

- On Day 1, Mr. Smith buys two contracts, which creates 2 in the volume column and creates two open interest, so 2 goes into the open interest column.
- On Day 2, Mrs. Green buys three contracts, which creates 3 in the volume column, and because 3 more contracts are open, 3 is added to the 2 from Day 1, making 5 open interest.
- On Day 3, Mr. Smith sells his two contracts, and Mr. Black buys back two of his contracts (effectively closing out 2 of his open contracts). This transaction creates volume of 2 and −2 open interest, which we net off Day 2's figure, taking open interest down to 3.

TABLE 2.1   Open Interest vs. Volume

Day	Activity	Volume	Open Interest
Day 1	Mr. Smith buys 2 contracts from Miss Jones	2	2
Day 2	Mrs. Green buys 3 contracts and Mr. Black sells 3 contracts	3	5
Day 3	Mr. Smith sells his 2 contracts and Mr. Black buys back 2 contracts	2	3
Day 4	Miss Brown buys 3 contracts from Mrs. Green	3	3

- On Day 4, Miss Brown buys three contracts from Mrs. Green, who closes out her trade. In this transaction, volume is 3 but open interest is unchanged. This is because Miss Brown's acquisition raises open interest by 3, but Mrs. Green's closing out of her three contracts reduces open interest by 3. The net-net for the day is zero, hence open interest remains at 3 from the day before.

Open interest is calculated daily and, being one of the components of the OVI, it means that the OVI is calculated on an end-of-day basis.

Implied Volatility   In the simplest terms, implied volatility is a measure of an option's expense. Option premiums are made up from intrinsic value and time value.

- We know that the intrinsic value for calls is the stock price minus the strike price.
- We know that the intrinsic value for puts is the strike price minus the stock price.
- We also know that the option premium is made up from intrinsic value and time value. At expiration there is only intrinsic value left. Intrinsic value cannot be manipulated as such.
- Time value is fuzzier in terms of its composition. The formula involves several factors. However, in practice much of it will depend on the floor specialist's perception of risk.

   Ultimately the floor specialist sells options to other traders. We already know that the option seller may be exposed to unlimited risk. Therefore when stock prices are volatile and unpredictable, the specialist will raise the price of the option premiums to compensate for the higher perceived risk. When stocks settle down and are more predictable, option premiums will be lowered.

With options there are seven core factors that affect the premium:

(i) The type of option (call or put)

(ii) The underlying stock price

(iii) Strike price

(iv) Time to expiration

(v) The risk-free interest rate

(vi) Dividends and stock splits

(vii) Volatility

The first six factors are known with certainty. The volatility element of the option premium has to be calculated in reverse with the hindsight that we already know the option premium being quoted. The resulting figure (or missing link) is known as "implied volatility" and only affects the time value portion of the premium. Implied volatility is distinct from the volatility figure of the stock price, which is known as "historical volatility."

Implied volatility therefore gives us a measure of how the specialists are pricing option premiums. If they're sensing danger or uncertainty, option premiums will rise, and vice versa. Therefore implied volatility may also give us a clue as to how savvy investors are viewing a particular stock.

Which Options Are Relevant for the OVI   Obviously this is part of the secret sauce of the OVI. Like the VIX, certain elements will be dynamic. Suffice it to say that some options are more relevant than others for our purposes and will therefore be weighted differently.

Typically, the biggest concentration of options trading activity occurs near the money—in other words, at the strike prices that are nearby the current stock price.

If you've traded options you may have noticed that the nearer out-of-the-money strikes generally have greater trading activity than the nearer in-the-money options. Why is this so? The reason is because there is also a lot of selling volume as well as buying volume at the nearer out-of-the-money strike prices. (*Out-of-the-money for puts is the lower strike, and out-of-the-money for calls is the higher strike.*)

As you've seen already, the OVI is closely correlated with medium-term trending price-action as it tends to be roughly in line with the major trend of the markets. The OVI is especially useful in sideways markets where it can often indicate the most probable direction of the breakout.

With choppy markets the OVI may be choppy as well, in which case we wait until we can get a clear indication.

WHEN TO USE THE OVI AND WHEN NOT TO USE IT

The OVI is not always going to be "readable," and the reality is that only the stocks with the most liquid and actively traded options are suitable for our trading purposes. Sometimes stocks come into and fall out of OVI fashion; a flurry of activity may be followed by relative inactivity. This is actually an advantage because you're going to be able to recognize immediately when a stock's OVI is relevant or not to your analysis.

The other factor is one you'll read, see, and hear from me over and over again like a mantra: We only use the OVI in conjunction with a tradable chart pattern. In our case it's flags, channels, and potential breakouts from support and resistance. The OVI will often reveal the likely direction of the breakout before the breakout materializes. Our trading plan involves placing a stop-limit order so that the trade is only triggered when the stock has broken out.

In this way the OVI can be seen as being a leading indicator, as described in Chapter 1. It is based on the latest daily data and not a sequence of past averaged data. This is another factor that distinguishes the OVI from traditional stock-based indicators like moving averages, MACD, and stochastics. Also, the OVI is not actually based on the stock, but rather the options transactions for the stock.

OVI Qualifying Stocks

Only stocks that have options can have an OVI reading for obvious reasons. Beyond that, these options must be liquid. In other words, there must be consistent and regular transaction activity together with a decent volume traded every day. This will translate itself into an OVI that is responsive and wiggles almost every day. This is what we want to see.

By definition, a stock with ample options liquidity will tend to be a big stock with actively traded shares as well.

In Figure 2.5 you can see that the OVI is responsive and moves virtually every day. There is not a prolonged series of days where the OVI is completely flat horizontal. Even during the time where it is relatively flat from mid-August to the end of September, it is still wiggling most days. It also

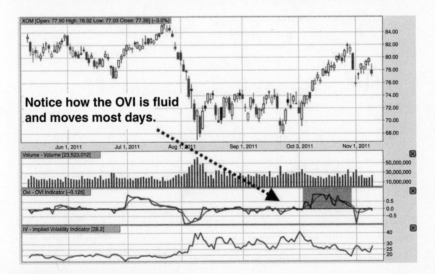

FIGURE 2.5 A Qualifying OVI
Source: OVI Charts. Courtesy of FlagTrader.com. Go to www.theinsideredge.com for more information.

helps that this is a chart of Exxon Mobil (XOM), which we know is very actively traded.

Notice also how the OVI breaks into positive territory at the beginning of October just before the stock break out of its two-month resistance. The OVI went positive a few days beforehand as the stock was drifting upward but before it actually broke out through $75.00.

When the OVI Is Unreadable

Sometimes a stock will have a reasonably responsive OVI, then for no apparent reason the options transactions dry up and the OVI will go horizontal along its zero line. In such cases you can easily see there is no OVI reading of note, so you move onto a stock that does have a responsive OVI.

In Figure 2.6, the stock (Iron Mountain Inc; IRM) has times where the OVI has been responsive and worked a treat followed by periods where it flatlines along its neutral line.

Some stocks have such thinly traded options that they'll never truly qualify for a decent OVI reading. These OVI readings are easy to spot, as they perennially hug the neutral line or go from one extreme to another with very little in the way of "wiggling" in between (see Figure 2.7).

Some stocks have OVIs that are mainly horizontal but swing from one extreme to another (see Figure 2.8).

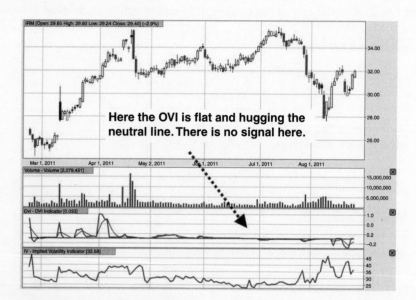

FIGURE 2.6 A Non-Qualifying OVI
Source: OVI Charts. Courtesy of FlagTrader.com. Go to www.theinsideredge.com for more information.

FIGURE 2.7 Persistently Flat OVI
Source: OVI Charts. Courtesy of FlagTrader.com. Go to www.theinsideredge.com for
more information.

FIGURE 2.8 Horizontal OVI
Source: OVI Charts. Courtesy of FlagTrader.com. Go to www.theinsideredge.com for
more information.

The OVI with Indices and ETFs

In general, we focus our OVI attention on liquid stocks that have liquid options. The rationale for focusing on stocks is that we're looking to identify stocks where there has been some "informed" trading activity in the options that hasn't yet filtered through to the stock price. The hope is that we will be able to spot those stocks that look most likely to break out from their trading range and that have correlating responsive OVI readings.

With this in mind, is it possible that the OVI could work with indices and exchange-traded funds (ETFs)? After all, how can one have information regarding an index or basket of securities? With certain ETFs, the OVI can work rather well. How is this? I can only surmise that in-the-know traders know about a lot of things. My reasoning is that (a) the OVI often works so well with the indices, and (b) in February 2008 I was told specifically to watch out for a stock market collapse in the late summer of that year. And we all know what happened in the late summer/early fall of 2008!

So yes, the OVI can work rather will with certain ETFs, albeit with caveats.

The main indices we follow are the S&P 500, the Dow Jones Industrial Average, and the Nasdaq Composite.

In the OVI world, we track the three corresponding ETFs for these indices, namely the SPY, the DIA, and the QQQ.

An ETF is an investment fund traded just like a stock on a stock exchange. For our purposes, the ETF is just like a stock, and we're only interested in the ones that are optionable. An ETF holds assets like stocks, commodities, or bonds, and trades close to its net asset value during the course of traded hours. Many ETFs track an index and will do so with such high correlation that it's the equivalent of trading the index itself, but in the guise of a stock.

The other main ETFs I like to track are GLD and SLV for gold and silver, respectively. Like the indices, these ETFs have reasonably readable OVIs for much of the time.

In terms of the indices, I've found that the SPY and QQQ are more useful than the DIA, which seems to have a bullish bias. It should also be emphasized that the OVI works best when the markets are either trending or are on the point of breaking out of a range and about to start a new trend.

In Figures 2.3 and 2.4 we saw how well the OVI correlated with the SPY chart, which was trending down and then up in 2008–2009.

There are many examples of the OVI working in conjunction with breakout patterns. Some are more obvious than others, but it's critical to display the opportunities that you could spot with the minimum of training.

As part of the bonuses that come with this book, there are video tutorials on the www.theinsideredge.com web site. This will help bring the OVI to life for you, as well as allow you to view the OVI charts for the main indices as well.

Let's take a look at a few charts of the indices to see the more obvious opportunities.

From May 2011 onward, the OVI for the SPY remained negative nearly all the way until mid-October 2011. The scene was set from May onward as the S&P started a downward descent, giving us opportunities to profit from downward breakouts.

In Figure 2.9, we can see the OVI has been predominantly negative for a few weeks after the high formed in May.

Two immediately obvious breakout points are shown by the dotted lines 1 and 2. Both lines are support. Both are eligible, though 1 is weaker than 2. As such, 1 is more likely to be broken, though at the same time it is also more likely to be hit on a snapback, too.

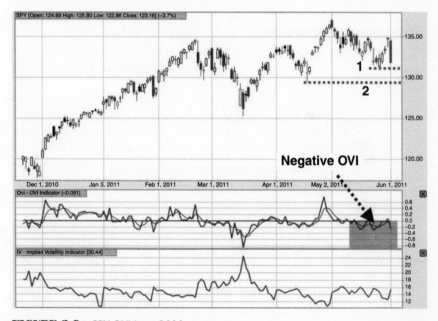

FIGURE 2.9 SPY OVI June 2011
Source: OVI Charts. Courtesy of FlagTrader.com. Go to www.theinsideredge.com for more information.

As you can see in Figure 2.10, the SPY broke through both supports and gave a decent trade on both, with minimal drawdown.

From here the SPY recovered toward the end of June 2011, before starting to wobble again in July.

Figure 2.11 is even more obvious than the June 2011 chart shown in Figure 2.10. We can see that volatility is increasing (see below the OVI), indicating that premiums for the SPY options are rising. We now have a support line at just below 130, with an OVI that is negative and that has only fleetingly flirted above the zero line.

A break of the support line could yield a decent move to the downside.

Look what happens next (see Figure 2.12). The SPY breaks down through 130 and through the next support level at 126, all the way down to a low of around 110. On the main index this represented a move of 200 big points in seven days. And not for the first time, the OVI gave the trade to us in advance.

As you can see, the SPY broke through both support levels and gave a great trade on both, with minimal drawdown.

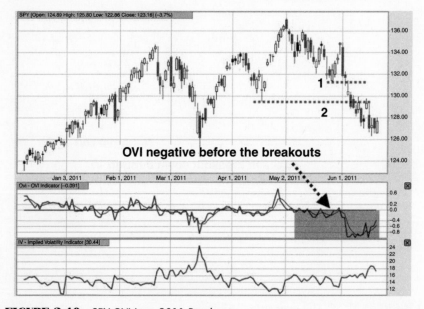

FIGURE 2.10   SPY OVI June 2011 Breakout
Source: OVI Charts. Courtesy of FlagTrader.com. Go to www.theinsideredge.com for more information.

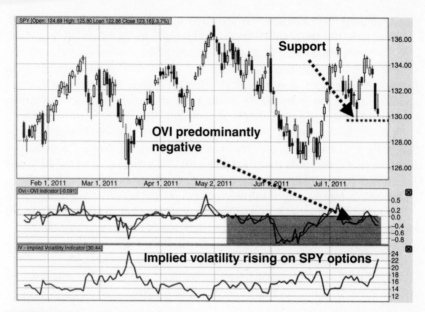

FIGURE 2.11   SPY OVI July 2011
Source: OVI Charts. Courtesy of FlagTrader.com. Go to www.theinsideredge.com for more information.

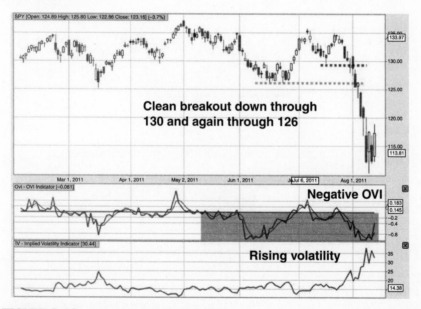

FIGURE 2.12   SPY OVI July 2011 Breakout
Source: OVI Charts. Courtesy of FlagTrader.com. Go to www.theinsideredge.com for more information.

The OVI and Divergence   In the next three charts (Figures 2.13–2.15) I'll show how the QQQ's ETF was at odds with those of the SPY and the DIA, yet how it ultimately was signaling a reversal.

Figure 2.13 shows the QQQ at the top of the market on April 26, 2010 (in the Introduction I showed you the SPY on this date). On this very day I e-mailed my private subscribers to tell them of impending volatility and a downturn I was concerned about.

The OVI hasn't quite turned negative; however, it's not blisteringly positive, either. Considering this was the market high following a good run since February, and also that the QQQ's OVI was divergent to the SPY and DIA OVIs, I found this to be intriguing, particularly as the QQQ had previously been rather prescient in December 2009 and again in January 2010.

At point 1 in Figure 2.13, the OVI is positive and the stock breaks up out of its sideways channel through resistance as you would expect.

At point 2, the OVI has turned negative and the stock breaks down from its sideways channel through support, again as you would expect.

At point 3, the OVI is negative while the QQQ is rising. This was unusual and divergent to the OVIs for the SPY and DIA at the time.

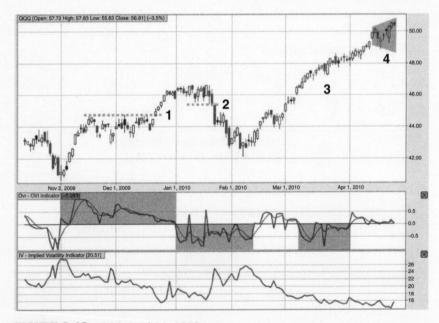

FIGURE 2.13   QQQ April 26, 2010
Source: OVI Charts. Courtesy of FlagTrader.com. Go to www.theinsideredge.com for more information.

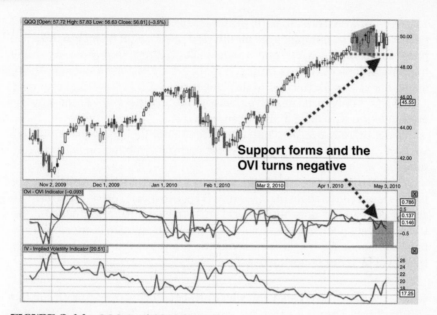

FIGURE 2.14   QQQ April 2010 Support
Source: OVI Charts. Courtesy of FlagTrader.com. Go to www.theinsideredge.com for more information.

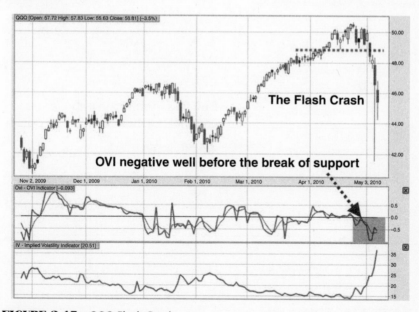

FIGURE 2.15   QQQ Flash Crash
Source: OVI Charts. Courtesy of FlagTrader.com. Go to www.theinsideredge.com for more information.

At point 4 on April 26, 2010, the OVI is drifting to neutral having turned positive at the beginning of the month. The QQQ is still rising but the price bars are becoming wider and a megaphone pattern is developing on all three main indices. It was on this date that I alerted my students. All we needed next was for the OVI to turn negative.

The OVI duly turns negative the next day and the stock forms a messy consolidation with a clear area of support.

From there it was just a matter of time until the stock broke through support. As it happened, the OVI–chart pattern combination was forerunning the "flash crash."

So, as you can see, the OVI can be used as a bellwether for the wider indices and even to trade them via the ETFs. However, I emphasize that you should stick to the most obvious and attractive opportunities that conform to our trading plan and breakout strategy. Obviously, the more stocks you have to choose from (within reason) the more you'll be able to trade, as there will be more opportunities.

GLD and SLV Even gold and silver present worthy opportunities in our OVI world. In Figure 2.16 we can see a clear bull flag for GLD, which is

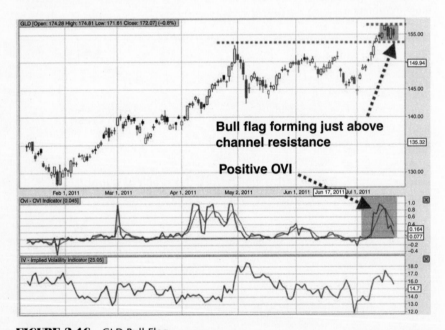

FIGURE 2.16 GLD Bull Flag
Source: OVI Charts. Courtesy of FlagTrader.com. Go to www.theinsideredge.com for more information.

forming just about a W-shaped channel breakout. The OVI is positive, and any move up beyond the bull flag high of $156.58 is likely to be accompanied by a strengthening OVI as well.

This was a no-brainer. GLD broke out of the flag and went on another run all the way to $184.82 (see Figure 2.17). The OVI stayed positive throughout the move. Remember: The OVI has nothing to do with the price chart, which makes this sort of correlation all the more remarkable. It shows that the options traders are in tune with the machinations of the markets and the underlying securities they're trading.

Of course, it must be said that the OVI doesn't always correlate like, this but it is very obvious when it both is and isn't correlating. Waiting for the most obvious opportunities is a perfectly legitimate strategy, even if it means a long wait.

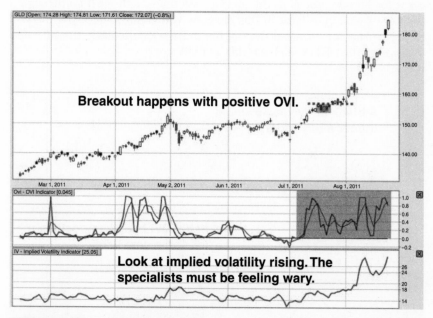

FIGURE 2.17 GLD Bull Flag Breakout
Source: OVI Charts. Courtesy of FlagTrader.com. Go to www.theinsideredge.com for more information.

Here's an obvious opportunity with SLV, which is forming a cup and handle pattern with the flag just below the December high of 30.44 (see Figure 2.18). A breakout above 30.55 would trigger a buy order here. The OVI has been positive for two weeks and this stock looks like it could go on a run if it breaks out.

In Figure 2.19, we can see the result of the breakout: a 50-percent gain in two and a half months—a massive move for a commodity ETF.

Notice how implied volatility rose sharply as SLV increased exponentially. This was a clear signal that the specialists did not have faith in the move's longevity. Indeed, when the bubble eventually burst for SLV in May and then September 2011, SLV collapsed back down to $32 and sub $28, respectively.

The OVI with Forex   We already know that the OVI can be highly relevant for certain stocks at the appropriate times, and we'll go through a number of examples later in this chapter. You can also see how the OVI can bear fruit for us when trading the indices (particularly the SPY and QQQ), and other ETFs such as GLD and SLV.

FIGURE 2.18   SLV Bull Flag
Source: OVI Charts. Courtesy of FlagTrader.com. Go to www.theinsideredge.com for more information.

FIGURE 2.19   SLV Bull Flag Breakout
Source: OVI Charts. Courtesy of FlagTrader.com. Go to www.theinsideredge.com for more information.

A question I'm often asked is whether the OVI works for Forex. Generally I'd say no to Forex with the OVI (and, besides, I'm no Forex expert). However, there are times where I've glanced at it and correctly deduced the direction of the next breakout.

It's tempting to include a few charts to illustrate this now, as long as it doesn't detract from the main use of the OVI, which is to trade stocks and a select few ETFs. The whole point of the OVI is that it gives us an edge because it follows what the savvy options traders are doing in certain stocks at certain times. With Forex no one knows with any more certainty than anyone else what is likely to happen next. There are no "insiders" per se with Forex, and the OVI is all about following informed traders and insiders.

With that understood, Figure 2.20 shows the FXE, which is the ETF of the euro/dollar. We can clearly see weakness in the euro reflected by a negative OVI reading, though, to be fair, the FXE's OVI was also rather negative in the preceding months as the euro was rallying.

However, in terms of trading the FXE, when it finally breaks down in September 2011 from its several-month range, because the OVI has already

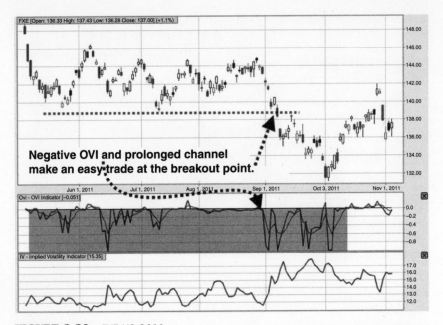

FIGURE 2.20   FXE H2 2011
Source: OVI Charts. Courtesy of FlagTrader.com. Go to www.theinsideredge.com for more information.

been negative for so long, it gives us a very easy trade on the breakdown. Remember: We don't need many of these easy trades to be successful.

The challenge is having the discipline and patience to bide our time, though that is made easier because we do have a number of stocks and ETFs to look at. This was an obvious opportunity, and it worked well, as the FXE broke down through 138 to 132 in only three weeks.

The actual breakout date was September 8, 2011. However the OVI had been negative for months already and plunged for a couple of days on September 1, 2011.

THE OVI WITH STOCKS

Now you're up to speed with how the OVI works and when to use it, it's a matter of being selective for the obvious opportunities. These will happen regularly enough to keep your attention, and you don't have to spend much time assessing each day. Much of the time it's enough to simply track just a few major stocks, which will take 10–20 minutes per day depending on how much trading there is to do.

In this section we'll go through a number of charts and see if you can spot the opportunity before we play it out. We'll start with an example we saw in Chapter 1 with Goldman Sachs (GS), which had formed a bear flag as part of a wider head and shoulders pattern in May 2011. The original chart was shown without the OVI in Figure 1.30 and was already compelling to the downside. Now let's look again, this time with the OVI in Figure 2.21.

We said before that this was a great setup without the OVI. With the OVI included the chart is even better. The OVI turned negative during the first half of April and stayed that way almost uninterrupted for over three weeks. We have a bear flag pattern forming that's highly attractive as a short if the stock can break through its support just below $150.

FIGURE 2.21 GS Head and Shoulders Setup
Source: OVI Charts. Courtesy of FlagTrader.com. Go to www.theinsideredge.com for more information.

This is exactly what happens (see Figure 2.22).

As we saw in Chapter 1, the opposite of a head and shoulders is a reverse head and shoulders. This sets the scene for a potential bullish resolution. What we like to trade, though, are flags and breakouts through support and resistance. With GS (Figure 2.22), we could trade that on a break of support. The head and shoulders set the scene for a bearish breakout and we simply had to wait for our chance to trade a bear flag or break of support.

In Figures 1.33, 1.34, and 1.35, we saw a reverse head and shoulders with Google (GOOG), which set the scene for a bullish breakout, which materialized with a bull flag.

Let's look at those GOOG charts again, but this time in the context of the OVI.

FIGURE 2.22 GS Head and Shoulders Breakout
Source: OVI Charts. Courtesy of FlagTrader.com. Go to www.theinsideredge.com for more information.

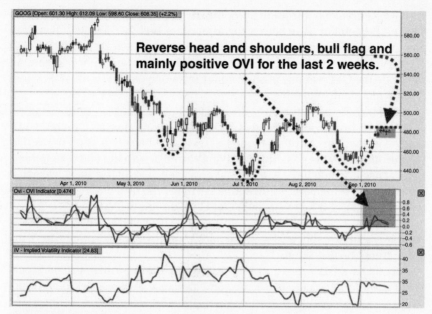

FIGURE 2.23 GOOG Reverse Head and Shoulders Setup 1
Source: OVI Charts. Courtesy of FlagTrader.com. Go to www.theinsideredge.com for more information.

As you can see in Figure 2.23, GOOG was forming a classic bull flag with a tight range, ideal for a low-risk trade. The OVI has been positive for all but one day in the last two weeks, and, although it's not the most compellingly positive OVI reading, it is a fantastic chart pattern—and remember: We only trade the breakout, anyway.

As we know already, the stock did break out to the upside and subsequently formed another bull flag in the wider context of the reverse head and shoulders and reverse cup and handle. This really is a "gimme" of an opportunity with very low risk.

GOOG breaks out from the first bull flag at $484.75 on September 17 to $520 on September 21, where it forms another bull flag. The OVI has been positive since September 3, except for just one day (see Figure 2.24).

From there GOOG duly breaks out again and soars to new highs. All the while the OVI remains positive apart from one day on October 4, where it turns marginally negative.

Earnings is on October 15. From the first bull flag up until earnings, GOOG rises by $60. At earnings GOOG gaps up another $60 though you'd only be in that part of the trade if you'd already banked a good portion of your profits and were effectively playing earnings with the market's money. In this case it would have worked out very well, and all the signs were that it would. Just remember, though, that earnings can be a bit of a gamble and typically requires a more specialist and non-directional strategy.

In Figure 2.25 you can see the entire move from start to finish, including our likely exit just above $600 in the middle of November. Notice where the rising trendline is broken.

So that's a $120 move in under two months on a high-priced stock. Putting it into perspective, it's the same percentage as a stock rising from

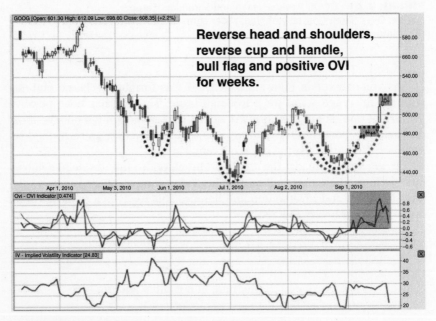

FIGURE 2.24   GOOG Reverse Head and Shoulders Setup 2
Source: OVI Charts. Courtesy of FlagTrader.com. Go to www.theinsideredge.com for more information.

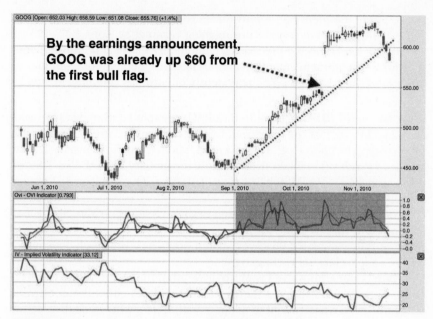

By the earnings announcement, GOOG was already up $60 from the first bull flag.

FIGURE 2.25 GOOG Reverse Head and Shoulders Breakout
Source: OVI Charts. Courtesy of FlagTrader.com. Go to www.theinsideredge.com for more information.

$48.50 to over $60. Both are impressive moves in a very short space of time. At the mid-range of stock prices from $15 to $50, it's not unusual to see prices double or halve in very quick time.

In recent years the higher priced stocks such as AAPL, GOOG, and Amazon (AMZN) have been fantastic to trade safely with obvious chart pattern and OVI combinations. So, try not to be put off by stocks with high share prices; just trade fewer of them at one time.

The OVI and Events

Inevitably it's the case that the OVI will often correlate with earnings reports, particularly when the markets are relatively stable. You saw as much from the above example with GOOG. However, trading directionally on an earnings announcement is something of a gamble and not something I encourage, even if all the planets are lining up.

In unstable markets with constant whipsaws, trading directionally over an earnings report would be akin to Russian roulette. One wrong move could be seriously bad for your trading account's health unless you know how to limit your risk during such times. That's not what this book is all about. There are plenty of opportunities to trade stocks that aren't imminently making announcements during most earnings seasons.

Just as the OVI often precedes a channel price breakout, it often does so prior to an announcement or event. Here are a couple of examples of this sort of thing happening independently of earnings announcements.

Bear Stearns (BSC)   Back to that BSC example I outlined in the Introduction. Let's look at the chart as it began to set up (Figure 2.26). You can see two support lines: One (1) is at $76.81, taken from the February 13 low, and the second (2) is taken from the low on January 22 at $68.18. BSC already breached (1) on March 3, and as of March 6 it's resting on $70, poised to breach (2).

The OVI slammed to its maximum negative reading on March 3 (3) and has stayed at that extreme for four days. This is unusual for such a liquid stock as BSC, which also had very liquid options. If the stock goes under $68 we have a clear short trade here.

There's something else I want to draw attention to here. When the OVI slams to the floor on March 3, there is no hint given by either the stock price or volume as to what's about to happen next. Here's where you can see the

FIGURE 2.26   BSC Support March 2008 Chart 1
Source: OVI Charts. Courtesy of FlagTrader.com. Go to www.theinsideredge.com for more information.

OVI at its impressive best, preceding any other potential signal. Volume is around 5.3 million shares, which was unremarkable, and BSC's share price is down about $2.50 from the previous day; there was nothing remarkable about that either (see Figure 2.27).

With the OVI in your armory you can see something is clearly wrong with BSC here. Without the OVI you wouldn't notice anything. What the OVI is telling us here is that a lot of options contracts are being traded with a negative bias. Essentially, this means put buying, though it could also include call selling.

The OVI in Figure 2.28 shows definitively how the options market was far ahead of the stock market in anticipating the fate of Bear Stearns. See how small that volume of 5.3 million looks now in the context of the volume surge that followed in the following few days. Similarly, look at how the price fell through the floor.

On the chart I've marked two horizontal support lines, and also two downward arrows linking a price bar with its corresponding volume bar. Volume on March 3 was around 5.3 million shares. On March 10, volume was over 32.4 million shares, taking the stock down to $62.30. Four days later, on Friday, March 14, when the fate of Bear Stearns was becoming reality, the stock plunged to $30.00 on volume of almost 186.6 million shares!

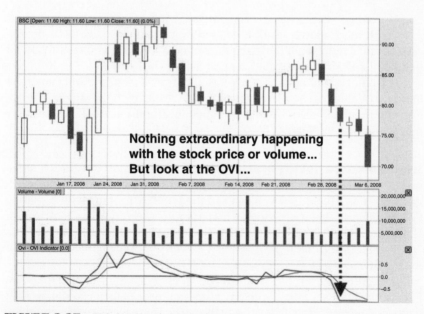

FIGURE 2.27 BSC OVI March 2008 Chart 2
Source: OVI Charts. Courtesy of FlagTrader.com. Go to www.theinsideredge.com for more information.

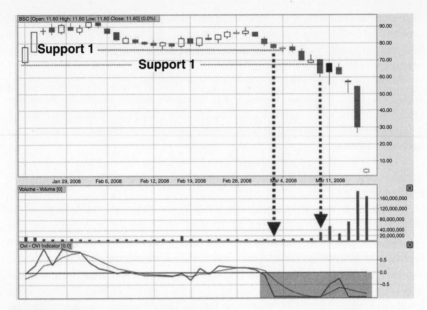

FIGURE 2.28 BSC March 2008 Chart 3
Source: OVI Charts. Courtesy of FlagTrader.com. Go to www.theinsideredge.com for more information.

On Monday, March 17, BSC gapped down and closed at $4.81 on volume of 166.2 million shares, having reached a low on the day of $2.84. At that point J.P. Morgan stepped in and rescued the company.

The point is that not one stock-based indicator gave investors any semblance of a clue that something was fatally wrong with this stock. The options market was where it was all happening, and the stock market only reacted several days later.

Iron Mountain Incorporated (IRM) This was an interesting situation, albeit one that was not capitalized upon because of the way the stock gapped up. In Figure 2.29 you can see the bull flag forming with a soaring OVI. In the past this was a stock where the OVI was too flat to be readable. However, it came up in my FLAG/OVI combination filter and, because the OVI had started to be more responsive over the previous two months, it looked like a potential opportunity.

In Figure 2.30, we can see how the stock gapped up the next day, on February 25. This rendered the buy stop-limit order unexecuted, but what happened next was intriguing to say the least. There was clearly something happening with the OVI as the stock bounced from its low on February 11 and the OVI turning sharply positive as the bull flag formed.

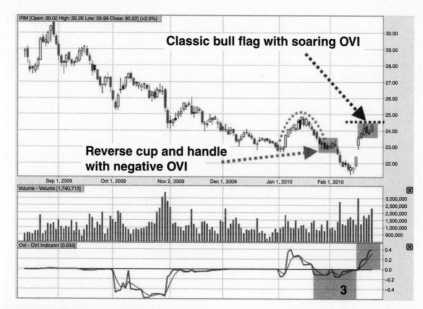

FIGURE 2.29   IRM Bull Flag Chart 1
Source: OVI Charts. Courtesy of FlagTrader.com. Go to www.theinsideredge.com for more information.

FIGURE 2.30   IRM Bull Flag Chart 2
Source: OVI Charts. Courtesy of FlagTrader.com. Go to www.theinsideredge.com for more information.

| **Iron Mountain Authorizes $150 Million Buyback** |
| 2/26/2010 6:46:00 AM - Investrend |

Feb 26, 2010 (FinancialWire via COMTEX) –

(Comment on this article at
http://www/financialwire.net/2010/02/26/iron-mountain-authorizes-150-milion-buyback/)

February 26, 2010 (Financial/Wire) – Iron Mountain Inc. (NYSE: IRM), an information management services firm, said that its board of directors approved a new share repurchase program authorizing up to $150 milion in repurchases of its common stock.

The buyback represents around 3% of the company's outstanding common stock based on the closing price on February 19, 2010.

Massachusetts-based Iron Mountain offers records management and data protection solutions to corporate clients throughout North America, Europe, Latin American and Asia Pacific.

FinancialWire(tm) is committed to serving the financial community through true journalism and providing relevant resources to investors. Standards-based, independent equity research on numerous public companies is available through the investrend Research Syndicate (http://www.investrend.com/reports) written by FIRST Research Consortium (http://www.investrend.com/FIRST) member-providers. Free annual reports and company fillings for companies mentioned in the news are available through the Investrend Information Syndicate (at http://investrend.ar.wlink.com/?level=279). FinancialWire(tm), in cooperation with the Investrend Broadcast Syndicate, also provides complete, daily conference call and webcast schedules as a service to shareholders and investors via the FirstAlert(tm) Network's "FirstAlert(tm) Daily" (http://www.financialwire.net/news-alerts/).

FinancialWire(tm) is a fully independent, proprietary news wire service. FinancialWire(tm) is not a press release service, and receives no compensation for its news, opinions or distributions. Further disclosure is at the FinancialWire(tm) website (http://www.financialwire.net/disclosures.php). Contact FinancialWire(tm) directly via inquires@financialwire.net.

http://www.financialwire.net

© 2010 Financialwire(TM): Div., Investrend Communications, Inc. All rights reserved. ....
As of Monday, 02-22-2010 23:59, the latest C

FIGURE 2.31   IRM News

It was only the day after the gap that news emerged that the company was doing a share buyback of around 3 percent of its outstanding common stock.

I'm not suggesting any impropriety on behalf of anyone connected with the company. However, whoever was trading the options on this stock did their main spate of buying just before the stock gapped up and certainly before any news announcement of the board's decision (see Figure 2.31).

Trade the Obvious Charts

Trade with the OVI when the opportunity looks obvious. We only ever use it in conjunction with tradable chart patterns and the benefits are clear to see. It will help your batting average if you focus on the really obvious opportunities. This means a clear chart pattern, as described throughout Chapter 1, and a clear OVI correlation in the direction of the chart pattern breakout.

Another major benefit with this type of trading is that you can focus on the large cap stocks, which are very liquid and household names. By all means, you can be adventurous and widen your search, but if time is precious you can focus on your top 30, which will only take a few minutes to monitor each day. A further bonus is that these stocks are cheap to trade in terms of commissions, tight bid-ask spreads, and little to no slippage.

The key is to stick with the obvious opportunities—in other words, stocks that are forming attractive chart patterns with a clear OVI reading, and that have shown a propensity to move in a big way. After all, it is movement that makes us profits.

Here I'm going to focus on a few large cap or household name stocks that we can all recognize. We've already seen examples with AAPL, AMZN, GS, GOOG, Bank of America (BAC), Research in Motion (RIMM), not to mention some of the major ETFs, so I'll pick a few different ones now.

Baidu (BIDU)   Here's BIDU forming a constructive chart pattern and OVI combinations in quick succession.

In Figure 2.32 we can see the stock gap up and forming into a flag that is supported by the November high. The gap up and consolidation after earnings is a classic bullish pattern. The OVI is also cooperating beautifully, so this is an opportunity that must be seized!

We'll get into the trading plan in detail in Chapter 3. For now, suffice it to say that a break above 119.50 or thereabouts would trigger a buy order with our stop underneath the bottom of the flag, our first profit target at just under $125, and a trendline managing the second half of the trade.

Let's see what happened next, in Figure 2.33.

The stock duly broke out to the upside and within four days had reached our first profit target just under $125.

At this point we typically draw a rising trendline, which determines our second profit. If the stock keeps trending then we can make windfall profits and add to our position on breakouts of new flags as and when they form.

From here the stock rose to above $130, and we have two possibilities. As the stock goes parabolic we can draw a steep trendline which dictates that we take profits at "A" just below $126.81. Or we can have a gentler trendline that has us wait too long in this case, and our second profit turns out to be less than the first as the stock gaps back down, opening at $123.53. Still, a profit is a profit.

Both profit-taking strategies are technically sound. We never have the benefit of hindsight, and when a stock goes parabolic in our favor it's

Gap up and consolidation immediately after earnings. This is a classic bullish pattern and the OVI is cooperating nicely here!

FIGURE 2.32 BIDU Bull Flag Chart 1
Source: OVI Charts. Courtesy of FlagTrader.com. Go to www.theinsideredge.com for more information.

First profit taken around $125

Second profit taken either at A or B

FIGURE 2.33 BIDU Bull Flag Chart 2
Source: OVI Charts. Courtesy of FlagTrader.com. Go to www.theinsideredge.com for more information.

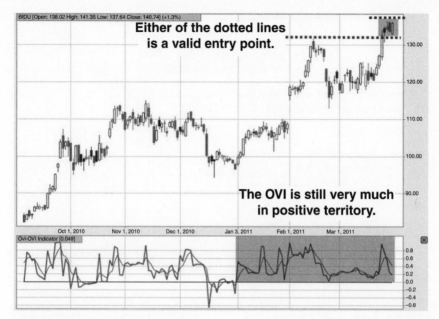

BIDU [Open: 138.02 High: 141.35 Low: 137.64 Close: 140.74] (+1.3%)

Either of the dotted lines is a valid entry point.

The OVI is still very much in positive territory.

FIGURE 2.34 BIDU Bull Flag Chart 3
Source: OVI Charts. Courtesy of FlagTrader.com. Go to www.theinsideredge.com for more information.

tempting to give it some leeway to see if it can keep going, or at least form new sideways flags on its trending journey.

In this case BIDU formed a second flag around the $130 area, and it was utterly reasonable to give it room to keep rising, but instead it gapped down severely, knocking us out of the second half of our trade at the open.

Let's now move the chart along about a month. We have two more opportunities to go long BIDU (see Figure 2.34). The OVI is still positive despite the steep retracement in February and if the stock rises beyond the February high ($131.63+) this would be a potential entry.

This materializes on March 23, with a steep rising bar that is subsequently followed by a bull flag, forming a cup and handle pattern at a high of $136.49. Both the breakout from the February high and the new cup and handle high are opportunities to enter the trade.

We'll go into the details of our trading plan in Chapter 3, but it's obvious that different entry points will generate different first profit targets. As a brief explanation at this point, we make our first profit target by extending the "flagpole" by around 30–38.2 percent in the direction of the trend. In both cases here that means a move of around $5 as the "flagpole" loosely starts from around $117 in mid-March.

FIGURE 2.35 BIDU Bull Flag Chart 4
Source: OVI Charts. Courtesy of FlagTrader.com. Go to www.theinsideredge.com for
more information.

If we trade the breakout of the February highs we don't have a flagpole
as such, but we can measure between the February high (131.63) and the
bottom of the new thrust (117.10), which is around $14.50. Five dollars is
approximately 35 percent of the $14.50 range, taking us to our profit target
of around $136.50.

If we trade the breakout of the cup and handle high at 136.49, our flagpole is over $19 from the base at 117.10. However, we don't want to be
overambitious, so a first profit target of $5.50 is reasonable, conservative,
and sensible. In this case our first profit target will be around $142.

From there BIDU goes on another run, albeit a bit bumpy. Nonetheless,
it's enough to get us from either breakout point to $145–150 within three to
four weeks.

We can see in Figure 2.35 that, while the stock does keep rising, it's
becoming quite jumpy as it does so, particularly by late April.

By this time the OVI has been solidly positive since the beginning of
January, and the stock has risen 50 percent since that time.

Honeywell (HON)   Figure 2.36 shows HON in July 2011. We can see that
the stock is trending down, is in a five-month head and shoulders pattern,
and has just broken the June low with the OVI turning negative. This is a

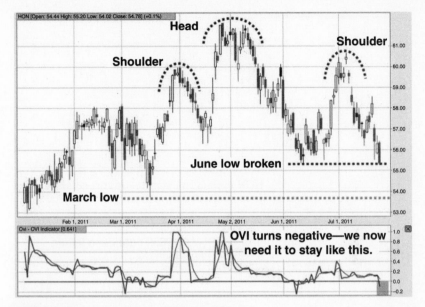

FIGURE 2.36 HON Break of Support Chart 1
Source: OVI Charts. Courtesy of FlagTrader.com. Go to www.theinsideredge.com for more information.

great setup, and a break of the March low below $53.74 would be an entry point if the OVI remains negative.

So we may have an entry point for a short trade if the stock breaks below the March low. Note: The March low is $53.74, but we need the break to be at a point below that—say $53.48.

The next day that level is broken (see Figure 2.37).

The move down is spectacular from here. The OVI remains negative and the stock falls precipitously down to below $42 in just a few weeks (see Figure 2.38).

In this case we use the head and shoulders to determine our first profit target. There are many theories about price targets from a head and shoulders pattern, but my view is to be pragmatic and take a conservative first profit target (P1).

You can either take the distance from the head to the neckline and project that down. Or you can take the distance from the right shoulder top to the neck down and project that distance down. In this case, the peak of the right shoulder is just above $60 and the neckline is just above $55. So let's call that distance $5. Projecting $5 from the neckline at $55 gives us a first profit target at $50 or just above $50 to be conservative.

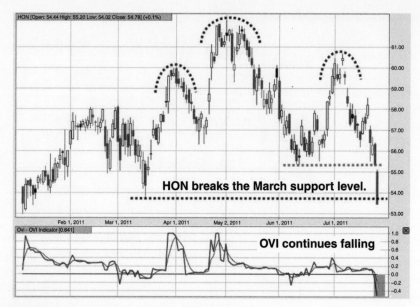

FIGURE 2.37 HON Break of Support Chart 2
Source: OVI Charts. Courtesy of FlagTrader.com. Go to www.theinsideredge.com for more information.

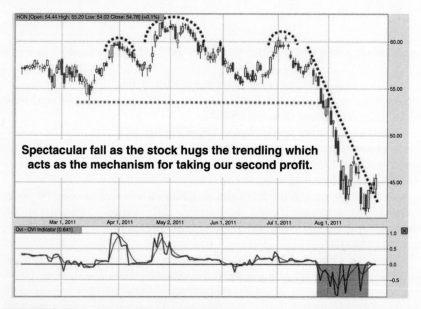

FIGURE 2.38 HON Break of Support Chart 3
Source: OVI Charts. Courtesy of FlagTrader.com. Go to www.theinsideredge.com for more information.

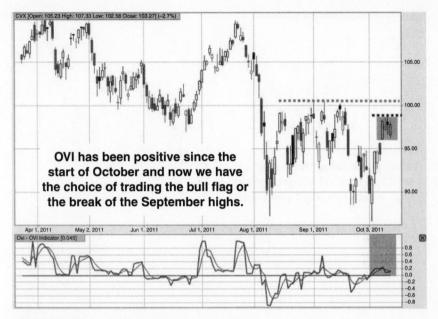

FIGURE 2.39 CVX Break of Resistance Chart 1
Source: OVI Charts. Courtesy of FlagTrader.com. Go to www.theinsideredge.com for more information.

Without a flag pattern in place we'll use the trendline as our stop loss along the way, and our second profit mechanism after we've taken our first profit. (We'll go through this in detail later in the book.)

Chevron (CVX) The next stock is an opportunity that came from a protracted sideways movement throughout the stock market between August and October 2011.

From Figure 2.39 you can see CVX forming a bull flag which is forming below the resistance, which is just above $100. The OVI has been positive for over a week, and while not spectacular it was relatively speaking positive in comparison with much of the market.

The brave might take a breakout from the bull flag itself, and the more conservative would enter after the stock breaks beyond the resistance formed by the September highs above $100.

If the stock breaks out then our first profit target (P1) is around 4.20 from the top of the flag or around 4.90 from the top of the resistance just above $100. This gives us a P1 of either $102.95 or $104.90 (lowered to be conservative).

FIGURE 2.40   CVX Break of Resistance Chart 2
Source: OVI Charts. Courtesy of FlagTrader.com. Go to www.theinsideredge.com for more information.

Remember: We take the length of the flagpole, multiply it by between 30 and 38.2 percent, and project that from the breakout point. (More details on this in Chapter 3.)

What actually happened was that the stock did break out and hit our P1 target, whether the trade was originated from the bull flag or the break of the September highs.

The second half of our trade was governed by the rising trendline, which was hit by a steep falling bar taking us out of the remainder of the trade at just above $105 (see Figure 2.40).

Caterpillar (CAT)   Here was a potential conundrum. In Figure 2.41 you can see CAT is forming a perfect cup and handle, and that the OVI has recently rocketed up but is now neutral.

In a case such as this you have to go for it. The pattern on its own is good enough if it breaks through the resistance. In this particular case there is some resistance from the high of April, though that particular bar closed at $71.65 and the highest close in August was $72.07, so I'd be inclined here to play the flag of the cup and handle. The high of the flag is $72.48 so a break of say $72.62 will see us in the trade.

FIGURE 2.41 CAT Cup and Handle Chart 1
Source: OVI Charts. Courtesy of FlagTrader.com. Go to www.theinsideredge.com for more information.

Our first profit target (P1) here is calculated as follows. The up-thrust of the cup and handle is from $63.33 to $72.48, let's say 9 points. Roughly a third of 9 points is 3 points, which is very conservative for this opportunity, so let's make a target of $75.62, which will give us three whole points from our entry at $72.62.

As you can see, there's a science to getting our P1, but there's also discretion. More about this later, but once we get to P1, we sell half the position and move our initial stop up to near breakeven. This ensures we shouldn't lose on the trade unless there's a severe gap against us. Because we're aware of the news events with any stock we trade, this should never happen unless there's a catastrophe outside of our normal control.

As you can see in Figure 2.42, the stock bursts upward and hits our P1 within three days. From here our rising trendline manages our trade. Note you can choose to give the stock some leeway from here if you choose. The prospects for CAT from here look very promising, and indeed the stock progressed upward 60 percent to $116. 25 by the end of April. The question is how much of that move you could have participated in without the benefit of hindsight.

FIGURE 2.42 CAT Cup and Handle Chart 2
Source: OVI Charts. Courtesy of FlagTrader.com. Go to www.theinsideredge.com for more information.

From Figure 2.43 you can see that with just one stock we have opportunities to go long at least four times, with three of them being certain winners with no drawdown and one (2) suffering a bit of drawdown. Throughout the entire uptrend the OVI remained positive, giving us extra confidence for each entry point.

Schlumberger Ltd (SLB) With SLB we had a potential breakout scenario in late September and also an earnings report on October 22, so the question was how to trade the first breakout that was looking likely toward the end of September.

Resistance had formed at $60.45 on September 13, and a break of this would trigger a trade, as the OVI had been consistently positive since the beginning of September.

From Figure 2.44, Point 1 is the level of the potential first entry from which you'd have to take partial profits before earnings. While SLB is trending upward, the individual bars are gapping at the open and leaving long shadows, so a conservative profit target before earnings is advisable here.

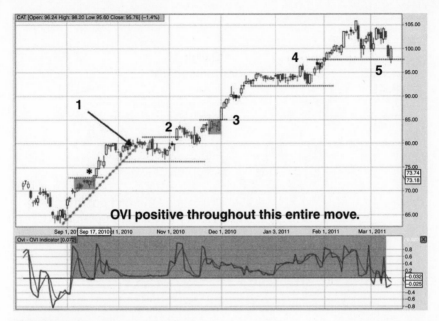

FIGURE 2.43 CAT Uptrend Chart

Key to Figure 2.43:

*	Our starting point where we traded the original cup and handle.
1	Likely P2 exit point from the original trade. The trendline gets hit at around $78.60.
2	With the OVI positive there's another chance to enter long at around $81.30. Notice that this breakout retraces to just below $80 before climbing back up to our next bull flag at 3.
3	Bull flag forms just below $85, prompting a long trade just above $85.
4	Prolonged sideways channel with positive OVI means the breakout is likely to be to the upside.
5	If profits haven't been taken above $100, then they should be taken as the stock breaks the February 23 low.

Source: OVI Charts. Courtesy of FlagTrader.com. Go to www.theinsideredge.com for more information.

Earnings is positive and the stock gaps up and forms a bull flag at just below $70 (Level 2). The OVI is positive, we have a great bull flag pattern, and earnings has just happened, so this is a perfect setup.

Within five days of the flag breakout the stock reaches $75, by which time first profits from this breakout have been taken.

FIGURE 2.44 SLB Breakout Chart
Source: OVI Charts. Courtesy of FlagTrader.com. Go to www.theinsideredge.com for more information.

Once the stock has hit our first profit target it's a matter of how far the stock can run without retracing too dramatically on us. In a situation like this, with an uptrend in place alongside a permanently positive OVI, you want to participate in the trend as much as possible. If the stock retraces steeply, we have no choice but to exit the second portion of the trade, as our diagonal trendline is bound to be hit. But when the stock resumes its trend (upward in this case) we may want to rejoin it or add to an existing position as it breaks new resistance points.

Looking at Figure 2.45, we can see how SLB continued to rise.

In this way you can see how the pattern/OVI combination can not only get us into trades but also manage them dynamically to stay in, get out, re-enter, or add more to an existing position. (More details on this in the next two chapters.)

Exxon Mobil (XOM) XOM formed one of the simplest opportunities we get to see in any kind of trading, particularly with the OVI at our disposal.

For a start, we're talking about the biggest company in the world by market capitalization. Second, it's in the oil business, for which the

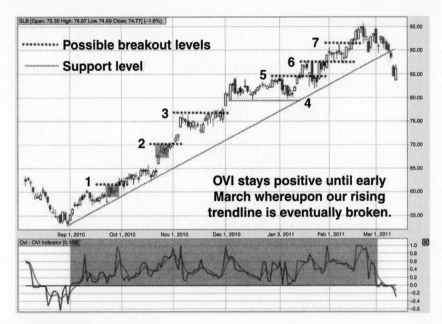

FIGURE 2.45 SLB Uptrend

Key to Figure 2.45:

1	Our first flag area at $60.45 a few weeks before earnings.
2	Our post-earnings bull flag at $70. This was irresistible.
3	The beginning-of-November highs form a resistance level that is breached toward the end of the month.
4	Support from mid-December holds as the stock meanders sideways, but with the OVI being positive a breakout to the upside is more likely and happens at point 5.
5	The breakout from the sideways channel.
6	Another breakout from the mid-January highs of $87.70.
7	The final breakout from the early-February high of $91.24.
	Ultimately the long rising trendline is hit at around $90. Along the way it may have been tempting to make it steeper, which is valid. In this case the Breakout at Point 5 had some drawdown but nothing too dramatic.

Source: OVI Charts. Courtesy of FlagTrader.com. Go to www.theinsideredge.com for more information.

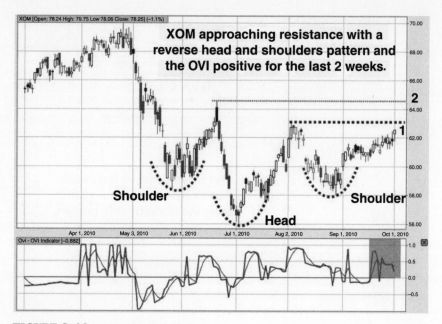

FIGURE 2.46 XOM Uptrend Chart 1
Source: OVI Charts. Courtesy of FlagTrader.com. Go to www.theinsideredge.com for more information.

prospects were continuing to be positive as oil itself is a scarce resource. Being so vast, XOM is as well placed as any other oil company to take advantage of this for the foreseeable future.

In terms of Figure 2.46, by the end of September we have a clear reverse head and shoulders pattern forming with resistance at $62.99 (Level 1) and $64.50 (Level 2). A breakout from either of these levels would see us go long as the OVI is already in positive territory. If we go for the lower entry point, we need to be mindful that there is some potential resistance from the June high at $64.50.

What happened next was similar to events with SLB in Figure 2.45; after all, both companies are in connected industries.

XOM bounded up and through Level 1 and within a few days was through Level 2 as well.

With earnings on October 28, the stock dipped and formed another mini resistance between October 21 and October 25, dipped down on October 27, and was primed for another breakout after October 29, at Level 3 in Figure 2.47.

As you can see, XOM bounded upward through Level 3.

FIGURE 2.47 XOM Uptrend Chart 2
Source: OVI Charts. Courtesy of FlagTrader.com. Go to www.theinsideredge.com for more information.

So in the case of XOM, we had the opportunity to grab profits before the earnings announcement, and we then, like with SLB, were fortunate to get another opportunity after the announcement as the stock retraced slightly, giving us a minor resistance level through which to trade.

Over the next few months XOM reached a high of $88.23 in February 2011, with a virtually uninterrupted uptrend and more chances for investors to jump onto the trend as short-term mini resistances were formed.

In Figure 2.48, you can see that at Level 4 a new high was formed in November, from which the stock retraced from $71.90 to $68.32. It then began to climb back up, giving us another opportunity to trade the stock, this time through the new resistance level. From here there were no new steep retracements until March 2011, when the rising trendline was well and truly broken.

When stocks go on a run like this we have the opportunity to make windfall profits. These examples are actually quite conservative but still illustrate the point eloquently. The stock market creates these opportunities better than any other financial instrument. They don't happen every day, and that's part of our challenge. When they happen you'll find

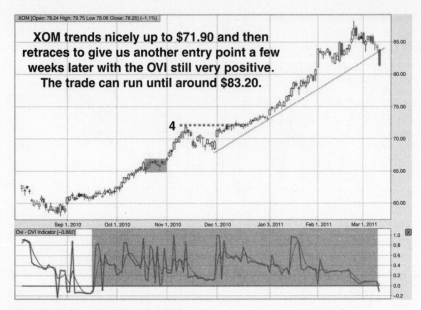

FIGURE 2.48   XOM Uptrend Chart 3
Source: OVI Charts. Courtesy of FlagTrader.com. Go to www.theinsideredge.com for more information.

a number of stocks qualifying unusually well, and that will be part of your wakeup call.

With trading like this, you won't make incremental daily, weekly, or even monthly profits. Instead you'll make profits in great bursts of trending activity. This is how it works. There may be periods of weeks without much activity and then all of a sudden everything goes crazy and the market is on a run. This is where you make your windfall profits.

The great thing is that you'll be able to see things developing almost in slow motion when a setup is forming. You'll see a channel developing with the OVI obstinately positive or negative, and you'll bide your time until a proper breakout occurs. The OVI-breakout combination will also greatly enhance your intuition with the markets.

Remember: Your main focus is to trade with the trend. There are creditable reversal strategies, but the big money is made trading with the meat of the trend.

Reversals

The OVI is designed to work best with breakouts from trading ranges and consolidation patterns. As such, reversals couldn't be the main focus of this book, and we generally don't look for the OVI to correlate with reversals per se. With the right stocks at the right times, the OVI is very obviously responsive, as you've seen, and we make our money from clear breakouts through support or resistance, not by trying to second-guess the ultimate high or low.

Over time some of our breakouts will go on to form the long-running trends that give us our windfall profits.

There are some great ways to trade reversals, but these do not involve the OVI unless the reversal happens to be in the direction of the dominant trend. Of course there are examples where reversals have tied in nicely with the OVI, but these are rare.

For a reversal signal I like to see an extreme in price (high or low) being made over a 20-day period, coupled with a Doji type of price bar. If we're really lucky we'll get a volume spike as well, but we generally settle for a 20-day high or low with a Doji happening within a day of that extreme price happening.

Trading reversals like this is a valid strategy, but it should not be your only strategy, nor indeed should it be your mainstay. That should be trading with the trend, even when it means having to be patient.

LEARNING POINTS

So you can now see how exciting the OVI is when you trade with it in its proper context.

Share traders have long been inundated with the standard indicators that are generally based on some sort of average of past prices. Who's to know whether the 50-day or 200-day moving average is the right one to use? Who's to know what MACD or stochastic setting to use over which time frame? Who's to know which Fibonacci ratio, Gann angle, or Elliott wave we should be using?

The OVI merges the components of options transactions data into a line that oscillates between −1 and +1. We use it with specific stocks at specific times with specific patterns.

Specialization in life—and in trading—is what leads to the most lucrative paychecks. We're specializing in one form of trading, and if you cherry-pick the most obvious opportunities with the liquid optionable stocks, you'll be well positioned.

The next thing you need is a robust and simple trading plan that keeps you safe if the market turns against you and includes the ability for windfall profits if the market cooperates. We've touched on this during some of the trading examples above. What we now need to do is to go through our trading plan in detail.

There is no question that some of the savviest investors congregate in the options markets. The OVI gives us an eye on what they're up to, provided we use it together with a chart pattern. On its own the OVI will not work, as we need to distinguish the motives of the options activity.

For example some options activity may be due to hedging or covering other positions. This happens frequently and therefore a pure OVI reading may be misleading. When we use the OVI and chart pattern combination we have a far better idea of what the OVI is actually saying. In the context of a sideways chart pattern, more often than not, if the OVI is positive, it's likely that the breakout will be positive; if the OVI is negative, it's likely that the breakout will be negative.

For everyday share traders to have an indicator that is based on options transaction data is a paradigm shift that will have hugely positive implications for those who understand how to use it as outlined in this chapter.

Remember the main points about the OVI:

- It has nothing to do with the stock price, and yet it correlates very well with trending price action of stocks with liquid options. The OVI tends to correlate best with medium-term trends.
- The chart pattern always comes first. We only use the OVI in conjunction with our favored chart patterns (namely flags, channels, and breakouts from support and resistance).
- Used with these breakout patterns and channels, the OVI will often precede the breakout. The OVI can give us extra confidence that the pattern will not fail.
- In broad terms, when the OVI is positive, we would focus on bullish chart patterns; when the OVI is negative, we would focus on bearish patterns.
- We do not have our trades executed before the price breaks out, but the OVI will get us ready to be positioned in the right place, at the right time, in the right direction. Our trades are only executed as the stock breaks through a predefined support or resistance level.
- It's best to focus on the obvious charts with clear OVI signals.
- Options traders are typically more experienced than just stock traders, but you don't need to know anything about options in order to use the OVI to trade stocks.

In the next chapter we're going to get into the detail of flags and breakout patterns. It's not enough to be able to recognize the pattern. You have to know the difference between a tradable pattern and one that is not suitable. We're also going to go into detail with the trading plan that you'll be using when you see these patterns. We'll do this precisely, but with the knowledge that in the real world you may use some discretion, depending on how the markets are behaving.

CHAPTER 3

Flags and Channel Breakouts in Detail

Focusing on the Patterns That Work Best with the OVI

In Chapter 1 you saw how various chart patterns can make for great trades, and in Chapter 2 you learned how certain OVI behavior can also be incredibly powerful.

In this chapter we focus in more detail on the most important chart patterns in the stock market: flags and channel breakouts. These are the patterns that can lead to the most explosive and profitable moves with very low risk if executed properly.

They're also the best patterns to use in combination with the OVI, as you'll soon discover (particularly in Chapter 4 where we stitch everything together into a coherent and robust trading plan that you can use over and over again).

A s you've already seen, most indicators are lagging because they use averages of past price and/or volume. These lagging indicators include the classics such as moving averages, MACD, stochastics, and so on. By contrast, the OVI is used as a *leading* indicator, particularly when used with the patterns we're focusing on here.

My favorite chart patterns are flags and channels from which a stock is poised to make a breakout. There are several reasons for this:

- If the stock doesn't break out, I cannot lose, as my entry is dependent on the breakout itself. Therefore I can be wrong and yet not lose a bean if my trade isn't executed. This automatically boosts my trading performance.

- These patterns lend themselves to low-risk trading plans with clear entry levels, small but sensibly positioned stop losses, and optimized profit targets that can accommodate windfall profits.
- Because these patterns work so well with a well-constructed trading plan, your trading psychology will benefit from the clarity and simplicity of the plan.

Before we get stuck in the detail of these patterns, it's important to understand that the profits you reap from them will not happen smoothly. Rather, your profits will occur in frenetic bursts, followed by relatively quiet periods.

The idea is that we benefit enormously from markets that are trending and don't get punished while the markets are churning sideways. The greatest fortunes in trading are made in bursts and by riding trending markets.

Given that we don't have hindsight as to whether we're in a trending market, we must have a trading plan that enables us to make the most of a trend while not leaving us to be slaughtered by rangebound or choppy markets.

Trading breakouts with a modest first profit target enables us to achieve all this elegantly, and we'll cover this in detail in Chapter 4.

Let's now go through our favored chart patterns.

BULL FLAGS

As we saw in Chapter 1, a bull flag occurs when the dominant trend is rising.

Remember that a flag pattern is made up of two parts: a thrusting surge or step (the flagpole), and the consolidation (flag). Our aim is to make money as the stock continues to rise in line with the dominant uptrend.

The Ideal Bull Flag

With bull flags we want the consolidation to be either sideways or drifting slightly downward against the main trend. This ensures we have an area of resistance that we can use in order to define our entry point. See in Figure 3.1 how we enter either at Level A, which is the top of the flag pattern, or at Level B, which is the top of the consolidation area, in the event that it has drifted downward.

If the consolidation drifts upward in line with the main trend, it is impossible to define an entry point based on a break of resistance. Therefore

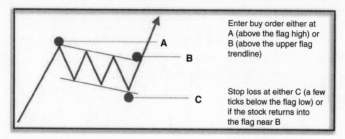

FIGURE 3.1   The Ideal Bull Flag

it is crucial for the consolidation to be either sideways or slightly *against* the direction of the dominant trend.

Here's the idealized bull flag as we saw earlier.

Our trade is only activated when the stock price rises through the resistance level of A or B in Figure 3.1.

- Level A is just above the highest part of the flag and is the most conservative entry point, because it requires a new high to be achieved.

    If the entry is activated, then we place our stop loss either just below Level B or at C.

- Level B is just above where the price would break out above the higher trendline of the flag pattern. This is more aggressive than Level A and is more suitable during a reliable bull market where volume is rising as the breakout occurs.

    If the entry is activated at Level B, we place our stop loss either just below B inside the flag, or at C just below the flag.

This is your basic trading plan for entering a bull flag trade, within the context of an upward trend.

Our ideal bull flag has the following qualities:

- It's neat and visually recognizable.
- The consolidation is reasonably tight. (As you'll see in Chapter 4, this is so that our stop placement isn't too far away.)
- The flagpole and breakout are accompanied by rising volume, while the consolidation is matched with reduced volume. (We'll address this later in this section.)
- The flag itself is either sideways or slightly down, countering the direction of the dominant uptrend.
- The OVI is positive during the consolidation phase.

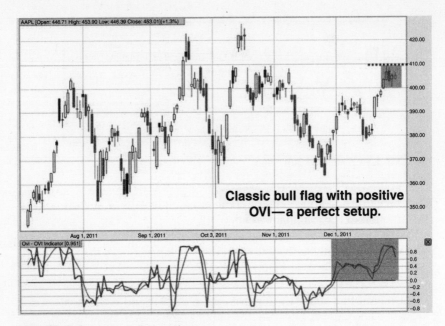

FIGURE 3.2   AAPL Bull Flag Chart
Source: OVI Charts. Courtesy of FlagTrader.com. Go to www.theinsideredge.com for
more information.

Now that we know what we're looking for, Figure 3.2 shows a great
example of a bull flag with a perfect OVI scenario.

In Figure 3.2 you can see how Apple (AAPL) is forming a textbook bull
flag while its OVI has been positive for around a month. This is a perfect
setup—easy to spot and easy to trade.

The pattern could actually be viewed as a cup and handle, but whatever
the case, this is an opportunity that cannot go begging.

As you can see in Figure 3.3, AAPL breaks out from the original bull
flag and consolidates again before gapping up immediately after earnings.
Although we would take partial (or more than partial) profits before earnings, what the chart demonstrates is the ability for this technique of trading flags, combined with the OVI, to make substantial profits very quickly.
(We'll discuss the precise trading plan in Chapter 4.)

Avoiding Market Manipulation   In Figure 3.3 the high point of the flag
is $409.09 and we need this point to be broken to the upside. However, our
buy order entry is slightly above this high—say $409.37 (an arbitrary num-
ber that is deliberately unrounded so it is not clumped along with other
orders at the exact same price). The fact that your lot size is likely to be

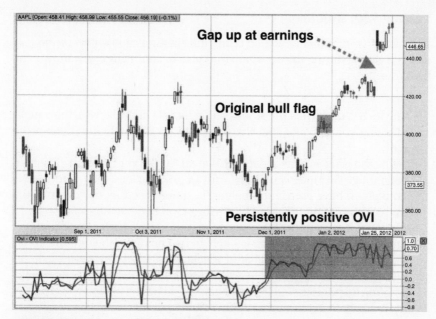

FIGURE 3.3 AAPL Bull Flag Breakout Chart
Source: OVI Charts. Courtesy of FlagTrader.com. Go to www.theinsideredge.com for more information.

comparatively small will indicate that this is a non-professional order anyway, but it's best that it's not clumped in with other obvious orders that may, for example, be amassed right on the flag high. Such clumps of orders in the same place are a sign to professionals that amateurs have conglomerated at the same position and could be there for the taking.

By this, I mean that a market maker may artificially walk up the price in order to trigger buy orders exactly where all the amateurs have placed their trades, right at the same price. A market maker makes his money when trades are matched. So when volume is light and he can see a bunch of amateur orders all at the same place, this is what could be considered low-hanging fruit. Having nursed the share price to the flag high, the prices are matched and the market maker has his fill. The stock is now at a price where there is no authentic demand.

And without authentic demand for the shares, the price must fall, leaving you with a false breakout—and a loss!

By positioning your buy order beyond the flag high and with an unrounded number that is unlikely to be accompanied by other breakout traders, you stand a much better chance of this false breakout (or even whipsaw) scenario not happening to you.

Volume with Bull Flags

In an ideal world volume will be rising during the flagpole part of the pattern, subsiding during the consolidation phase, and rising again during the breakout.

- The idea is that when the stock is moving, it is doing so with the benefit of rising volume, meaning there is likely to be conviction behind the move.
- While the price is consolidating it's ideal for the volume to also be consolidating. This means that any drift in price against the main trend is unlikely to have conviction behind it, thereby setting up the potential for a continuation breakout in the direction in the main trend.
- It's most favorable to have the breakout accompanied by rising volume since this means there is likely to be conviction behind the move, which increases the chances of a sustained move. As discussed earlier, it also means there is less likelihood of market makers artificially walking up prices to the key resistance point (such behavior is typically more likely to occur during a low volume period).

From the diagram in Figure 3.4, you can see how volume is higher during the thrusting phase of the pattern at the first point (A), also representing aggressive bidding that forces the stock price higher. It's worth noting that prices can rise even with falling volume if the buying (bidding) is aggressive enough.

For example, with a stock at $50.00, if bids are coming in at $50.03 and those bids are matched, then the price will rise. Similarly, if bids are coming in at $49.97 and those bids are matched, then the price will fall.

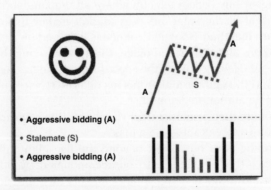

FIGURE 3.4   Ideal Volume Consolidation with Ideal Bull Flag

Even during a few seconds the stock price may fluctuate to reflect all this happening. When a greater number of higher bids are coming in for the stock, then the price will rise and stay higher—and vice versa, of course. A greater volume for the stock during the surge suggests a healthy demand. This is a good first step for the pattern.

As the stock price settles into the consolidation phase (S), it's ideal that the volume also consolidates. This indicates that even while the price is drifting sideways or down against the main trend there is not a great conviction to sell off. Effectively there's a stalemate between buyers and sellers during this consolidation phase.

Later, when the stock price starts to rise again at the second point (A), it's useful if volume is rising again, indicating a conviction of healthy demand for the stock as it breaks the pattern's resistance levels. This suggests a greater likelihood for the move to be sustained long enough for us to make profit on the trade as the price breaks out.

Avoid Rising Wedges with Bull Flags

Some bull flags will manifest with the consolidation drifting up with the dominant trend. This often presents itself as a "rising wedge," which itself can be bearish (see Figure 3.5).

However, the main problem with this type of flag (which will also be captured by filtering software such as my FlagTrader) is that as the consolidation drifts upward in line with the dominant uptrend, there is no identifiable resistance at which to enter your buy order.

So now we don't have a clear or logical entry point; we have no basis for a sensible and low-risk trading plan. Remember: A trading plan must have an entry point, stop loss, and profit target(s) built in. Without our entry point we don't have a plan at all.

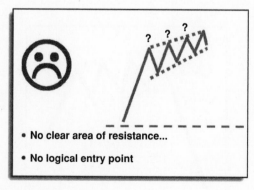

FIGURE 3.5 Rising Wedge

Rounded Tops

Rounded tops occur when a bull flag doesn't break out (see Figure 3.6). The result is that we don't lose any money because your entry is dependent on a breakout. No breakout, no losses! This is infinitely better than a false breakout where the price breaks in our favor and triggers our buy order, only to retreat straight back down again.

Sometimes even the most beautiful flags don't break out, and all we lose is an opportunity. What we gain is the fact that we didn't lose even though we were "wrong" about the trade. To not lose when we're wrong is a pretty good place to be in trading. There are plenty of people who get the direction right and still lose money in trading. Either they've tried to be too clever with options without truly understanding them, or they got stopped out just before the stock resumed its trend.

Let's take a look at an example of a rounded top.

In Figure 3.7 Chipotle Mexican Group, Inc. (CMG) is forming a cup and handle with a perfect bull flag at the end. The price has thrust up past resistance and formed a tight bull flag with volume also consolidating. Earnings has just passed, and this is primed for the next leg up.

You'd bet this was going to burst upward, wouldn't you? Well, there's a reason why we must have a breakout past resistance in order to trade a bull flag, and that is because not all bull flags—even the best-looking ones—are destined to break out upward.

In Figure 3.8 you can see how the bull flag fails, yet because the price never breaks past the flag high, we're not punished.

Bull Flag Summary

You should be getting a good idea that we're looking for neatly formed bull flags, preferably with a positive OVI reading.

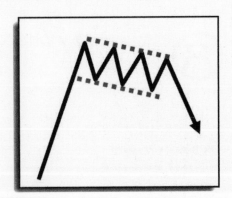

FIGURE 3.6   Rounded Top

FIGURE 3.7 CMG Rounded Top Formation Chart
Source: OVI Charts. Courtesy of FlagTrader.com. Go to www.theinsideredge.com for more information.

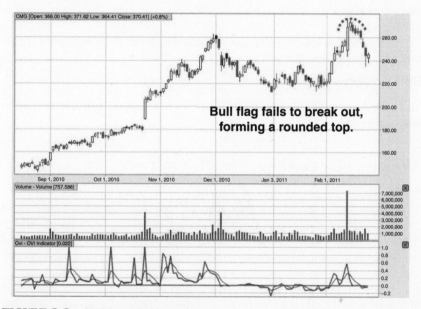

FIGURE 3.8 CMG Rounded Top Chart
Source: OVI Charts. Courtesy of FlagTrader.com. Go to www.theinsideredge.com for more information.

The setup, as described above, prepares us for a low-risk trade with great potential for a windfall profit if the stock price gets on a trend. In Chapter 4 you'll see how we pick off modest profits even if the stock doesn't get on a trend. Our trading plan must cover all eventualities and yet be simple and clear to understand.

Remember the ideal qualities for our bull flag. We may not always trade ones with them, but this is what we're really looking for:

- Neat and visually recognizable.
- The flag part itself is reasonably tight.
- Volume consolidates with the price consolidation.
- The bull flag itself is sideways or gently counters the direction of the dominant uptrend.
- The OVI is positive during the bull flag consolidation phase.

Now let's look at the detailed criteria for bear flags.

BEAR FLAGS

As we saw in Chapter 1, a bear flag occurs when the dominant trend is down.

A bear flag works exactly the same as a bull flag except that the directions are flipped upside down.

The bear flag pattern is made up of two parts: a downward thrusting surge or step (the flagpole), and the consolidation (flag). Our aim is to make money as the stock continues to fall in line with the dominant downtrend.

The Ideal Bear Flag

With bear flags we want the consolidation to be either sideways or drifting slightly upward *against* the main trend. This ensures we have an area of support that we can use in order to define our short entry point. See in Figure 3.9 how we enter either at point (A), which is the bottom of the flag pattern, or at point (B), which is the bottom of the consolidation area in the event that it has drifted upward.

If the consolidation drifts downward in line with the main trend, it is impossible to define an entry point based on a break of support. Therefore it is crucial for the consolidation to be either sideways or slightly *against* the direction of the dominant trend.

Here's the idealized bear flag as we saw earlier.

Our trade is only activated when the stock price falls through the support level of A or B in Figure 3.9.

- Level A is just below the lowest part of the flag and is the most conservative entry point for shorting, because it requires a new low to be achieved.

    If the short entry is activated, then we place our buy stop loss either just above B or at C.

- Level B is just below where the price would break down through the lower trendline of the flag pattern. This is more aggressive than Point A and is more suitable during a technical bear market where volume is rising as the breakout occurs.

    If the entry is activated at B, we place our buy stop loss either just above B inside the flag, or at C just above the flag.

This is your basic trading plan for entering a bear flag trade, within the context of a downward trend.

As with the bull flag, the ideal bear flag shares similar qualities:

- It's neat and visually recognizable.
- The consolidation is reasonably tight. (As you'll see in Chapter 4, this is so that our stop placement isn't too far away.)
- The flagpole and breakdown are accompanied by rising volume, while the consolidation is matched with reduced volume. (We'll address this later in this section.)
- The flag itself is either sideways or slightly up, countering the direction of the dominant downtrend.
- The OVI is negative during the consolidation phase.

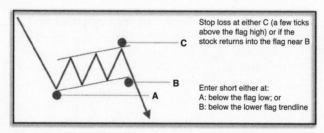

FIGURE 3.9 The Ideal Bear Flag

Now that you know what we're looking for, Figure 3.10 is a great example of a bear flag with a perfect negative OVI scenario.

Here I've chosen a stock that isn't one of our usual favorites. This was picked up in a filter for neat bear flags with a negative OVI for the last five days. In Figure 3.10 you can see how Shutterfly, Inc. (SFLY) is forming an easily recognized bear flag while its OVI has clearly turned negative. This is another great setup—easy to spot and easy to trade.

It's interesting how often flags are part of other patterns, and this one could be viewed as a reverse cup and handle. Regardless of that, this is another opportunity that should be seized upon, should the price break to the downside.

As you can see in Figure 3.11, SFLY breaks down from our original bear flag at $35, consolidates again into another bear flag, and keeps sliding until a partial recovery around $25. This represents a "gettable" move of $10 or around a 30 percent move on the trade.

In Chapter 4 I'll show you exactly how we take our profits on a move like this. We take a conservative partial profit and let the rest ride as the stock price continues to fall.

FIGURE 3.10   SFLY Bear Flag Chart
Source: OVI Charts. Courtesy of FlagTrader.com. Go to www.theinsideredge.com for more information.

FIGURE 3.11 SFLY Bear Flag Breakout Chart
Source: OVI Charts. Courtesy of FlagTrader.com. Go to www.theinsideredge.com for more information.

A move of 10 points on a $35 stock is significant. Proportionately it's the same as a $100 move on a $350 stock . . . and that would certainly have you purring!

Avoiding Market Manipulation with Bear Flags The same concepts apply with bull and bear flags when it comes to managing your orders with your broker.

In the SFLY chart the low point of the bear flag is $35.38. We need this point to be broken to the downside.

Indeed our order here is to short only when the stock falls slightly below this low (in fact, below $35 in this case—say $34.88). This is a psychological thing with a stock that clearly isn't as liquid as say AAPL.

We want to ensure that the flag is decisively resolved to the downside, so I want the comfort of having both the flag low and the round number of $35 taken out.

Our short here is a sell stop limit to open at $34.88, or a conditional order to open a short at that level. If the stock trades *through* this level, our order is triggered. If it gaps through it, your order will not be triggered. This type of order protects us from gaps that may put us into a trade that's not at our ideal price. The concern is that gaps are often filled, and we don't want to be gapped in, only for the price to reverse on us and fill its gap.

Remember: We set our orders at deliberately unrounded numbers away from others that are likely to be placed by amateur traders. While our order is relatively small and likely to be recognized as a private trade, it's typically only when lots of small orders are clumped together where a market maker will deem it worth gobbling them all up at the same place, only to then reverse the price.

Markets are manipulated, but if you play the game intelligently you'll be fine. Remember: Only a small number of private traders bother to get any form of proper education—and even then they're often seduced by poorly devised strategies that are simply very well marketed.

In the case of lots of different small sell orders accumulated in the same vicinity, in the event of a low-volume period, the market maker can walk the price down and match the sell orders with buy orders. Once that's done, with no more authentic sell orders at that price or below, the price will start to rise again, causing a problem for those who sold short.

With your order placed intelligently away from the amateur noise, you are far less likely to be taken to the cleaners by this sort of activity.

Volume with Bear Flags

Bear flags work in the same way as bull flags. In an ideal world, volume will be rising during the flagpole part of the pattern, subsiding during the consolidation phase, and rising again during the breakout.

- The idea is that when the stock is moving, it is doing so with the benefit of rising volume, meaning there is likely to be conviction behind the move.
- While the price is consolidating it's ideal for the volume to also be consolidating. This means that any drift in price against the main trend is unlikely to have conviction behind it, thereby setting up the potential for a continuation breakout in the direction in the main trend.
- It's optimal to have the breakout accompanied by rising volume since this means there is likely to be conviction behind the move, which increases the chances of a sustained move. As discussed earlier, it also means there is less likelihood of market makers artificially walking prices down to the key support point (such behavior is typically more likely to occur during a low volume period).

In the idealized diagram in Figure 3.12, you can see how volume is higher during the thrusting phase of the pattern at the first point (A), also representing aggressive offers (to sell) that force the stock price lower.

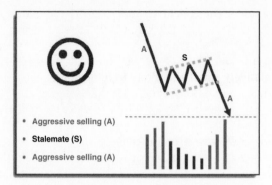

FIGURE 3.12 Ideal Volume Consolidation with Ideal Bear Flag

It's worth noting that prices can fall even with falling volume if the selling offers are aggressive enough.

For example, with a stock at $40.00, if offers are coming in at $39.96 and those offers are matched, then the price will fall. Similarly, if offers are coming in at $40.03 and those offers are matched, then the price will rise.

Even during a few seconds the stock price may fluctuate to reflect all this happening. When a greater number of lower offers are coming in for the stock, then the price will fall and stay lower—and vice versa, of course. A greater volume for the stock during the surge suggests there are more sellers than buyers. This is a good first step for the pattern if we want it to continue falling.

As the stock price settles into the consolidation phase (S), it's ideal that the volume also consolidates. This indicates that even while the price is drifting sideways or upward against the main trend there is no great demand for the stock. Effectively there's a stalemate between buyers and sellers during this consolidation phase.

Later, when the stock price starts to fall again at the second point (A), it's useful if volume is rising again, indicating excess supply for the stock as it breaks the pattern's support levels. This suggests a greater likelihood for the move to be sustained long enough for us to make profit on the trade as the price breaks down.

Avoid Descending Wedges with Bear Flags

Some bear flags will manifest with the consolidation drifting down with the dominant trend (see Figure 3.13). This often presents itself as a "descending wedge," which itself can be bullish.

However, the main problem with this type of flag (which is also captured by filtering software such as my FlagTrader) is that as the

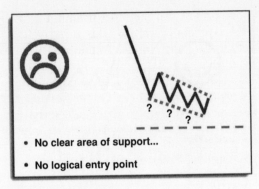

FIGURE 3.13 Descending Wedge

consolidation drifts downward in line with the dominant downtrend, there is no identifiable support at which to enter your short order.

So now we don't have a clear or logical entry point; we have no basis for a sensible and low-risk trading plan. Remember: A trading plan must have an entry point, stop loss, and profit target(s) built in. Without our entry point, we don't have a plan at all.

Rounded Bottoms

Rounded bottoms occur when a bear flag doesn't break down (see Figure 3.14). The result is that we don't lose any money, because our short entry is dependent on a breakout. No breakout, no losses! This is infinitely better than a false breakout where the price breaks in our favor and triggers our short order, only for it to bounce straight back up again.

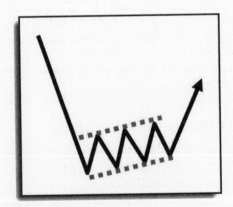

FIGURE 3.14 Rounded Bottom

As before, sometimes even the most beautiful bear flags don't break out, and all we lose is an opportunity. In this way we can be "wrong" about the trade and yet not lose any money. To not lose when we're wrong is a good place to be in trading.

Let's take a look at an example of a rounded bottom:

Here's AAPL again in Figure 3.15. (I'm deliberately using some of the same stocks over and over again so you can see that you don't have to look too hard over thousands of stocks to find examples of chart patterns occurring over and over again.)

AAPL is in the middle of a head and shoulders type of bearish pattern. In Figure 3.15, you can see it has two heads and two shoulders on either side. In this bearish context, the last three bars indicate a bear flag, though the OVI isn't quite corroborating at this juncture.

Although this looks more bearish than bullish, remember it is AAPL we're talking about in late 2011, when it's still a darling of the stock market. In this sort of scenario, I'm commenting that you'd be a brave person to bet against the company and there are better propositions out there to short! However, it's a nice chart to showcase a rounded bottom.

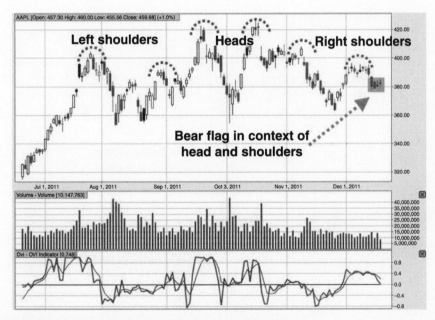

FIGURE 3.15 AAPL Rounded Bottom Formation Chart
Source: OVI Charts. Courtesy of FlagTrader.com. Go to www.theinsideredge.com for more information.

Remember: We only trade the breakout. In the case of bear flags, we need the stock price to continue downward past the flag's support.

In Figure 3.16 you can see how the bear flag fails, yet because the price never breaks down through the flag's support, our conditional order won't be triggered and we don't lose any money.

Notice also how in this case the OVI never ventured into negative territory and in fact rebounds strongly into positive territory as the bear flag fails. Soon a bull flag will form here, setting up the simplest of trades, which proved very successful.

Bear Flag Summary

Once again, we're looking for neatly formed bear flags, preferably with a negative OVI reading.

The setup prepares us for a low-risk trade with great potential for a windfall profit if the stock price gets on a downtrend. In Chapter 4 you'll see how we pick off modest profits even if the stock doesn't get on a trend. Our trading plan must cover all eventualities, and yet be simple and clear to understand.

FIGURE 3.16   AAPL Rounded Bottom Chart
Source: OVI Charts. Courtesy of FlagTrader.com. Go to www.theinsideredge.com for more information.

Remember the ideal qualities for our bear flag. We may not always trade ones with them, but this is what we're really looking for:

- Neat and visually recognizable.
- The flag part itself is reasonably tight.
- Volume consolidates with the price consolidation.
- The bear flag itself is sideways or gently counters the direction of the dominant downtrend.
- The OVI is negative during the bear flag consolidation phase.

FLAGS WITH A STRONG OVI SIGNAL

Securities often move in undistinguishable patterns, in which case they are untradeable in any meaningful sense. Messy, ugly charts are a lottery, and therefore untradeable.

Recognizable chart patterns are a first step toward trading with a coherent trading plan that improves our odds of success. Neat flags are the ultimate for me, but they're even better if we have a way of qualifying them. By this, I mean we want a way to distinguish which flags are more likely to break out in our favor.

Some critics argue that flags can be prone to make false breakouts, particularly in sideways markets. This is both valid and harsh, as during sideways markets flags will often fail to break out at all, thereby protecting us from any losses.

However, while flags on their own have made fortunes for many ordinary traders over the years, I still wanted to refine them in order to up my batting averages. This is where the OVI comes into play.

A Strong OVI Signal

A strong OVI signal while the flag is forming can be invaluable to increasing the odds of breakout happening in our favor.

For example:

- When you have the OVI noticeably positive for say five days and a good-looking bull flag, then you have a greater chance of a meaningful upside breakout, because the options market is positioned bullishly.
- When you have a clearly negative OVI for five days and a neat bear flag, then you have a greater chance of a meaningful downside breakout, because the options market is positioned bearishly.

When I say "meaningful," I mean a breakout that will be big enough to create a profitable trade—in other words, not a false breakout that triggers our order only to rebound straight back.

The flag/OVI combination is my favorite setup. But there's another setup that is also very good, and that is the breakout from a sideways channel.

CHANNEL BREAKOUTS

A sideways channel can form in the wider context of rising, falling, or non-trending markets.

These patterns can form for weeks or months at a time, where they form reasonably distinguishable areas of support and resistance. These are identified by lows and highs achieved during the channel's formation.

The Ideal Channel

What makes a tradeable channel is how well formed the support and resistance areas are.

Aesthetics are only pleasing because they give us the parameters for our trading plan. We need the support and resistance areas to be clearly defined by way of previous highs and/or lows. If an extreme has been approached more than once, this lends weight to its importance.

For example, looking at Figure 3.17, if a high made early in the channel formation is approached again (perhaps more than once) but not broken, then resistance (R) is seen to be strengthened.

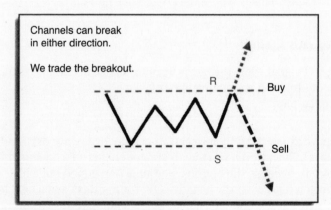

FIGURE 3.17   The Sideways Channel

Similarly, if a low made earlier in channel formation is approached again but not broken, then support (S) is seen to be strengthened.

In either case, if support or resistance is breached, it's likely that a decent move is more likely, which means profit for us! (We'll cover the trading plan in full in Chapter 4.)

Our long trade will only be activated when the stock price breaks *beyond* the resistance (R) level, as shown in Figure 3.17. Remember: The price has to trade through and above the resistance in order to not be clumped with other obviously placed amateur trades, which are more likely to be right at that resistance level.

Our short trade will only be activated when the price breaks down past the support (S) level as shown in Figure 3.17. Remember: The price has to trade through and below the support in order to not be clumped with other obviously placed amateur trades, which are more likely to be right at that support level.

This is our basic trading plan for entering a sideways channel breakout, either long or short.

Our ideal sideways channel has the following qualities:

- It's neat and visually recognizable with clear levels of support and resistance, defined by previous lows and highs within the channel itself.
- The channel contains other support and resistance levels inside. This will help to ensure our stops are sensibly placed (more about this in Chapter 4).
- As the price starts to drift toward its breakout, the OVI corroborates in the same direction.

   If the price starts to rise within the channel, it's helpful if the OVI becomes positive before the breakout. This increases the probability of a sustained move to the upside, enough to bag us a profit.

   If the price starts to fall within the channel, it's helpful if the OVI becomes negative before the breakdown. This increases the probability of a sustained down move.

Now that you know what we're looking for, let's look at a couple of charts showing channels with corroborating OVIs.

From Figure 3.18, you can see how Exxon Mobile (XOM) is forming a two-month sideways channel from August to September 2011.

- The resistance is well formed, having been initiated by the high at R1 before the pattern became a channel. At this point the snapback was merely a retracement.
- At R2, at the end of August, the level of $75 is tested before pulling back into what is now becoming a channel.
- This level is tested again at R3, with the OVI barely responding. The stock pulls all the way back into the channel and almost back to the August lows.
- At R4 the stock approaches the channel highs again before pulling back into the channel again for a couple of days.
- A couple of days later the stock is in the vicinity of the resistance again, but this time with a difference: The OVI has jumped into positive territory. At this point you can enter a buy stop limit order at $75.27, or a conditional order equivalent with deep in-the-money calls, an options spread, or just plain stock.

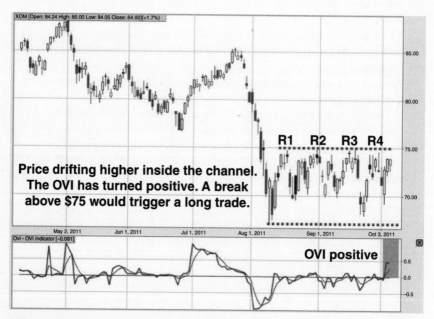

FIGURE 3.18   XOM Sideways Channel Chart
Source: OVI Charts. Courtesy of FlagTrader.com. Go to www.theinsideredge.com for more information.

From Figure 3.19, you can see how the OVI had turned positive before XOM broke the resistance to the upside. The stock then glides up into the 80s before pulling back steeply and breaking our rising trendline. This causes us to exit the trade . . . with a good profit.

Not all channels are as clear-cut as this; some do slant up or down. The key is to remain true to the principles of keeping things simple.

Figure 3.20 shows an example with Goldman Sachs (GS). The stock is channeling with steady highs just below $140 and slightly lower lows. The overall context is that of a longer-term downtrend.

Our resistance is just below $140, and GS fails to breach this level before taking a leg down toward its July low of $125.50. At the same time the OVI gets back into negative territory, so a break below this—say $125.18— would trigger a short trade.

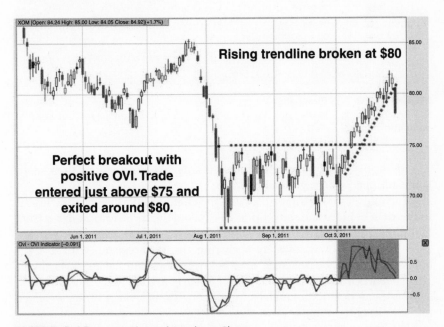

FIGURE 3.19 XOM Channel Breakout Chart
Source: OVI Charts. Courtesy of FlagTrader.com. Go to www.theinsideredge.com for more information.

FIGURE 3.20 GS Channel Chart
Source: OVI Charts. Courtesy of FlagTrader.com. Go to www.theinsideredge.com for more information.

GS is poised to break down below its July low, does so, and then keeps going, ultimately falling to below $85.

You may notice in Figure 3.20 that the channel lows keep getting lower, rather than being at the same price. I've linked the three lows starting from early June to mid-July.

While these lower lows are occurring, the $140 resistance level keeps holding. So what we're seeing here is lower lows and flat to lower highs. This is bearish, and by the time we get to early August with the July low in sight, we can position ourselves for a short if this level is broken—hence the $125.18 entry point.

In Chapter 4 you'll learn how to take profits as we complete our trading plan. We take a partial profit at a conservative target, and with the remainder we ride the trend for as long as possible, even adding to our position as the stock continues to make new flags and entry points.

Here, although GS falls to below $84, our second profit is more likely to be taken at around $100, as the downward trendline is broken in October (see Figure 3.21). This still represents a profitable down move of around $25 from our support break entry at $125.18.

FIGURE 3.21   GS Channel Breakdown Chart
Source: OVI Charts. Courtesy of FlagTrader.com. Go to www.theinsideredge.com for
more information.

Avoiding Market Manipulation with Channels   As with flags, remember there is an art to where you place your trades, to position them
away from the herd of amateurs.

Essentially this means we don't place our orders bang on support or
resistance levels but close to them.

Trading breakouts, when the price is rising and we go long, we want to
position our buy order slightly above the resistance level.

When the price is falling and we go short, we want to position our short
sell order slightly below the support level.

Channels Summary

Channels and imperfect, extended flag-type formations can be lucrative
patterns when they form with clear areas of support and resistance. As
you do with flags, you're looking for a breakout, preceded by a corroborating OVI.

The ideal qualities for our channels are:

- The channel is neat and visually recognizable.
- The channel has horizontal support and resistance levels defined by
  multiple highs and lows.

- The channel itself contains mini areas of support and resistance around which we can place our stops (we'll cover this in Chapter 4).
- The OVI is positive as the price rises toward resistance, and negative as the price declines toward support.

You can also consider stocks that aren't necessarily channeling, but that are approaching a key level of support or resistance. Again, a corroborating OVI will greatly enhance the chances of a breakout that will at least bring you to our first profit target.

Talking of which, we now need to identify our first profit target in the context of trading these patterns. As you'll see in Chapter 4, our trading plan identifies:

- Entry.
- Stop loss.
- First profit target (P1).
- Second profit using a trendline (P2).

Arguably the most difficult of these to define is our first profit target, and yet it is crucially important. Make it too ambitious and we risk not achieving a profit at all, even if the stock price goes in our favor, so it's vitally important to get this right.

SETTING THE FIRST PROFIT TARGET

What sets my best students apart from the others is that my best students religiously take partial profits at conservative targets, as I'm about to outline.

The One to One (1:1) Theory

The one to one (1:1) theory is also known at the equal drive pattern or simply the 1:1. The pattern gained notoriety among intraday S&P e-mini traders and is loosely based on Elliott Wave and Gann theory, neither of which I'm enthused by!

The premise of 1:1 is that a price makes an impulse move in the direction of the dominant trend and retraces a bit before then making a second move in the direction of the dominant trend. The theory is that the second move will match the magnitude of the first impulse move (see Figures 3.22 and 3.23).

While this theory is clearly flawed, we can modify it for the purposes of identifying a conservative and achievable first profit target after a breakout occurs.

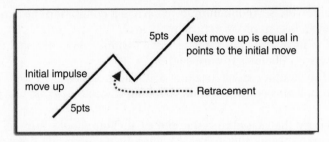

FIGURE 3.22   One to One (1:1) Up

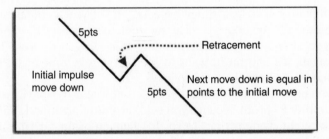

FIGURE 3.23   One to One (1:1) Down

Before we modify the theory to create our first profit target, it's important to emphasize why it's so important to have a first profit target in the first place.

The Need for a First Profit Target

The first question many of my students ask is: Why bother having a first profit target? It's a good question—and my answer draws upon an experience that every trader has experienced. It's all about psychology.

Nearly all traders have experienced this at least once!

Imagine you're a novice investor and you've just bought a stock for $50. The stock rises to $55 and you're very happy—but you don't take any profit off the table.

The next day you see the stock is now at $53, and you're still quite happy, but you're now thinking: "I won't sell until its back at $55."

The next day the stock is at $51. You now feel aggrieved at a measly $1 profit, so there's no way you're selling until it's back up again to at least $53!

Two days later the stock is at $49. What?! "There's no way I'm selling until I get back to breakeven."

The next day the stock is at $46; you're now holding a $4 loss!

I'm sure you get the picture . . . you've just committed the cardinal sin of allowing a decent profit to turn into a loss.

So, the next time this happens, let's assume you've learned from the experience.

You buy another stock, again at $50. The stock rises to $55—and this time you sell the entire position, banking a healthy $5, or 10 percent, profit.

In theory that should be the end of it. You should now be moving on to the next trade. But you're a human being, with emotions and ego, and most amateur traders don't have a trading strategy they can rely on, anyway!

So what do you do by instinct (especially if you're not confident enough in your method)? You take a peek at the stock to see where it is now—even though you already exited your position! Why do you do this? Because, being human, it's natural to want to see if you sold your position at the right place, capturing the most profit.

What happens next? You see the stock is now at $60! You've just missed out on another $5 profit because you sold the entire position at $55.

Being smart, you vow not to let that happen again. So what happens next time? You risk repeating the first scenario all over again, allowing a decent profit to turn into a loss.

This is typical of the psychological battles that can rage in your mind while you're trading. This is why you need a simple but clever trading plan that allows you to take a conservative first profit and yet still leave money on the table to ride a trend if the price keeps moving in your favor.

Some people say: Why have the first profit target at all? Why not just raise your initial stop and ride the trend that way? The answer is because if the stock gaps against you, then you've lost all your profits, which could be psychologically very damaging.

But if you took some off the table at a logical first profit target, even if the stock gaps a bit against you, you're still likely to walk away with an overall profit.

The basis of my trading plan is to keep you psychologically sound and balanced at all times. If you achieve this, then you're on your way to being a good trader, and my trading plan does ensure this.

Modifying the 1:1 to Create the First Profit Target (P1)

So while we accept that the 1:1 theory in itself is a flawed concept, with a slight modification we can make use of it to create a safe and achievable first profit target for our breakout trades.

Identifying our first profit target is a mixture of science and art. The 1:1 is partly derived from Gann and Elliott theory. Gann, Elliott, and Fibonacci are not so much divine indicators as they are self-fulfilling prophecies.

Some computer-automated trading programs are set to enter and exit trades based on the different Gann/Elliott/Fib levels, which means that different levels are going to be hit by price action on a seemingly uncanny frequency. But what you don't know is which levels may be hit in advance! Remember: We don't have hindsight with trading, though it doesn't stop people from being clever after the event.

Remember also that there are umpteen different levels for Gann/Elliott/Fib, so picking out which one is going to be the ultimate turning point for a particular move is as much guesswork as anything else. Do not be seduced by systems claiming they know which level will be hit in advance. I studied these theories for years to the cost of my sanity!

Calculating the First Profit Target (P1) So how do we use the concept of 1:1 for our first profit target? First we measure the initial impulse move. Let's say the stock thrusts up by $8.

Then we take a rough 0.382 ratio of that move: $0.382 \times 8 = 3.06$.

Then we add that figure to the breakout point to determine our first profit target (P1).

If there is other resistance (including round numbers) in the way, or we feel the target is too far away, we can always bring it closer and therefore easier to achieve. Remember: No one ever went broke by banking a profit!

In the example in Figure 3.24 shows a stock that moves up $8 to a high of $50 (this now forms resistance). The stock then retraces say by $2 down to $48.

The stock now starts to climb, and as it breaks above $50 your buy order is activated.

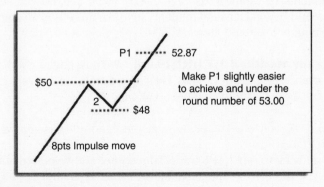

FIGURE 3.24 Modified One to One Up

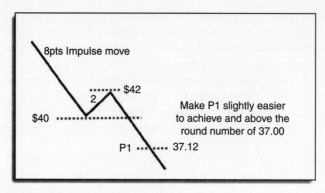

8pts Impulse move

2

$42

$40

Make P1 slightly easier
to achieve and above the
round number of 37.00

P1 ···· 37.12

FIGURE 3.25 Modified One to One Down

Our calculated target P1 is $50 + 3.06 = 53.06$. However, as you can see, this is just above and beyond a round number, so let's make this easier to achieve and bring the target closer and under \$53.00. Let's make it \$52.87.

Figure 3.25 shows a similar example in reverse, with the impulse being an \$8 move down.

This time let's say the stock thrusts down by \$8.

Then we take the approximate 0.382 ratio of that move: $0.382 \times 8 = 3.06$.

Deduct that figure from the breakout point to determine our first profit target (P1).

Again, if there is other support (including round numbers) in the way, or we feel the target is too far away, we can always bring it closer.

In Figure 3.25, the stock falls by \$8 to a low of \$40 (this now forms support). The stock then retraces say by \$2 up to \$42.

The stock then starts to fall again, and as it breaks below \$40 our sell short order is activated.

Our calculated target P1 is $40 - 3.06 = 36.94$. As you can see this is just below and beyond a round number, so make this easier to achieve and bring the target closer and above \$37.00. Let's make it \$37.12.

Applying the Modified 1:1 with Flags   We now have a good idea how to create our P1 first profit targets. Let's now take a look at real examples of a bull flag, bear flag, and channel breakout.

Bull Flags   We set our P1 for bull flags in exactly the same way as described in Figure 3.24.

Let's go back to our AAPL trade from earlier and calculate our P1. Remember: The aim is to set a reasonable and achievable first profit target, at which point we'll close out half of our position.

In Figure 3.26, you can see that the base of the impulse move (B) is at \$377.68. The top of the impulse move forms resistance (R) at \$409.09, making the impulse move 31.41 points.

Multiply this figure by 0.382 to arrive at the amount we're looking for the stock to move beyond the top of the bull flag.

$$0.382 \times 31.41 = 11.99 \text{ points}$$

Next, add this figure to the top of the bull flag to calculate our P1:

$$409.09 + 11.99 = \$421.08$$

So, \$421.08 is our first profit target. There's nothing wrong with this, though we can always bring it closer if we like. In this case, we could set it under \$421.00, or bring it under \$420.00 if we like. There's nothing ostensibly wrong with the calculated target. The point is we want to achieve it, so we can bank our profits so even if the stock retraces against us afterward, we'll still end up with a profit.

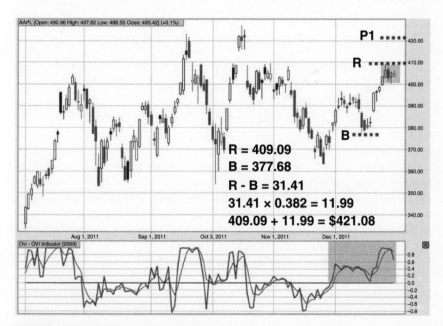

FIGURE 3.26 AAPL Bull Flag P1 Setup
Source: OVI Charts. Courtesy of FlagTrader.com. Go to www.theinsideredge.com for more information.

FIGURE 3.27   AAPL Bull Flag P1
Source: OVI Charts. Courtesy of FlagTrader.com. Go to www.theinsideredge.com for more information.

In this example, the stock rises past our P1 by a few points, before then stalling and forming another bull flag around our P1 area. This is not an uncommon phenomenon.

In Figure 3.27 you can see how our P1 is hit within just four days of the bull flag breakout.

Bear Flags   We set our P1 for bear flags in exactly the same way as described in Figure 3.25.

Let's return to our SFLY trade and calculate our P1. Again, the aim is to set a reasonable and achievable first profit target, at which point we'll close out half of our position.

In Figure 3.28 you can see that choosing the top of the impulse move isn't obvious, as there are effectively two levels to choose between. We can either take the start of the entire move (A) in October of $49.53, or the next resistance level down, which is marked (B) at $43.00 at the beginning of November. It depends on how confident you are of SFLY falling after you've done your calculations. The bottom of the bear flag (S) is at $35.38.

Let's compare the size of move that would be required for the two scenarios.

FIGURE 3.28 SFLY Bear Flag P1 Setup
Source: OVI Charts. Courtesy of FlagTrader.com. Go to www.theinsideredge.com for more information.

Using (A), the very beginning of the impulse move is at $49.53, and the bottom of the bear flag is at $35.38. This is a move of 14.15. Multiply this by 0.382, and we're looking for a further move of $5.40 from the bear flag low.

Subtract this figure from the bottom of the bear flag to calculate our P1:

$$35.38 - 5.40 = \$29.98$$

In this scenario, since we're being slightly aggressive with our P1, I would suggest bringing it nearer by raising it above $30.00. Something like $30.23 would be a suitable P1.

Using (B), the beginning of the impulse move is at $43.00, and the bottom of the bear flag is at $35.38. This is a move of 7.62. Multiply this by 0.382, and we're looking for a further move of $2.91 from the bear flag low.

Subtract this figure from the bottom of the bear flag to calculate our P1:

$$35.38 - 2.91 = \$32.47$$

So, which P1 are you going to choose here? To make a fully informed decision you'd have decided where your initial stop loss is going to be. Way back in Figure 3.9, we saw how you can place a stop above the bear flag consolidation area, but in reality you can choose to place it inside the flag if you're nervous about having such a wide stop. Remember, though: The tighter the initial stop, the more chance there is of being stopped out.

As you'll see in Figure 3.29, you'd have been happy with (A) or (B), as SFLY broke down beautifully. It only took two days for SFLY to hit (B) at $32.47. At this point, you close half of your position—meaning you take profits on that half—and then move your initial stop to near the bear flag breakout (S).

In this way you guarantee your profit on the entire trade unless there is a spectacular gap up past the newly adjusted stop. This would be highly unusual. Note, with this trade, that you have the trend (down) in your favor, you have the stock moving down in steps and bear flags, you have a negative OVI, and earnings has already passed. Having achieved even your modest P1 at (B), it would be astonishing for the stock to now gap up significantly.

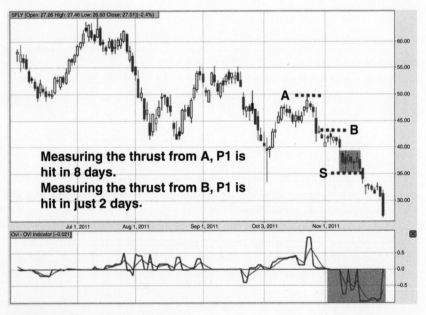

FIGURE 3.29   SFLY Bear Flag P1
Source: OVI Charts. Courtesy of FlagTrader.com. Go to www.theinsideredge.com for more information.

With the (A) target P1 at $30.23, it took six more days for the stock to reach that level. Again, the procedure is that once the P1 has been achieved, you take half profits and then adjust the stop to near the breakeven point (S). Even if the stock retraces from here, you'd simply break even on the second half of the trade while having made a profit on the first half of the trade.

We'll cover the entire trading plan in full in Chapter 4, but you're already getting an idea now of why P1 is an important part of the plan. It enables you to be rewarded for making a good trade, even if the stock then rebounds. Psychologically this is extremely important.

When the markets are not trending, many trades will rebound after hitting P1. Taking no reward for your good trade is a dangerous first step to bad trading habits. Take the partial reward at P1 and you'll feel good no matter if the stock rebounds against you, or if it keeps going in your favor and makes you a windfall profit on the second half of the trade.

Applying the Modified 1:1 with Channels   The modified 1:1 works in just the same way for channel breakouts. We can make money when the channel breaks in either direction. Let's look at a couple of examples.

Channels with Upward Breakouts   We set our P1 for channels with upward breakout in exactly the same way as described in Figure 3.24 above.

Let's return to our XOM trade and calculate our P1. The aim is to set a reasonable and achievable first profit target, at which point we'll close out half of our position.

In Figure 3.30, you can see that the channel has support at $67.03 and resistance at $74.98.

$$74.98 - 67.03 = 7.95$$

Multiply this figure by 0.382 to arrive at the amount we're looking for the stock to move beyond the resistance.

$$0.382 \times 7.95 = 3.04 \text{ points}$$

Add this figure to the top of the channel to calculate our target P1 for an upward breakout:

$$74.98 + 3.04 = \$78.02$$

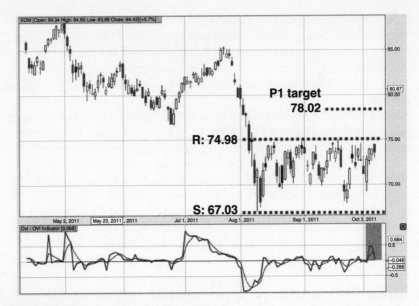

FIGURE 3.30 XOM Channel P1 Setup
Source: OVI Charts. Courtesy of FlagTrader.com. Go to www.theinsideredge.com for more information.

So our P1 target of $78.02 is conservative, reachable, and below the potentially psychological resistance of $80.

As you can see in Figure 3.31, this is achieved in just five trading days.

Calculating our P1 for upward channel breakouts is very simple, and we use the same method in reverse to calculate our target P1 for a downward channel breakout.

Channels with Downward Breakouts   We set our P1 for channels with downward breakout in exactly the same way as described in Figure 3.25 above.

Let's revisit our GS trade and calculate our P1. Again, the aim is to set a reasonable and achievable first profit target, at which point we'll close out half of our position.

In Figure 3.32, you can see that the channel has support at $125.50 and resistance at $139.25.

$$139.25 - 125.50 = 13.75$$

Multiply this figure by 0.382 to arrive at the amount we're looking for the stock to move beyond the support level.

$$0.382 \times 13.75 = 5.25 \text{ points}$$

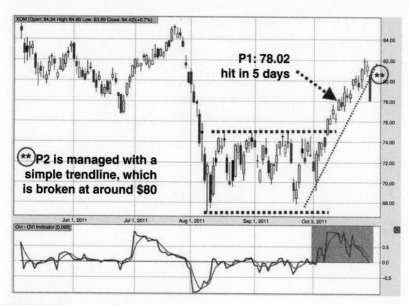

FIGURE 3.31 XOM Channel P1

Source: OVI Charts. Courtesy of FlagTrader.com. Go to www.theinsideredge.com for more information.

FIGURE 3.32 GS Channel P1 Setup

Source: OVI Charts. Courtesy of FlagTrader.com. Go to www.theinsideredge.com for more information.

FIGURE 3.33 GS Channel P1
Source: OVI Charts. Courtesy of FlagTrader.com. Go to www.theinsideredge.com for more information.

Subtract this figure from the bottom of the channel to calculate our target P1 for a downward breakout:

$$125.50 - 5.25 = \$120.25$$

So our P1 target of \$120.25 is just over 5 points away. This is conservative; it's reachable and closer than the potentially psychological resistance of \$120.00.

As you can see in Figure 3.33, this is achieved in just two trading days.

LEARNING POINTS

You can now see how exciting the OVI is when you trade with it in its proper context. For our purposes we're now focused on four main chart patterns:

- Bull flags
- Bear flags
- Channel breakouts (up)
- Channel breakout (down)

These patterns work well in conjunction with the OVI. Perhaps the most powerful use of this combination is where the OVI has been positive for a few days while a bull flag is forming or where the OVI has been negative for a few days as a bear flag is forming.

The same applies to channels. A powerful combination is where a rangebound sideways channel is forming and the OVI is positive for a few days as the stock price drifts up toward resistance before breaking out to the upside.

Similarly, we also look for where a rangebound sideways channel is forming and the OVI is negative for a few days as the stock drifts down towards support before breaking out to the downside.

Regardless of these four patterns, and regardless of the respective OVI position, our trade should only become active as the stock breaks out beyond support or resistance.

No doubt over time different traders will combine the OVI with other price patterns and indicators; that's the beauty of the OVI. Right now, I favor it with breakouts from consolidation patterns, but this was my preferred way of trading, anyway, so perhaps I'm biased!

In this chapter we've also learned to be discerning about the quality of patterns that we trade. We don't just trade any old flag; it has to conform so that we can construct a robust trading plan around the pattern with entry levels clearly defined. This enables us to set realistic and achievable first profit (P1) targets.

Taking an early first profit keeps your trading psychology sound. This is vital for a long and prosperous trading experience. While some initially question the wisdom of taking partial profits early, they soon discover its merits. It keeps you on the straight and narrow and gives you crucial early reward for a good trade, while still enabling you to make a windfall if the stock continues to trend in your favor.

With our style of trading, profits will come in bursts. In fact, the same goes for any style of end-of-day trading. Remember: What made shrewd observers suspicious of Bernie Madoff years before he was found out was the unusual consistency of his reported returns, month after month. Real-world investing and trading simply don't work like that.

The markets move in cycles, and different cycles may exhibit different characteristics at different times. Some cycles involve choppiness, which is challenging to trade, and some involve bursts of trending activity, which are a delight.

Our job is to tick along during the choppy times, and make serious hay during the trending times. The greatest trading fortunes are made during trending markets, so learn to love trading *with* the tide, not against it.

If you were going to ask me for the most ideal set up I would say a flag pattern occurring a few days after a stock has reported earnings—ideally as part of a shallow cup and handle, and preferably with the OVI positive for bull flags and negative for bear flag setups.

Figure 3.34 illustrates an example of this. AAPL forms its first bull flag at the end of December (F), a month before its earnings announcement.

It then gaps after its earnings announcement (E) and forms a new bull flag. The cup part of the entire pattern could be shallower in order to be completely ideal, but it's still very good! At the same time, the OVI has been persistently positive for two months. This is a near-perfect setup.

At this point AAPL drifts up and out of the bull flag, and immediately forms another miniature bull flag. So if you missed the first one, you can certainly get in if the second one breaks out—which it does (see Figure 3.35).

It bursts out above $460, all the way to $526 before retracing back to the trendline at around $500.

Figure 3.36 is a great example of another basing stock with a shallower cup but with no OVI reading, as it was a nonoptionable stock.

I don't typically look at penny stocks, but this was too hard to resist. Pacific Ethanol. Inc. (PEIX) was forming the bowl pattern over a three-month period, with the flag forming just under $0.80 (Figure 3.37). A break above $0.80 would trigger a buy order.

FIGURE 3.34   AAPL Post Earnings Bull Flag Setup
Source: OVI Charts. Courtesy of FlagTrader.com. Go to www.theinsideredge.com for more information.

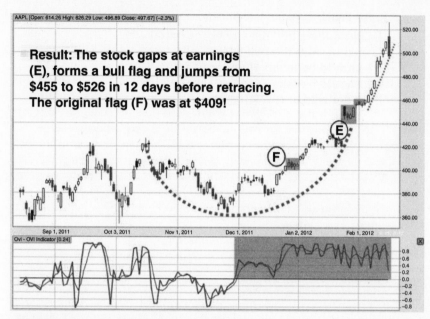

Result: The stock gaps at earnings (E), forms a bull flag and jumps from $455 to $526 in 12 days before retracing. The original flag (F) was at $409!

FIGURE 3.35 AAPL Post Earnings Bull Flag
Source: OVI Charts. Courtesy of FlagTrader.com. Go to www.theinsideredge.com for more information.

This stock has no OVI but was discovered due to the bull flag. In context with the shallow cup and handle, this is a fantastic pattern.

FIGURE 3.36 PEIX Cup and Handle Setup
Source: OVI Charts. Courtesy of FlagTrader.com. Go to www.theinsideredge.com for more information.

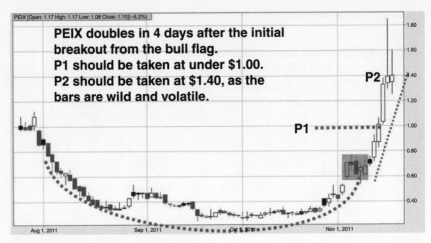

FIGURE 3.37   PEIX Cup and Handle
Source: OVI Charts. Courtesy of FlagTrader.com. Go to www.theinsideredge.com for
more information.

The stock now breaks out and has hit our P1 at just under $1.00 in just
two days.

Within four days, PEIX has more than doubled in a violent surge before
settling back down around $1.40.

If only we could find these setups every day!

In Chapter 4 we bring everything together to create the full trading
plan, including how to take our second profit (P2).

Our hope is that the stock trends well past P1 so that our P2 yields a
far greater profit.

If the stock doesn't fly, P2 can end up being the same as P1, which is
fine. If the stock were to hit our P1 and then snap back to our entry point,
we could have a scenario where we only break even on our P2.

However, even in those cases we still make a profit on the entire trade
because we had the discipline to take partial profits at P1 when it was up
for grabs.

This is the beauty of this simple but elegant trading plan.

CHAPTER 4

The Trading Plan

The Complete Trading Plan

In Chapter 3 we focused on the best chart patterns for breakout trading, and saw how powerful they are when combined with a clear OVI signal. The clearest OVI signal is where the OVI has been decisively positive or negative for several successive days.

We also started to create the ultimate trading plan for this type of trading.

In this chapter we complete the trading plan—a plan that is simple, safe, and yet enables you to make windfall profits if the stock price trends after the breakout.

Most people express their goal in trading as to "minimize risk and maximize reward," but this is a rather hackneyed and obvious statement. The real goal is to minimize risk and take partial profits when they're available, while also allowing for windfall profits, all within the same trading plan.

These are the steps we need to take:

(i) Find the trade according to our preferred criteria (consolidations, preferably with a corroborating OVI). Neat patterns with clear areas of support and resistance are the best ones to focus on.

(ii) Check the news to ensure an earnings announcement isn't about to happen with the stock we're looking to trade. Opening a trade right before the company announces earnings is tantamount to gambling, and that's not what we're about!

(iii) Decide the strategy (are you trading stocks or options?).

(iv) Place the trade.

(v) Manage the trade.

Let's get into more detail with points (iv) and (v) above in order to formulate our trading plan.

Placing and managing the trade consists of the following steps:

1. Enter just above resistance (when we're going long) or just below support (when we're shorting).

2. Set the initial stop loss at the same time.

3. Take half profits at the first profit target (P1). This means you exit half your stake at the P1 level, and leave the remaining half on.

4. Adjust the initial stop to near your initial entry point for the remaining half of the stake. This will now become a trailing stop if the stock continues to trend. For the trailing stop we typically use a diagonal trendline. (For uptrends our trendline rises diagonally just under the lows of the price bars. For downtrends our trendline falls diagonally just above the highs of the price bars. When the prices retrace sufficiently, our trendline is hit and our trailing stop is activated, meaning the second half of our trade is exited.)

5. Monitor and adjust the trailing stop as the price trends until you're stopped out for the second profit (P2).

As you'll see in the detailed trades below, you can use some discretion with your trendline to manage your P2 profit. This discretion includes being able to change the trendline angle and even pause it horizontally as the stock is retracing or forming new flags and channels.

The possible outcomes are as follows:

- No breakout means no losses because our trade isn't triggered in the first place.
- The price breaks out, triggering our entry, but then reverses before hitting our P1 target. In this case we're stopped out at our initial stop loss.
- The price breaks out, triggering our entry, reaches P1 for the first profit on half our stake, and then reverses. In this scenario we make the P1 for half our stake. Depending on how vicious the reversal is, our P2 could turn out to be the same as P1, less than P1, or even just a breakeven if the reversal goes all the way back to our initial entry point.

- The price breaks out, triggering our entry, reaches P1 for the first profit on half our stake, and then continues the direction of the dominant trend. In this scenario our P2 will be greater than our P1, potentially significantly so. There may even be the opportunity to add a new trade if the stock keeps making pauses as it trends. Where a price keeps trending, this is where we make our windfall profits seemingly effortlessly.

With this trading plan we already have the odds in our favor. Because we only enter on a breakout, and because we set a modest first profit target at P1 and immediately adjust our initial stop to near breakeven, we're already using basic probabilities to work for us. We're also ensuring that our mindset will stay on the straight and narrow.

ORDER TYPES

To make our trading plan as user-friendly as possible it's important that we're not stuck to our screens all day ensuring our orders are placed correctly. To make this possible we can take advantage of the different types of order that are available with brokers.

The Stop-Limit Order to Open

To enter our trades, with a traditional online broker we can use a stop-limit order. This combines the features of a stop order with those of a limit order. Let's look at these two orders and how they are combined to give us maximum control and safety with our order to open.

- A stop order is defined as an order to buy or sell a security when its price surpasses a particular level. Once the price surpasses the predefined entry point, the stop order becomes a market order.

  In the case of a bull flag, our buy stop to open would be placed just above the resistance as the price rises out of the consolidation.

  In the case of a bear flag, our sell stop to open would be placed just below the support as the price falls below the consolidation.

  We're on the right track with this, but the stop order is not a guarantee of getting the desired entry point. For example, with our bull flag scenario, if we place a buy stop to open at $50.35, and the price gaps up beyond $50.35, our stop order will trigger where the stock has gapped up to, not the stop price of $50.35 as we specified. If the stock gapped up significantly, we've now bought at a much higher price than we wanted, and then the chances are that the price could soon retrace against us as it fills the gap, leaving us nursing a nasty drawdown.

We need to prevent this scenario from happening, and luckily we can by combining a limit order with the stop order.

Before we get to the limit order, let's consider the same gapping scenario with a bear flag where we activate a sell stop to open. So if we place a sell stop to open at $39.87, and the price gaps down below $39.87, our stop order will trigger where the stock has gapped down to, not the stop price of $39.87 we specified. If the stock gapped down significantly we've now shorted at a much lower price than we wanted, and then the chances are that the price could soon retrace against us as it fills the gap, leaving us nursing a nasty drawdown.

So now let's look at how the limit order can help us:

A limit order is defined as an order to buy or sell a security at a specified price or better. So if our limit to buy is $50.35, then $50.35 will be the maximum price we'll pay. If our limit to sell is $39.87, then $39.87 is the lowest price at which we'll sell.

Let's combine the stop and the limit to create the stop-limit order:

- A buy stop-limit order combines both elements to ensure we buy when a price has been surpassed (the stop part), but we control the maximum price at which we buy (the limit part).

    Similarly, a sell stop-limit ensures that we sell when a price has been surpassed (on the way down; this is the stop part), but we control the minimum price at which we sell (the limit part).

In summary, a stop-limit order will be executed at a specified price (or better) after a given stop price has been reached. Once the stop price is reached, the limit prevents us from entering beyond the limit price.

Buy Stop-Limit to Open Expanding on our example above, we have a bull flag with a high of $50.30. If we want to buy the stock at $50.35 but no higher, we place a buy stop-limit order to open with both parts at $50.35. This means the stock must trade through $50.35 for our trade to become activated (the stop part). If it gaps up beyond that level then the trade is not executed (the limit part).

Let's now say we're happy to buy if the stock reaches $50.35, but we're also happy to buy it at any price up to $50.88. In this case we set up our buy stop-limit order with the stop at $50.35 and limit at $50.88. This ensures that the trade will trigger at $50.35 at best. However, if the stock gaps up beyond this level, the trade can still be executed between $50.35 and $50.88, but no higher.

Sell Stop-Limit to Open Repeating the exercise for the bear flag, it has a low of $40.02. If we want to short the stock at $39.87 but no lower, we place a sell stop-limit order to open with both parts at $39.87. This means the stock must trade down through $39.87 for our short trade to become activated (the stop part). If it gaps down beyond that level then the trade is not executed (the limit part).

Let's now say we're happy to short if the stock reaches $39.87, but we're also happy to short it at any price down to $39.44. In this case we set up our sell stop-limit order with the stop at $39.87 and limit at $39.44. This ensures that the trade will trigger at $39.87 at best. However, if the stock gaps down beyond this level, the trade can still be executed between $39.87 and $39.44, but no lower.

THE TRADING PLAN

So our trading plan can be summarized as follows:

- Entry.
- Initial stop loss.
- Take profits on half the stake at P1.
- Adjust the initial stop.
- Monitor and adjust the trailing stop for P2.

This basic plan will be used for bull flags, bear flags, and channel breakouts both up and down.

Bull Flag Trading Plan

Let's remember the ideal bull flag we should be familiar with by now in Figure 4.1.

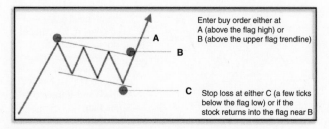

FIGURE 4.1 The Ideal Bull Flag

The bull flag potentially has two resistance levels. If the bull flag has consolidated sideways, then the only possible entry point is at Level A, just above the flag high.

If the bull flag has retraced downward, then the most recent point of the upper trendline is the other. Level B is just above this.

Bull Flag—Entry   We can enter our buy stop-limit order at Level A or Level B. Level A is more conservative, as it is higher. Because it is above the highest resistance level for the entire pattern, if the stock price reaches it, the chances of a double top occurring are lower.

In rampantly bullish trending markets, Level B would be appropriate as a more aggressive entry point.

If the top of the flag is $50, then Level A will be slightly above this—say around $50.17.

Bull Flag—Initial Stop Loss   With a tight, neat bull flag we typically place our initial stop loss under the base of the consolidation at Level C in Figures 4.1 and 4.2.

There is an alternative, however, especially where the flag is not so tight.

If our entry is at Level A (just above the entire pattern) then you could have a stop just below Level B at Level C1 (see Figure 4.2). So, if a stock price breaks out to trigger our trade at Level A, only to reverse back into the flag consolidation, then you could have your initial stop loss within the consolidation itself around Level C1.

Having the stop here means your bear less risk on the trade, but because your stop is now nearer your entry point, your risk of being stopped out in the first place is higher.

At this point I should nail my colors to the mast and say that I typically prefer to enter at Level A, and, provided the flag is tight, I'm usually okay with my initial stop at Level C.

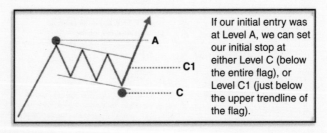

If our initial entry was at Level A, we can set our initial stop at either Level C (below the entire flag), or Level C1 (just below the upper trendline of the flag).

FIGURE 4.2   Bull Flag Initial Stop (a)

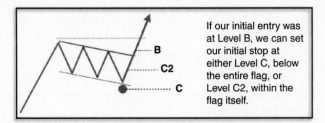

If our initial entry was at Level B, we can set our initial stop at either Level C, below the entire flag, or Level C2, within the flag itself.

FIGURE 4.3   Bull Flag Initial Stop (b)

If your entry is at Level B (just above the upper trendline of the flag) then you can have your initial stop loss either just below the base (Level C), or within the actual flag itself—just below the halfway point of the consolidation around Level C2 (see Figure 4.3).

Bull Flag—First Profit Target (P1)   Our first profit target is where we exit half our stake, taking profits on that portion of the trade. When we do this we'll also have to adjust the initial stop (we'll cover that shortly). The remaining half of the trade is still active as the price hopefully continues trending in our favor.

We covered how to calculate our P1 in Chapter 3.

Entering at Level A   If we enter the trade at Level A (just above the very top of the flag), we take the length of the flagpole, extend it upward by 0.382 beyond the high point of the flag pattern. Then round down as appropriate to set an easier target to reach.

In Figure 4.4 our flagpole is 8 points. So the move we're looking for beyond the breakout is:

$$8.00 \times 0.382 = 3.06$$

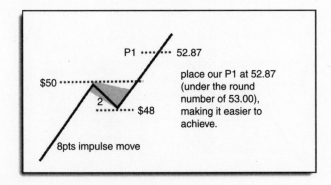

place our P1 at 52.87 (under the round number of 53.00), making it easier to achieve.

FIGURE 4.4   Bull Flag First Profit Target (a)

If our top-of-flag resistance is at $50, then we add 3.06 to this figure to calculate our P1:

$$3.06 + 50 = 53.06$$

But let's make our target easier to reach by setting it under the round number of $53.00 at say $52.87.

Remember: We can always bring our P1 in closer and therefore easier to achieve.

In this example below, we have a stock that moves up $8 to a high of $50. The stock then retraces by $2 to $48. This $2 retracement could have taken the form of a flag.

As the stock then resumes its ascent, our buy order is activated as it trades through our stated entry point of $50.17.

With P1 at $52.87, the amount of our first profit is:

$$52.87 - 50.17 = 2.70$$

Don't be disappointed that this first profit seems quite small. Remember, that's the point, and it's only part of your potential profit in this trade. Bagging the first profit secures a quick reward for us that also enables us to modify our initial stop loss into a trailing stop, thereby protecting what we already have.

Entering at Level B   Looking next at Figure 4.5, if you entered your trade at Level B (just above the flag's upper trendline), then you can use the same P1 as we did for Figure 4.4, or you could bring the calculated P1 target nearer to our Level B entry point.

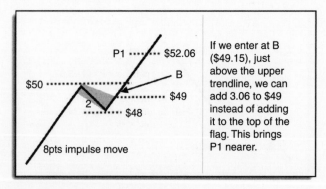

FIGURE 4.5   Bull Flag First Profit Target (b)

For our entry at Level B we'll use the same length of flagpole at 8 points. So the move we're looking for beyond the breakout is the same as before:

$$8.00 \times 0.382 = 3.06$$

If the most recent point of the flag's upper trendline resistance is at $49.00, then we can add 3.06 to this figure to calculate our P1:

$$3.06 + 49.00 = 52.06$$

Using the same example as in Figure 4.4, the only difference now is that we're entering at Level B, just above $49.00 (say at $49.15), rather than Level A ($50.17), which was just above the top of the entire flag pattern.

As the stock then resumes its ascent, our buy order is activated as it trades through our stated entry point of say $49.15.

With P1 at $52.06, the amount of our first profit is:

$$52.06 - 49.15 = 2.91$$

Bull Flag—Adjusting the Initial Stop   Now that we've secured our first profit, we need to adjust our initial stop (see Figure 4.6).

Remember: If we bought 200 shares in the first place, our initial stop would be with respect to those 200. Once we close half our position (100 shares) the stop now only relates to our remaining 100 still open.[1]

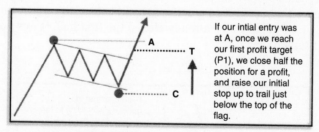

If our intial entry was at A, once we reach our first profit target (P1), we close half the position for a profit, and raise our initial stop up to trail just below the top of the flag.

FIGURE 4.6   Bull Flag Adjusting the Initial Stop (a)

---

[1]If you'd chosen to buy options contracts, then the same principle applies. If you'd bought 10 call contracts in the first place, you'd now be taking profits on 5 and keeping 5 open. Ideally you'd be buying deep in-the-money calls whose entry was contingent on the stock breakout and where the first profit was taken as the stock reached P1.

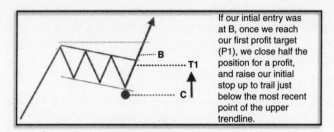

If our intial entry was at B, once we reach our first profit target (P1), we close half the position for a profit, and raise our initial stop up to trail just below the most recent point of the upper trendline.

FIGURE 4.7 Bull Flag Adjusting the Initial Stop (b)

So now we need to raise the level of the stop so it's at or just below our initial entry point. Placing it just below our entry point enables the stock price to test the breakout level without stopping us out.

If our initial entry point was at Level A (above the entire flag), then we raise the stop to trail just below this at Level T.

If our initial entry point was at Level B (above the most recent point of the upper trendline of the flag), then we raise the stop to trail just below this at Level T1 (see Figure 4.7).

Bull Flag—P2 Trailing Stop So far, so good—and now it's just a matter of managing the second half of the trade with a trailing stop (see Figure 4.8).

- From here, if the stock price reverses to below our entry point, hitting our adjusted stop, we'd make a tiny loss (or break even, depending on where you adjusted it to) on the second half of the trade, but overall we're up because we've already closed the first half of our position at the P1 target.

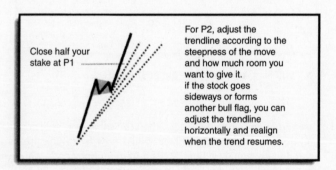

Close half your stake at P1

For P2, adjust the trendline according to the steepness of the move and how much room you want to give it. if the stock goes sideways or forms another bull flag, you can adjust the trendline horizontally and realign when the trend resumes.

FIGURE 4.8 Bull Flag Trailing Stop

- If the price meanders sideways, our adjusted stop holds firm horizontally until the stock either breaks down or resumes the uptrend.
- If the price resumes the uptrend, then we manage this with a simple rising trendline.

We draw a rising trendline under the bar lows as higher lows are made.

There is some room for discretion when it comes to managing your P2 profits with the rising trendline. If the stock price rises beyond P1 and then starts to form what might become another bull flag, you may want to adjust the trendline horizontally for a while to see if the price can make another burst upward.

Trends occur in steps and flags. Our windfalls depend on riding trends, so we need to give ourselves a chance to do so without being stopped out prematurely. At the same time, safety is our mantra.

Furthermore, you can always add another entry to each new flag and repeat the trading plan, thereby adding to your position in a very safe way, taking P1 targets each time, and potentially having several P2s running all at the same time.

Prevailing market conditions will have a bearing on how aggressively you manage your trendline for P2. In a choppy market you may keep it tight, especially if the stock rises very steeply before retracing just as severely.

In a low-volatility, stable, trending market you may want to keep the trendline quite loose in order to give the stock price room to keep trending. It's in trending markets where we make our windfall profits, and, once you've been trading this method for a while, you'll get a feel for which type of market we're in.

Also, by trading in this way, you only need one or two rockets to really boost your batting averages. If you just stick with prime OVI-flag combinations you'll have fewer trades, but the quality will be phenomenal, and you'll have more chance of picking up one of these . . .

Bull Flag Example—Apple (AAPL)   We've already seen part of this trade with AAPL, so let's complete the picture by outlining the entire trading plan. This has all been happening while I've been writing this book. It didn't require hindsight and it's the kind of setup you should be focusing on from now on.

Entry and Initial Stop Loss   So, AAPL forms a classic bull flag OVI combination at the very end of December 2011 (see Figure 4.9).

The flag high is at $409.09, so our entry level can be at say $409.37. I've simply picked a non-rounded number beyond the resistance of the top of the flag.

Because the flag pattern is so well defined and the OVI has been consistently positive for over a month by this time, we can place the initial stop loss below the low of the flag. The flag low here is at $400.51, so we'll place our initial stop below $400—say nicely out of the way at $399.87.

The difference between our entry and our stop is the risk we take on the trade.

$$409.37 - 399.87 = 9.50$$

This may seem like a lot of risk, but in context it's around 2.3 percent of the stock price. Remember: For our trade to be activated the stock price must break beyond the flag resistance. We also have a fantastic OVI here, so there's reason to be quietly confident. Of course, this must also be placed in the context of where we set our first profit target (P1).

So you enter a buy stop limit order with the stop and limit components at $409.37, meaning the price has to trade through this level in order to activate the trade. A gap above this level will not trigger the order unless the price then retraces back through it. On the protection side of things, your initial (sell) stop loss is at $399.87.

In this case, AAPL gaps up to $409.40 at the open on January 3, and retraces back to $409.00 before starting to climb up again. Our stop limit

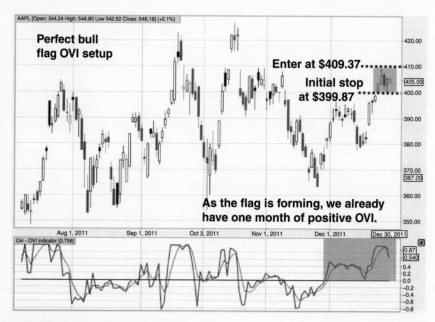

FIGURE 4.9 AAPL Bull Flag
Source: OVI Charts. Courtesy of FlagTrader.com. Go to www.theinsideredge.com for more information.

order has prevented us from being filled at the open, but we are filled as the price trades through $409.37. In this case it occurs as the price is falling from initial opening gap level, but happily the drawdown here is only 37 cents before AAPL resumes its climb.

P1–First Profit Target   The next step is to determine our P1. We learned about this in Chapter 3, where we also went through this particular example.

To set our P1, we extend the impulse move (or flagpole) by around 0.382 beyond the resistance we use to enter the trade.

In Figure 4.10 the base of the impulse move (B) is at $377.68. The top of the impulse move (and indeed the top of the bull flag) forms resistance (R) at $409.09, making the flagpole 31.41 points in length.

We now multiply this figure by 0.382, to arrive at the amount we're looking for the stock to move beyond the top of the bull flag.

$$0.382 \times 31.41 = 11.99 \text{ points}$$

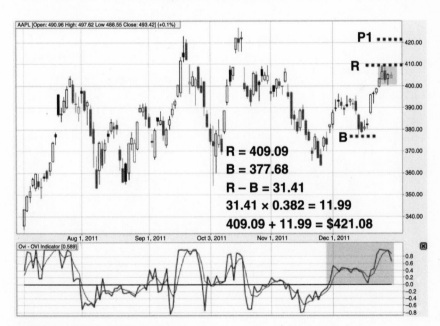

FIGURE 4.10   AAPL Bull Flag P1
Source: OVI Charts. Courtesy of FlagTrader.com. Go to www.theinsideredge.com for more information.

Now we add this figure to the top of the bull flag to calculate our P1:

$$409.09 + 11.99 = \$421.08$$

Remember from Chapter 3 we noted that we could bring the P1 target slightly closer by adjusting it down from $421.08 to under $421.

We can see in Figure 4.10 that this level is comfortably below the September and October highs (which could form future resistance), so I'm happy with $421.08 as our P1.

In Figure 4.11 you can see how our P1 is hit just four days after the breakout.

So far, so good. This was a relatively clean breakout with a minimal drawdown due the opening gap, and now we need to manage the remainder of our position.

We close half of our position for a profit at P1 ($421.08) and will have to manage the remaining stake.

Adjust the Initial Stop and Manage Trade for P2 Profit   Our first job is to adjust the initial stop by raising it to near our entry level. This means

FIGURE 4.11   AAPL Bull Flag P1
Source: OVI Charts. Courtesy of FlagTrader.com. Go to www.theinsideredge.com for more information.

that if the stock retraces below this point, the second half of our trade may yield nothing or even a very slight loss, but overall we still make profit on the trade.

Our entry level here was $409.37, so having reached P1, we can now raise the stop from its original level of $399.87 to just below the top of the flag—say at $408.87. This means that if the stock falls and tests the flag high we can still be in the trade if it bounces straight back up from the flag high level (see Figure 4.12).

Having achieved our P1 target, sometimes we can raise the initial stop beyond the breakeven level and directly under the rising trendline. In this case with AAPL, it seems sensible to track the stock as it trends upward, but we need to be mindful of a couple of things in this particular case.

First, AAPL has earnings after the close on January 24 (just over two weeks away) and we need to decide how to play this. Either we can bank all our profits before earnings, or we can decide to keep something on the table.

With the OVI so positive, the trend so strong, and because it's AAPL, provided the stock doesn't retrace too severely, it's probably worth keeping

FIGURE 4.12 AAPL Bull Flag—Adjusting the Initial Stop
Source: OVI Charts. Courtesy of FlagTrader.com. Go to www.theinsideredge.com for more information.

some skin in the game here. It would have to be a shockingly disastrous earnings report to wipe out our banked P1 profits here.

This leads to the second point. If a stock does continue to trend after surpassing the P1 target, it is likely to do so in surges and steps on the way up, interspersed with retracements and sideways pauses. In our pursuit of the windfall P2 profit, the art is to only be stopped out by a severe retracement, and not a sideways move, unless the sideways price action takes too long (weeks).

Let's track this AAPL trade and trace how you'd trade it step by step. Remember: After P1 you've already banked profit. Now it's a matter of maximizing the situation by giving yourself every chance to ride the trend if it does materialize. Remember that this is AAPL in January 2012. From what I can see it looks good, and I want to be part of any upside.

Figure 4.13 shows AAPL forming a new bull flag as of January 13. Earnings is on January 24. This looks like a decent flag, so it's worth keeping your stop underneath it.

As you can see, managing the P2 does have a discretionary element to it. The old saying goes that no one ever went broke making a profit, and

FIGURE 4.13　AAPL Bull Flag—P2

Source: OVI Charts. Courtesy of FlagTrader.com. Go to www.theinsideredge.com for more information.

I subscribe to that sentiment. However, when you have an opportunity as good as this staring you in the face, the only way I want to be taken out of it is in the event of a major retracement going against me.

With this in mind we need to give AAPL some room to breathe. It's currently forming another bull flag right before earnings, so our trailing stop should pause horizontally under the lows of this flag, and we'll see what happens. If the price falls further then we're out, but if it stabilizes we're still in the hunt for a windfall.

Your alternative is to simply keep your remaining stop at breakeven— that is, at $409.37, where we opened the trade in the first place. If the second half of our trade is stopped out here, we still win overall.

Remember: We entered at $409.37 and we took our first profit at $421.08, meaning for half our stake we've banked 11.71 points. Over the next few days, AAPL churns up and down as the earnings announcement looms. Provided the stock doesn't gap down to under $397.66, we're still making a profit on the entire trade.

In Figure 4.14 you can see, as it stands on earnings day, AAPL closes at $420.41 with the announcement due after the close.

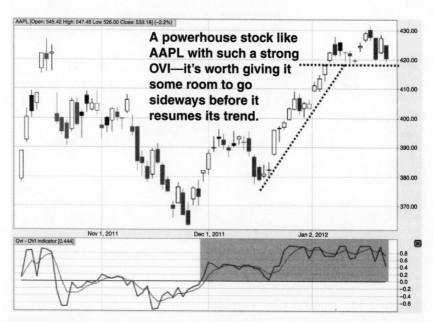

FIGURE 4.14   AAPL Bull Flag—Before Earnings
Source: OVI Charts. Courtesy of FlagTrader.com. Go to www.theinsideredge.com for more information.

With the OVI so positive, the trend unambiguously upward, the stock in question being such an earnings powerhouse, it would be a big surprise if it gaps down. So we're taking an informed and calculated position here.

What happens next vindicates our position. AAPL gaps up after earnings and then makes our dreams come true by consolidating again ... twice!

This is as perfect as it gets, and we can even add to our position by entering long into the new bull flag. (There are actually two beside each other, shaded above the earnings gap (E) in Figure 4.15.)

Even if we don't add to our position, we're in great shape with a good chance that the stock will continue to trend in our favor.

We can now move our trailing stop in any number of ways. In Figure 4.15 you can see how the dotted line (our P2 trailing stop) zigzags with the stock price, and I've extended it horizontally after the earnings gap. This is to allow for the price to fill the gap, but you may prefer to trail the stock with a continuing rising trendline.

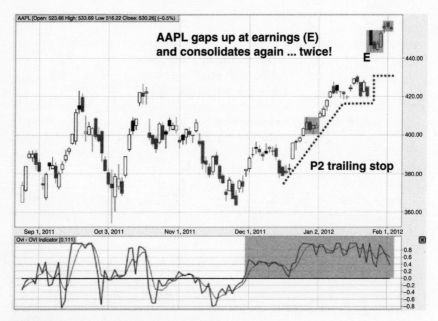

FIGURE 4.15   AAPL Bull Flag—After Earnings
Source: OVI Charts. Courtesy of FlagTrader.com. Go to www.theinsideredge.com for more information.

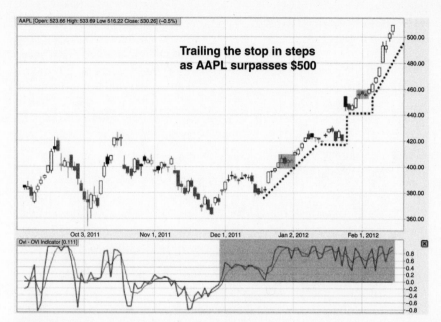

FIGURE 4.16 AAPL Bull Flag—Riding the Trend
Source: OVI Charts. Courtesy of FlagTrader.com. Go to www.theinsideredge.com for more information.

My feeling here is that we have a stock with very strong fundamentals, very strong technicals, and a very strong OVI, and at this time the market was also strong. This creates a perfect storm for windfall profits.

Once again our stance is vindicated as AAPL roars ahead to break new highs, taking out the $500 barrier (see Figure 4.16).

Surely now this stock must take a rest! And indeed it does, for all of two days, albeit that the two days were the result of profit taking rather than weakness in the stock. Regardless, we have to set our trailing stop without the benefit of hindsight, and that means a sensible place would be under $500.

Unless we choose to give AAPL room to retrace seriously steeply, we're finally stopped out of this trade on February 15 at $499.72, which is $90.35 higher than our initial entry point (see Figure 4.17). With no leverage, that's 22 percent in just six weeks! Even with deep in-the-money call options, you'd have made around 70 percent in profit. Given that the OVI is derived from options transaction activity, it's a fair assumption that there were many happy AAPL options traders.

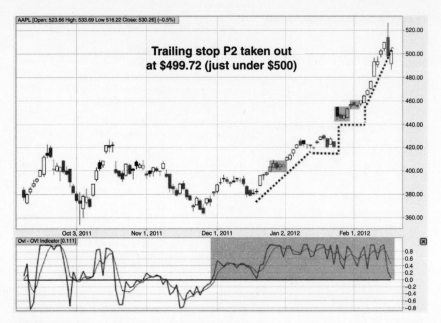

FIGURE 4.17   AAPL Bull Flag—P2 Stopped Out
Source: OVI Charts. Courtesy of FlagTrader.com. Go to www.theinsideredge.com for
more information.

As it happens, during the two-day retracement AAPL plunges to a low
of $486.63, which at the time looks like it justifies our decision to take prof-
its. But there's more to come.

Within a few days it's clear that the two-day retracement was a short-
term blip, and with AAPL being one stock we look at regularly, it's only a
matter of time until the next opportunity comes along (see Figure 4.18).

AAPL forms a new bull flag at $548.21, which looks like it's failing on
March 6 and 7, but immediately turns back up again, and breaks the resistance on March 12.

Within another few weeks the stock reached $621.45, for another 70 +
points of profit (not included in the results here). So, we may have missed
out the 50-odd points from around $499.72 to $548.21, but we were able
to grab the next opportunity when it came in March. Regardless of that,
for the main trade we didn't have hindsight that it was going to go on and
on, and yet we still picked up a meaty chunk of the rise from January to
February.

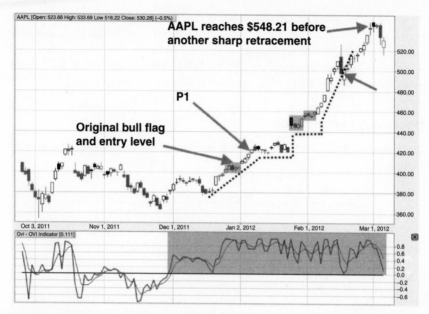

FIGURE 4.18 AAPL Bull Flag—Post Trade Action

Source: OVI Charts. Courtesy of FlagTrader.com. Go to www.theinsideredge.com for more information.

Summary of Original AAPL Trade

Action	Price	Comment
Entry	$409.37	Flag high at $409.09. Buy stop limit at $409.37 on January 3.
Initial stop loss	$399.87	Under the bull flag low ($9.50 or 2.32% risk on the trade).
First profit target (P1)	$421.08	0.382 upward extension of flagpole beyond the flag high. This was a reasonable and achievable target given the favorable conditions. 11.71 points profit.
Trailing stop		Stepped rising trendline as AAPL continued to trend.
P2 Level	$499.72	Rising trendline broken on February 15. 90.35 points profit.
Profit		• 11.71 points (2.86%) for the first half of the stake in just four days.
		• 90.35 points (22.1%) on the second half.
		• 51.03 points average profit (12.47% in just six weeks).
		• Annualized compounded profit: 177%.

This is an astonishing share price performance, especially when you consider at the time that AAPL, at the time of writing, is the most valuable corporation in the United States.

That takes us through the AAPL bull flag trade in real detail. We're now going to cover a bear flag trade and two channel breakouts (up and down).

Bear Flag Trading Plan

Let's recall the ideal bear flag, which we should be familiar with by now, in Figure 4.19:

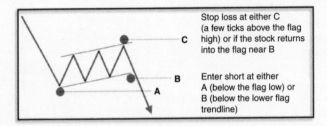

FIGURE 4.19   The Ideal Bear Flag

The bear flag potentially has two support levels. If the bear flag has consolidated sideways, then the only possible entry point is at Level A, just below the flag low.

If the bear flag has retraced upward against the dominant trend, then the most recent point of the lower trendline is the other. Level B is just below this.

Bear Flag—Entry   We can enter our sell stop-limit (to open) order at Level A or Level B. Level A is more conservative, as it is lower. Being below the lowest support level for the entire pattern, if the stock price reaches it, the chances of a double bottom occurring are lower.

In technical bearish trending markets, Level B would be appropriate as a more aggressive entry point, though I emphasize the word "technical" as distinct from a volatile news-driven bear market.

If the bottom of the flag is $40, then Level A will be slightly below this— say around $39.87.

Bear Flag—Initial Stop Loss   With a tight, neat bear flag we typically place our initial stop loss above the top of the consolidation at Level C in Figure 4.19.

There is an alternative, however, especially where the flag is not so tight.

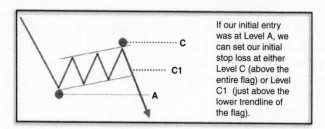

If our initial entry was at Level A, we can set our initial stop loss at either Level C (above the entire flag) or Level C1 (just above the lower trendline of the flag).

FIGURE 4.20 Bear Flag Initial Stop (a)

Looking at Figure 4.20, if our entry is at Level A (just below the entire pattern) then you could have a stop just above Level B at Level C1. So, if a stock price breaks out to trigger our trade at Level A, only to reverse back into the flag consolidation, then you could have your initial stop loss within the consolidation itself around Level C1.

Having the stop here means your bear less risk on the trade, but, because your stop is now nearer your entry point, your risk of being stopped out in the first place is higher.

Similar to the bull flag earlier, I typically prefer to enter just beyond the extreme of the flag, and, provided the flag is tight, I'm usually okay with my initial stop just beyond the other extreme.

If your entry is at Level B (just below the lower trendline of the bear flag) then you can have your initial stop loss either just above the top (Level C) or within the actual flag itself—just above the halfway point of the consolidation around Level C2 (see Figure 4.21).

Bear Flag—First Profit Target (P1) You're now fully aware that our first profit target is where we exit half our stake, taking profits on that portion of the trade. Remember that we'll also have to adjust the initial stop (more on that shortly). The remaining half of the trade is still active as the price hopefully continues trending (down here) in our favor.

We learned how to calculate our P1 in Chapter 3.

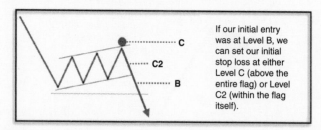

If our initial entry was at Level B, we can set our initial stop loss at either Level C (above the entire flag) or Level C2 (within the flag itself).

FIGURE 4.21 Bear Flag Initial Stop (b)

Entering at Level A If we enter the trade at Level A (just below the very bottom of the flag), we take the length of the flagpole, and extend it downward by 0.382 beyond the low point of the flag pattern. Then round down as appropriate to set an easier target to reach.

In Figure 4.22 our flagpole is 8 points. So the move we're looking for beyond the breakout is:

$$8.00 \times 0.382 = 3.06$$

If our bottom-of-flag support is at $40, then we subtract 3.06 from this figure to calculate our P1:

$$40 - 3.06 = 36.94$$

We can make our target slightly easier to reach by setting it above the round number of $37.00—say $37.14.

Remember: We can always bring our P1 in closer and therefore make it easier to achieve.

In the example below, we have a stock that moves down $8 to a low of $40. The stock then retraces by $2 to $42. This $2 retracement may have taken the form of a bear flag.

As the stock then resumes its descent, our sell-to-open order is activated as it trades through our stated entry point of $39.87.

With P1 at $37.14, the amount of our first profit is:

$$39.87 - 37.14 = 2.73$$

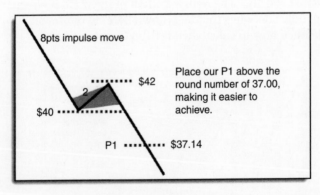

FIGURE 4.22   Bear Flag First Profit Target (a)

Remember: Once we've secured and banked our first profit, we can modify our initial stop loss into a trailing stop, thereby protecting what we already have.

Entering at Level B Looking next at Figure 4.23, if you entered your trade at Level B (just below the flag's lower trendline), then you can use the same P1 as we did for Figure 4.22 above, or you could bring the calculated P1 target nearer to our Level B entry point.

In Figure 4.22 our flagpole is 8 points. So the move we're looking for beyond the breakout is the same as before:

$$8.00 \times 0.382 = 3.06$$

If the most recent point of the flag's lower trendline support is at $41.00, then we can subtract 3.06 from this figure to calculate our P1:

$$41.00 - 3.06 = 37.94$$

Using the same example as in Figure 4.22, the only difference now is that we're entering short at Level B, just below $41—say at $40.87—rather than Level A ($39.87), which was just below the bottom of the entire flag pattern.

As the stock then resumes its descent, our sell-to-open order is activated as it trades through our stated entry point of say $40.87.

With P1 at $37.94, the amount of our first profit is:

$$40.87 - 37.94 = 2.93$$

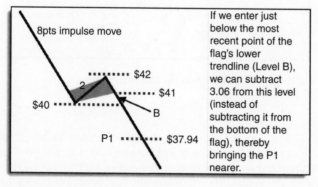

FIGURE 4.23 Bear Flag First Profit Target (b)

Bear Flag—Adjusting the Initial Stop   Now that we've secured our first profit, we need to adjust our initial stop (see Figure 4.24).

If we shorted 200 shares in the first place, our initial stop would be with respect to those 200. Once we close half our position (100 shares) the stop loss now only relates to our remaining 100 still open.[2]

So we need to lower the level of the stop so it's now at or just above our short entry point. Placing it just above our entry point enables the stock price to test the breakout level without stopping us out.

If our initial entry point was at Level A (below the entire flag), then we lower the stop to trail just above this at Level T.

If our initial entry point was at Level B (below the most recent point of the lower trendline of the flag) then we lower the stop to trail just above this at Level T1 (see Figure 4.25).

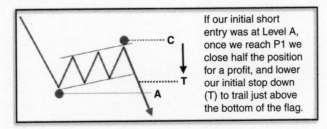

FIGURE 4.24   Bear Flag Adjusting the Initial Stop (a)

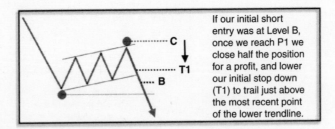

FIGURE 4.25   Bear Flag Adjusting the Initial Stop (b)

---

[2]If you'd chosen to buy put options, then the same principle applies. If you'd bought 10 put contracts in the first place, you'd now be taking profits on 5 and keeping 5 open. Ideally you'd be buying deep in-the-money puts whose entry was contingent on the stock breakdown and where the first profit was taken as the stock reached P1.

Bear Flag—P2 Trailing Stop So far, so good—and now it's just a matter of managing the second half of the trade with a trailing stop (see Figure 4.26).

- From here, if the stock price reverses to above our entry point, hitting our adjusted stop, we'd make a tiny loss (or break even, depending on where you adjusted it to) on the second half of the trade, but overall we're in profit because we've already closed half of our position at the P1 target.
- If the price meanders sideways, our adjusted stop holds firm horizontally until the stock either reverses upwards or resumes the downtrend.
- If the price resumes the downtrend, then we manage this with a simple descending trendline.

A descending trendline will follow the highs as lower highs are made.

As before, there is some room for discretion when it comes to managing your P2 profits with the descending trendline. If the stock price falls beyond P1 and then starts to form what might become another bear flag, you may want to adjust the trendline horizontally for a while to see what happens.

With trends typically manifesting by way of steps and flags, you can always add to your position by entering each new flag and repeating the trading plan. In this way you can add to your position safely, taking P1 targets each time and potentially having several P2s running all at the same time.

Market conditions will have an impact on how you manage your trendline for P2. In a choppy market you may keep it tight, as retracements may be very steep.

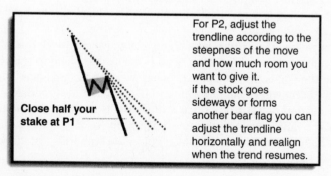

For P2, adjust the trendline according to the steepness of the move and how much room you want to give it.
if the stock goes sideways or forms another bear flag you can adjust the trendline horizontally and realign when the trend resumes.

Close half your stake at P1

FIGURE 4.26 Bear Flag Trailing Stop

In a low-volatility, technically trending market you may want to keep the trendline quite loose in order to give the stock price room to keep trending down. This is where we make our windfall profits.

Remember: You only need one or two rocket rides to really boost your trading performance. If you stick with just prime OVI-flag combinations you'll have fewer trades, but the quality will be high.

Bear Flag Example—Shutterfly (SFLY)   We saw the AAPL trade through from start to finish, so let's do the same for SFLY. As I mentioned in the last chapter, I found this one by simply applying a filter that searched for a bear flag combined with a negative OVI for the previous five days.

It just so happens that I'm aware of Shutterfly, as I'd subscribed to their services many years ago. While I was out of date in terms of my information on the company, my recollection was that you can put up your photos on the site and buy personalized products like calendars, mugs, and t-shirts, all with your chosen images on them.

While having an opinion is dangerous when it comes to trading, I had wondered over the last few years how Shutterfly would survive the social media onslaught, where people put up their photos and other media creations for free on Facebook, YouTube, and so on.

So when I see the stock floundering in a downtrend, stepping down in bear flags, and having a negative OVI for the previous 5 days (see Figure 4.27), I'm naturally intrigued!

Entry and Initial Stop Loss   SFLY is forming a classic bear flag OVI combination in November 2011. The only slight concern here is that the flag itself is quite deep, having a low of $35.38 and a high of $39.32, both of which were achieved on November 10. This makes a range of almost $4.00 on a stock in the mid-30s. That's around 11 percent, so we'll have to consider this when we come to set our initial stop loss.

With the flag low at $35.38 our short entry level can be below this at say $35.23.

Because the flag pattern is relatively deep, we can place the initial stop loss within the flag itself. All we need is a sensible place to position it. In this case the flag is moving sideways, so we need to find some support or resistance somewhere behind which to hide the initial stop loss.

The current bar is a down bar whose low is near the flag pattern low. So a good solution is to tuck our stop just above this current bar's high. The bar high is $37.70, so we'll place our initial stop loss just above this at $37.95 (see Figure 4.28).

FIGURE 4.27 SFLY Bear Flag

Source: OVI Charts. Courtesy of FlagTrader.com. Go to www.theinsideredge.com for more information.

FIGURE 4.28 SFLY Bear Flag Initial Stop

Source: OVI Charts. Courtesy of FlagTrader.com. Go to www.theinsideredge.com for more information.

The difference between our entry and our stop is the risk we take on the trade:

$$37.95 - 35.23 = 2.72$$

We've managed to get our risk down to 7.7 percent. This is still quite high for my taste, but remember the context here. First, we're not in the trade unless the stock breaks down past our entry point, which is lower than the flag itself. Second, we have good pattern here: a bear flag in the context of a downtrend and a negative OVI. It's not the best OVI pattern I've seen, but in this context it looks like a winner.

So you enter a sell stop limit order to open with the stop and limit components at $35.23, meaning the price has to trade down through this level in order to activate the trade. A gap below this level will not trigger the order unless the price then retraces back through it. On the protection side of things, your initial (buy) stop loss is at $37.95 (see Figure 4.29).

FIGURE 4.29 SFLY Bear Flag Short Entry and Stop
Source: OVI Charts. Courtesy of FlagTrader.com. Go to www.theinsideredge.com for more information.

You may notice from Figure 4.29 that there is a bear flag right before the one we're playing. Why didn't we start with that one? Well, the truth is I didn't see it, because the OVI hadn't been negative for five days at that stage, so it didn't appear on the filters I was focusing on at the time. That said, it is a worthy bear flag and one I would have been tempted by had I seen it.

So, what happens next? Well, SFLY drops straight through our entry level at $35.23, forms another bear flag, and keeps going for the next month or so. Really, this is one of the easiest and lowest maintenance trades you'll ever encounter.

P1—First Profit Target   To set our P1, we extend the impulse move (or flagpole) by around 0.382 beyond the support we use to enter the trade.

The challenge here is to determine what to use as our flagpole.

- Do we take the high from October 24 at $49.53 to the bottom of our flag at $35.38 (14.15 points)?
- Or do we take the high from the previous bear flag on November 3 at $43.00 to the bottom of our flag at $35.38 (7.62 points)?

Remember how we determine our P1 profit target. We take the flagpole and extend it by 0.382.

- In the first scenario our P1 target is $14.15 \times 0.382 = 5.40$ points below $35.38, which equals $29.98. Round this up above $30 to say $30.25.
- In the second scenario our P1 target is $7.62 \times 0.382 = 2.91$ points below $35.38, which equals $32.47.

How do you choose between the two? It really boils down to a few factors:

- The quality of the chart pattern.
- The quality of the OVI.
- The overall market.
- Your risk on the trade itself.
- Your intuition for the trade given the above factors.

With this trade, the flag is sound, but its depth is around 11 percent of the share price, which has given us a slight challenge with positioning our initial stop loss. The OVI is also sound in that it's been negative for five days, but it has spiked up to near neutral twice during the formation of this bear flag. The overall market at this time was looking like it had made a false breakout to the upside after three months of serious volatility.

My intuition for the trade was that it was worth taking, but on the basis that I take profits at the earliest opportunity when they're given to me and that I not be too greedy.

In Figure 4.30 we can see the main components of the trade. The bottom of the flag support is at \$35.38, while the top of the flagpole (T) is at \$43.00.

With the flagpole at 7.62 points, our target is 2.91 points further down from the flag low (S).

Our P1 target here is at \$32.47, and remember: Our sell stop-limit to open is at \$35.23. This makes our P1 profit 2.76 points, whereupon we'll protect the trade by lowering our stop to near breakeven.

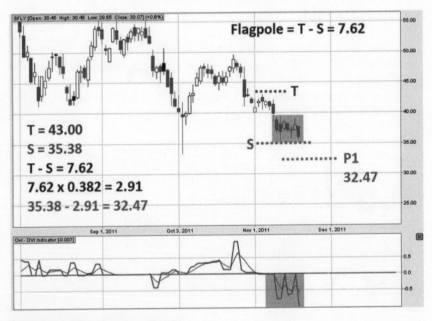

FIGURE 4.30   SFLY Bear Flag P1
Source: OVI Charts. Courtesy of FlagTrader.com. Go to www.theinsideredge.com for more information.

In Figure 4.31 you can see how our P1 target is hit the day after the breakout! At this point you're either very happy, as we've already banked profit, or you're wondering if our P1 target was too conservative. You have no way of knowing in advance, so be happy with the first profit and even happier that you're executing a trading plan that gives you an opportunity for a windfall profit if the stock keeps trending.

This was a completely clean breakout with no drawdown, so now we need to manage the remainder of our position.

We close half of our position for a profit at P1 ($32.47) and now we manage the remaining stake.

Adjust the Initial Stop and Manage Trade for P2 Profit Our first job is to adjust the initial stop by lowering it to near our entry level. This means that if the stock retraces above this point the second half of our trade may yield nothing or even a very slight loss, but overall we still make profit on the trade.

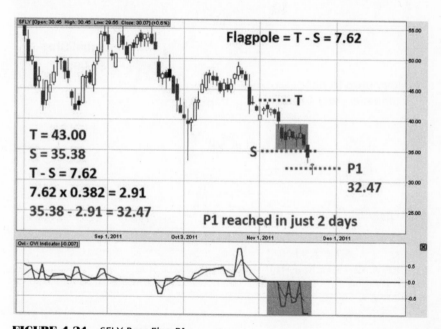

FIGURE 4.31 SFLY Bear Flag P1
Source: OVI Charts. Courtesy of FlagTrader.com. Go to www.theinsideredge.com for more information.

Our entry level here was $35.23. Having reached P1, we can now lower the stop from its original level of $37.95 to just above the bottom of the flag, say at $35.57. This means that if the stock rises and tests the flag low, we can still be in the trade if it bounces straight back down from the flag low level (see Figure 4.32).

In this example with SFLY, the price is already forming a nice downward trend, and it's easy to draw a well-fitting trendline that joins the high from October to the lower high in November. We'll use this to manage our P2 profits.

Remember: After P1 you've already banked a profit. Now it's a matter of maximizing the situation by giving yourself every chance to ride the trend if it does materialize.

FIGURE 4.32   SFLY Bear Flag—Adjusting the Initial Stop
Source: OVI Charts. Courtesy of FlagTrader.com. Go to www.theinsideredge.com for more information.

Figure 4.33 shows how the stock trends downward until December 23, where it reverses sharply with a spinning top bar. This bar breaks our downward trendline and therefore takes us out of the trade—with a very healthy and safely taken profit, so no complaints!

Also note how the price forms another bear flag around our P1 target. This gives us an opportunity to add to our position as it breaks down from this on November 30. We won't include that in this particular trading plan, but you can see clearly that the down bar on November 30 would take the new bear flag trade into its own P1.

In this example it's a very easy P2 to manage, because the stock trends downward in steps, and there aren't any severe retracements to navigate around until we're stopped out on December 23.

With the AAPL bull flag trade I pandered to our vanity and showed the post-trade action. With SFLY I won't do that, but I will say that we pretty much exited at the right time. The stock bumbled around for a month or so, before rising back into the mid-30s.

FIGURE 4.33 SFLY Bear Flag—P2 Stopped Out
Source: OVI Charts. Courtesy of FlagTrader.com. Go to www.theinsideredge.com for more information.

Summary of SFLY Trade

Action	Price	Comment
Entry	$35.23	Flag low at $35.38. Sell stop limit to open at $35.23 on November 18.
Initial stop loss	$37.95	Just above the high of the down bar on November 17 ($2.72 or 7.7% risk on the trade).
First profit target (P1)	$32.47	0.382 downward extension of flagpole beyond the flag low. This was the most conservative target from a choice of two possible flagpoles. 2.76 points profit.
Trailing stop		Stepped falling trendline as SFLY continued to trend. Even the chance of entering on another bear flag breakout on November 30.
P2 Level	$25.15	Falling trendline broken on December 23. 10.08 points profit.
Profit		• 2.76 points (7.83%) for the first half of the stake in just two days. • 10.08 points (28.61%) on the second half. • 6.42 points average profit (18.22% in just five weeks). • Annualized compounded profit: 470%.

This is a sound trade that turned into a great trade, one that you'll be repeating with ease if you use the OVI-flag combination like this.

Let's now cover a bullish channel breakout.

Channel Breakout Trading Plan (Up)

Remember from Chapter 3 that a sideways channel can break either to the upside or the downside. Ideally the channel will give us clear lines of support (S) and resistance (R) from which to create our trading plan (see Figure 4.34).

Remember from Chapter 3 that our ideal sideways channel has the following qualities:

- It's neat and visually recognizable with clear levels of support and resistance, defined by previous lows and highs within the channel itself.
- The channel contains other support and resistance levels inside. This will help to ensure our stops are sensibly placed.

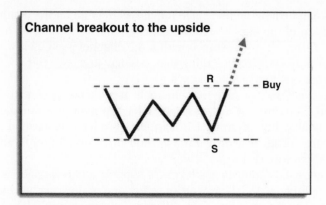

FIGURE 4.34 The Channel Upside Breakout

- As the price starts to drift toward its breakout, the OVI corroborates in the same direction.

     If the price starts to rise within the channel, it's helpful if the OVI becomes positive before the breakout. This increases the probability of a sustained move to the upside, enough to bag us a profit.

     If the price starts to fall within the channel, it's helpful if the OVI becomes negative before the breakdown. This increases the probability of a sustained down move.

Right now we're focusing on the channel break to the upside.

Channel Up Breakout—Entry We enter our buy stop-limit order (or conditional order) at the break of a clear resistance level. If it's not clear, then you may want to reconsider the trade. Clarity of the trading plan is sacrosanct.

Typically, the clear resistance level of the channel will be the high of the range, so our entry point for a buy order will be slightly above this level.

If the high of the range is say $50, then our entry point for the buy order will be say $50.27, depending on what other support and resistance levels are in the vicinity. Obviously this will be on a case-by-case basis. With some examples you may want to enter aggressively at just above the resistance—say $50.07—and with others you may want a larger clearance above the high of the channel range.

Channel Up Breakout—Initial Stop Loss Most channels are too deep to place the initial stop loss underneath the entire channel support, so we have to find somewhere within the channel itself to place it.

This can be a bit ad hoc since much will depend on the depth and the composition of the bars within the channel, but what we're looking for is an area of support or resistance within the channel itself, below which to place our initial stop loss. Failing that, we may just have to pick a high or low of a bar below which to place it.

In this way you can see that channels aren't quite as clean to trade as flags, and therefore not quite as desirable. However, their breakouts can be spectacular, like an animal in captivity suddenly unleashed and able to roam free! They're worth trading—and often you'll find fantastic OVI opportunities with them.

In Figure 4.35 you can see levels of support and resistance within the channel numbered 1, 2, 3, 4. We can select one of these as our initial stop loss level. The figure shows four different levels that could be used. As a rule I wouldn't want the stop to be much below Level 2 in Figure 4.35. (This is about one third of the channel down from the high.)

Channel Up Breakout—First Profit Target (P1)   The P1 for channels is straightforward.

We take the depth of the channel, multiply it by 0.382, and (in the case of channel breakouts to the upside) add that figure to arrive at the P1.

In Figure 4.36 the channel range is 6 points (50 − 44). So the move we're looking for beyond the breakout is:

$$6.00 \times 0.382 = 2.29$$

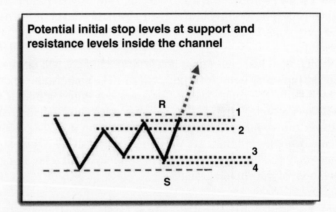

FIGURE 4.35   The Channel Up Initial Stop Loss Placement

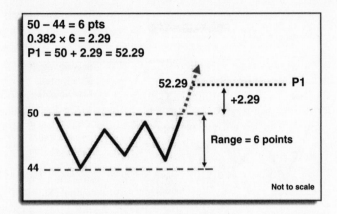

FIGURE 4.36 The Channel Up First Profit Target P1

If our channel high resistance is at $50, then we add 2.29 to this figure to calculate our P1:

$$2.29 + 50 = 52.29$$

Remember that you can always bring our P1 in closer if you wish.

Channel Up Breakout—Adjusting the Initial Stop Now that we've secured our first profit, we adjust our initial stop the same way we did for the bull flag.

So, if we bought 100 shares in the first place, our initial stop would be with respect to those 100. Once we close half our position (50 shares), the stop now only relates to our remaining 50 still open.

Once we've taken the partial profits at P1, we raise the level of the initial stop so it's at or just below our initial entry point. Placing it just below our entry point enables the stock price to test the breakout level without stopping us out.

Of course, we could have placed the initial stop just below the top of the channel in the first place, in which case we don't need to adjust it once we hit P1.

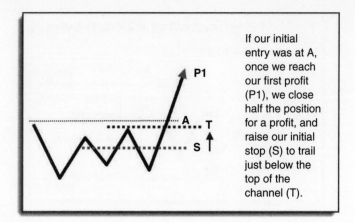

FIGURE 4.37   Channel Up Adjusting the Initial Stop

In Figure 4.37 if our initial entry point was at Level A (just above the channel), then we raise the stop from S to trail just below this at Level T.

Channel Up—P2 Trailing Stop   Now we just have to manage the second half of the trade with a trailing stop.

- From here, if the stock price reverses to below our entry point, hitting our adjusted stop, we'd make a tiny loss (or break even, depending on where you adjusted it to) on the second half of the trade, but overall we're up because we've already closed the first half of our position at the P1 target.
- If the price meanders sideways, our adjusted stop holds firm horizontally until the stock either breaks down or resumes its ascent.
- If the price resumes its ascent, then we manage this with a simple rising trendline.

To trail the stop we draw a rising trendline under the bar lows as higher lows are made (see Figure 4.38).

As before, there is some room for discretion when it comes to managing your P2 profits with the rising trendline. If the stock price rises beyond P1 and then starts to form what might become a bull flag, you may want to adjust the trendline horizontally for a while to see if the price can make another burst upward.

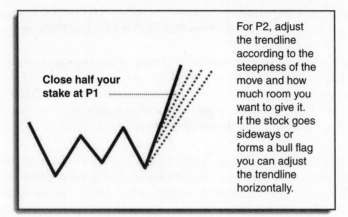

For P2, adjust the trendline according to the steepness of the move and how much room you want to give it. If the stock goes sideways or forms a bull flag you can adjust the trendline horizontally.

Close half your stake at P1

FIGURE 4.38 Channel Up Trailing Stop

Remember: Our windfall profits depend on riding trends, so we need to give the stock a chance to do so without being stopped out prematurely. At the same time, safety is our primary focus and we don't want to sacrifice our P1 profit, either.

As a reminder from earlier, prevailing market conditions will have a bearing on how aggressively you manage your trendline for P2. In a choppy market you may keep it tight, especially if the stock rises very steeply before retracing just as severely.

In a low-volatility, stable, trending market you may want to keep the trendline quite loose in order to give the stock price room to keep trending. It's in trending markets where we make our windfall profits. Once you've been trading this method for a while, you'll get a feel for which type of market we're in.

You only need one or two rocket rides to really boost your batting averages.

Earlier I mentioned if you just stick with prime OVI-flag combinations you'll have fewer trades, but the quality will be phenomenal. You can add to this OVI-channel combinations where, with bullish breakouts, the OVI has been positive for some time and where, with bearish breakouts, the OVI has been negative for some time.

Channel Up Breakout Example—Exxon Mobile (XOM) Revisiting our XOM trade from Chapter 3, we can see that the stock price is range-bound and forms a clear line of resistance as the price drifts upward and the OVI turns from neutral to positive. In Figure 4.39 we can see the resistance just below $75, clearly defined by four successive highs within a few pennies of each other.

We can also see that the stock is drifting upward toward this resistance again, but this time the OVI has popped from neutral to positive. Although I'd have preferred several consecutive days of clear positive OVI while the stock was rangebound, this is still a good signal in the context that the OVI has been neutral and is now seemingly making a statement.

Entry and Initial Stop Loss   Our entry is around $75.27 (just above the channel high resistance) so we need somewhere logical to place our initial stop. The most obvious support is just below $70.00, where we've seen some bounces off lows in August and September. But that's too far away for my liking. Can we put our stop loss a bit nearer our entry point?

One solution is to have a stop just below the high of the channel. That way, if the price breaks out, only to return to the channel, we bail out quickly. This would keep any loss on the trade to a minimum.

Another solution is to find a high or low of a bar (or bars) that will work as a natural barrier, below which we'll place our initial stop.

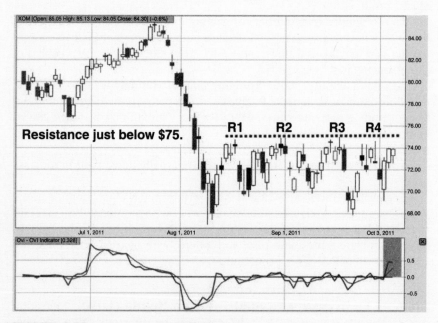

FIGURE 4.39   XOM Sideways Channel Chart
Source: OVI Charts. Courtesy of FlagTrader.com. Go to www.theinsideredge.com for more information.

The latest two bars both have highs at $74.00. How about we place our initial stop under this at say $73.78?

Or you could opt for under the low of the two latest bars, which would be under $72.21.

You can see the slight challenge we have with channels, yet we must make a decision. In this case I go for $73.78. It's reasonably tight without being overly so, and it gives the price a bit of room to move. If the stock price does break out only to return, then I'd be okay with conceding defeat at this level, knowing my loss would be small (see Figure 4.40).

The range of the channel is determined here by the low on August 9 (67.03) to the high on September 20 (74.98)—that is 7.95 points. We now need to determine our P1 profit target.

P1—First Profit Target To set our P1, we measure the channel range (7.95), multiply it by 0.382, and then extend that beyond the resistance level ($74.98).

$$7.95 \times 0.382 = 3.04 \text{ points}$$
$$\text{P1 First Profit Target} = 74.98 + 3.04 = \$78.02$$

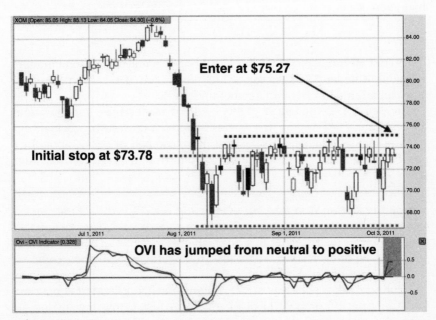

FIGURE 4.40 XOM Entry and Initial Stop Loss
Source: OVI Charts. Courtesy of FlagTrader.com. Go to www.theinsideredge.com for more information.

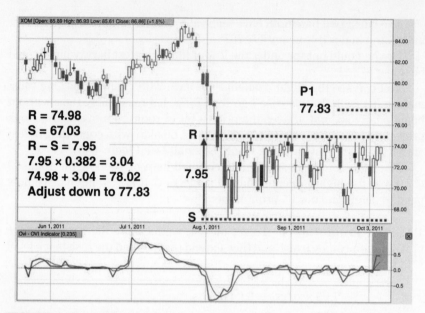

FIGURE 4.41   XOM Channel P1
Source: OVI Charts. Courtesy of FlagTrader.com. Go to www.theinsideredge.com for more information.

So our P1 target is $78.02, but let's bring this under the round number by taking it under $78.00 to say $77.83 (see Figure 4.41). Again, I've just taken an arbitrary non-round number under $78.

In Figure 4.42 you can see how our P1 is reached just five days after the breakout. Furthermore, this occurred with no drawdown whatsoever.

You're now familiar with the drill. We close half of our position for a profit of $2.56 at P1 ($77.83), and now we have to manage the remaining stake for P2.

Adjust the Initial Stop and Manage Trade for P2 Profit   First, we adjust the initial stop by raising it to near our entry level. This means that if the stock retraces below this point the second half of our trade may yield nothing or even a very slight loss, but overall we still make profit on the trade.

Our entry level here was $75.27. Having reached P1, we can now raise the stop from its original level of $73.78 to just below the top of the channel—say at $74.75. This means that if the stock falls and tests the channel high, we can still be in the trade if it bounces straight back up from the channel high level (see Figure 4.43).

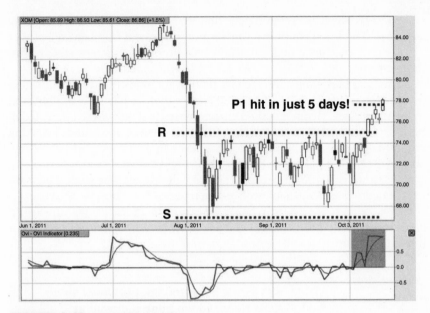

FIGURE 4.42 XOM Channel P1
Source: OVI Charts. Courtesy of FlagTrader.com. Go to www.theinsideredge.com for more information.

FIGURE 4.43 XOM Channel—Adjusting the Initial Stop
Source: OVI Charts. Courtesy of FlagTrader.com. Go to www.theinsideredge.com for more information.

So XOM has broken out nicely, and we're now trailing it with a rising trendline. The price continues to rise until it forms a Doji bar on October 27, where it reaches a high of $82.20, and promptly reverses steeply two days later.

The Doji bar is our alert, telling us that the odds of a reversal are increased, so we need to take heed and ensure that we have our trailing stop in the right place. Given that the Doji bar closes just below $82 on the October 27, and given that the stock has made a significant move since breaking out, it makes sense for our trailing stop to be tucked away just below $80, so we place it at $79.87 (see Figure 4.44).

On October 31, XOM reverses sharply, taking out our stop, which we can consider was positioned well as the reversal bar closes at $78.09.

Our P2 here is easy to manage because the stock trends upward in steps before making a Doji high and promptly reversing sharply, taking out our trailing stop.

FIGURE 4.44 XOM Channel—P2 Stopped Out
Source: OVI Charts. Courtesy of FlagTrader.com. Go to www.theinsideredge.com for more information.

While I don't want to fuel our vanity, my weakness as a human being—and my hunch that you're intrigued—compels me to yield to the inevitable and tell you what happened next after the trade! Well, XOM gapped down to close at $75.94 the day after we were taken out of the trade at $79.87. Over the following weeks it made a further low of $73.90 before recovering strongly.

If you'd hung on you'd have eventually been rewarded for doing so, but the key word is "eventually," and there were no guarantees. What would certainly have happened is that you'd have missed other opportunities if you'd retained your position in XOM without any proper plan.

Summary of XOM Trade

Action	Price	Comment
Entry	$75.27	Channel high at $74.98. Buy stop limit at $75.27 filled on October 10.
Initial stop loss	$73.78	Under the latest two bars shared high ($1.49 or 1.98% risk on the trade).
First profit target (P1)	$77.83	0.382 upward extension of the channel range beyond the channel high, and then adjusted down below $78 for a non-round number. 2.56 points profit.
Trailing stop		Rising trendline as XOM continued to rise.
P2 Level	$79.87	Rising trendline broken on October 31. 4.60 points profit.
Profit		• 2.56 points (3.40%) for the first half of the stake in just five days. • 4.60 points (6.1%) on the second half. • 3.58 points average profit (4.75% in just three weeks). • Annualized compounded profit: 113%.

On the face of it the trade doesn't look spectacular. But consider that it lasted just 16 traded days, and you'll see that this simple trade, compounded weekly, represents an annualized return of 113 percent.

The spectacular trades will come, but in the meantime we can enjoy these "nibbles," which on closer scrutiny are much more significant than just nibbles.

Let's now cover a bearish channel breakout.

Channel Breakout Trading Plan (Down)

As I mentioned earlier, it's preferable that the channel will give us clear lines of support (S) and resistance (R) from which to create our trading plan (see Figure 4.45).

Just as a reminder, our ideal sideways channel has the following qualities:

- It's neat and visually recognizable, with clear levels of support and resistance, defined by previous lows and highs within the channel itself.
- The channel contains other support and resistance levels inside. This will help to ensure our stops are sensibly placed.
- As the price starts to drift towards its breakout, the OVI corroborates in the same direction.

    If the price starts to rise within the channel, it's helpful if the OVI becomes positive before the breakout. This increases the probability of a sustained move to the upside, enough to bag us a profit.

    If the price starts to fall within the channel, it's helpful if the OVI becomes negative before the breakdown. This increases the probability of a sustained down move.

This time we're focusing on the channel break to the downside.

Channel Down Breakout—Entry   We enter our sell stop-limit order to open (or conditional order) at the break of a clearly defined support level.

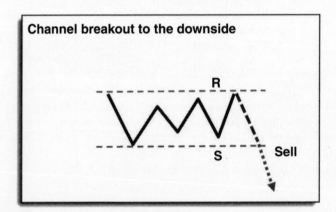

FIGURE 4.45   The Channel Downside Breakout

Typically, the clear support level of the channel will be the low of the range, so our entry point for a short order will be slightly below this level.

If the low of the range is say $40, then our entry point for the short order will be, say $39.87, depending on what other support and resistance levels are in the vicinity. Obviously this will be on a case-by-case basis. With some examples you may want to enter aggressively at just below the support—say $39.92—and with others you may want a larger clearance below the low of the channel range.

Channel Down Breakout—Initial Stop Loss   Most channels are too deep to place the initial stop loss above the entire channel resistance, so we have to find somewhere within the channel itself in which to place it.

As with the channel up breakout scenario, much will depend on the depth and the composition of the bars within the channel. What we're looking for in this situation is an area of support or resistance inside the channel itself, above which to place our initial stop loss. Failing that, we may just have to pick a high or low of a bar above which to place it.

In Figure 4.46 you can see levels of support and resistance within the channel designated (i), (ii), (iii), (iv). We can select one of these as our initial stop loss level. The figure shows four different levels that could be used. As a rule, I wouldn't want the stop to be much above Level (ii) in the diagram. (This is about one third of the channel up from the low.)

Channel Down Breakout—First Profit Target (P1)   You're now familiar with how we determine the P1 for channels.

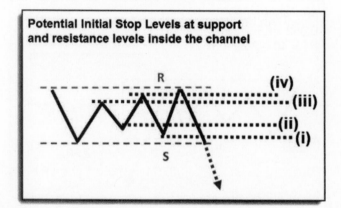

FIGURE 4.46   The Channel Down Initial Stop Loss Placement

We take the depth of the channel, multiply it by 0.382, and (in the case of channel breakouts to the downside) subtract that figure to arrive at the P1.

In Figure 4.47, the channel range is 6 points ($46 - 40$). So the move we're looking for beyond the breakout is:

$$6.00 \times 0.382 = 2.29$$

If our channel low support is at \$40, then we subtract 2.29 from this figure to calculate our P1:

$$40 - 2.29 = 37.71$$

Remember: You can always bring our P1 in nearer if you wish.

Channel Down Breakout—Adjusting the Initial Stop   Now that we've secured our first profit, we adjust our initial stop the same way we did for the bear flag.

So, if we shorted 100 shares in the first place, our initial stop would be with respect to those 100. Once we close half our position (50 shares) the stop now relates to only our remaining 50 still open.

Once we've taken the partial profits at P1, we lower the level of the initial stop so it's at or just above our initial short entry point. Placing it just above our entry point enables the stock price to test the breakout level without stopping us out.

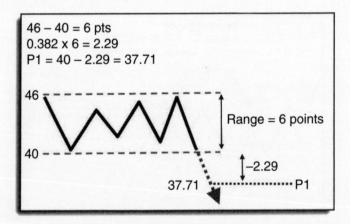

FIGURE 4.47   The Channel Down First Profit Target P1

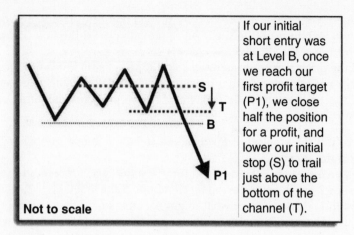

If our initial short entry was at Level B, once we reach our first profit target (P1), we close half the position for a profit, and lower our initial stop (S) to trail just above the bottom of the channel (T).

FIGURE 4.48 Channel Down Adjusting the Initial Stop

Of course, we could have placed the initial stop just above the bottom of the channel in the first place, in which case we don't need to adjust it once we hit P1.

In Figure 4.48, if our initial entry point was at Level B (just below the channel) then we lower the stop from S to trail just above this at Level T.

Channel Down—P2 Trailing Stop Now we just have to manage the second half of the trade with a trailing stop (see Figure 4.49).

- From here, if the stock price reverses to above our entry point, hitting our adjusted stop, we'd make a tiny loss (or break even, depending on

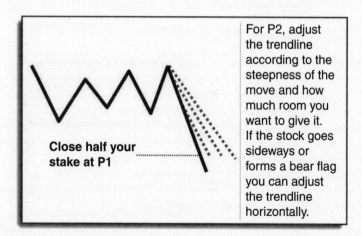

For P2, adjust the trendline according to the steepness of the move and how much room you want to give it. If the stock goes sideways or forms a bear flag you can adjust the trendline horizontally.

FIGURE 4.49 Channel Down Trailing Stop

where you adjusted it to) on the second half of the trade, but overall we're still in profit because we've already closed the first half of our position at the P1 target.

- If the price meanders sideways, our adjusted stop holds firm horizontally until the stock either breaks to the upside or resumes its descent.
- If the price resumes its descent, then we manage this with a simple downward trendline.

To trail the stop we draw a falling trendline above the bar highs as lower highs are made.

As before, there is some room for discretion when it comes to managing your P2 profits with the falling trendline. If the stock price falls below P1 and then starts to form what might become a bear flag, you may want to adjust the trendline horizontally for a while to see if the price can make another burst downward.

Remember that our windfall profits depend on riding trends, so we need to give the stock a chance to do so without being stopped out prematurely. At the same time, safety is our primary focus, and we don't want to sacrifice our P1 profit, either.

As already mentioned, prevailing market conditions will have a bearing on how aggressively you manage your trendline for P2. In a choppy market you may keep it tight, especially if the stock falls very steeply before the shorts cover, causing a severe retrace.

In a technical, non-news-driven downward market you may want to keep the trendline quite loose in order to give the stock price room to keep trending down. We want to give ourselves a decent chance of riding a trend up or down, just not at the expense of our P1.

Earlier I mentioned that OVI-channel combinations can be great to trade. In this situation we're talking about a bearish channel breakout. With these it's ideal to find channels where the OVI has been negative for some time—like a few consecutive days.

Channel Down Breakout Example—Bank of America (BAC)   For this example we're going to look at BAC, which I was publicly bearish about from late March 2011. The opportunity is very obvious, which is why I'm including it here.

As you can see from Figure 4.50, the OVI turns negative around March 24 as the stock is breaking down (see the downward pointing dotted arrow) and remains negative virtually uninterrupted until late August.

What happens over the next few months is a series of breakdowns from trade-worthy bear flags and channels. In Figure 4.50, I've highlighted the obvious tradeable areas with numbers 1–4.

(1) is a classic break of support where the OVI has been negative for several weeks by then.

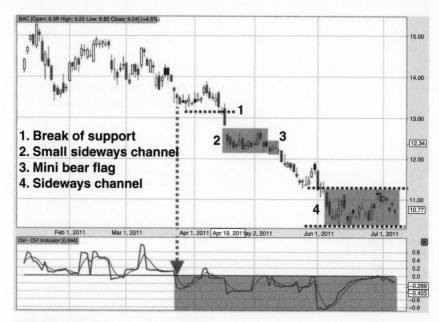

FIGURE 4.50 BAC Breakouts Chart
Source: OVI Charts. Courtesy of FlagTrader.com. Go to www.theinsideredge.com for more information.

(2) is small sideways channel that started life as a bear flag but kept going sideways.

(3) is a mini bear flag tacked on the end of (2)

(4) is the sideways channel that we're going to focus on for our bearish channel example.

Now that you've gotten to this point in the book, you could easily have spotted and traded each of these opportunities with BAC.

Let's now take a closer look at this chart. We can see the channel from early June to July 2011. It forms a low (support) of 10.41 on June 10 and a high (resistance) of $11.25 on June 29.

This high on June 29 takes the form of a Doji bar, which is very useful in telegraphing a potential reversal. What makes it even better is it's occurring in the context of a bearish stock, in a downtrend, and with a negative OVI. Granted, the OVI is in recovery by June 29, but it has been negative for three months and is virtually solid by that time.

If you were inclined to trade reversal patterns from Doji bars, a break of that Doji's low would be a potential short trade. As it is, we're now given

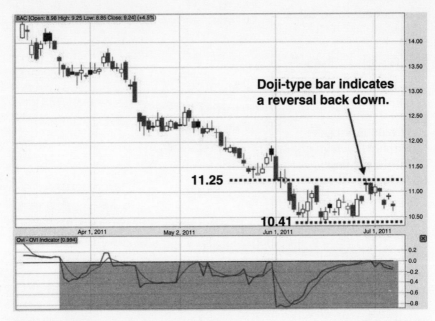

FIGURE 4.51 BAC Bearish Channel Chart
Source: OVI Charts. Courtesy of FlagTrader.com. Go to www.theinsideredge.com for more information.

a tipoff that this stock continues to look weak, as we observe the chart in Figure 4.51.

So, we're looking for a break of the support line below $10.41.

Provisional Entry and Initial Stop Loss For reasons that will shortly become apparent, I've labeled this heading "Provisional." But let's go through it normally and see where it takes us first.

Our short entry is just below the channel low support, so we'll have this at around 10.27. Now we need a logical place for our initial stop.

The range of the channel is $0.84, which is around 8 percent of the current stock price. This channel doesn't present us with an obvious natural support or resistance level inside itself, and 8 percent is quite a big hit to take.

I would say, in this case, if the stock breaks to the downside and triggers our short, if it returns back into the channel I would take the signal to bail out. I suggest we make our initial stop at $10.67. This gives us a risk of $0.40, which is under 4 percent for the trade (see Figure 4.52).

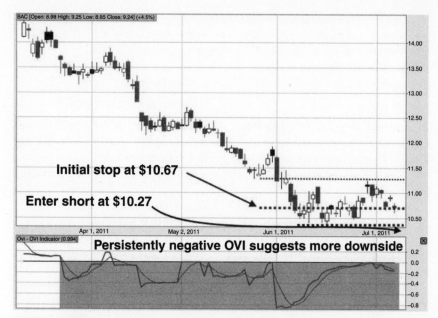

FIGURE 4.52 BAC Provisional Entry and Initial Stop Loss
Source: OVI Charts. Courtesy of FlagTrader.com. Go to www.theinsideredge.com for more information.

Remember: Our order would only be filled if the stock breaks down through $10.27. In this "provisional" setup, our entry is at $10.27 and our initial stop is at $10.67.

The range of the channel is determined here by the low on June 10 ($10.41) to the high on June 29 ($11.25)—that is, 0.84 points. We now need to determine our P1 profit target.

Provisional P1—First Profit Target   To set our P1, we measure the channel range (0.84), multiply it by 0.382, and then extend that below the support level ($10.41).

$$0.84 \times 0.382 = 0.321 \, \text{points}$$
$$\text{P1 First Profit Target} = 10.41 - 0.321 = \$10.09$$

So our provisional P1 target is $10.09. The only problem with this is that it's so near our entry point of $10.27. Our P1 profit in this trade would only be $0.18. The question is whether this is enough, even though it is just for our P1.

One thing to consider here is that BAC is a low-priced stock. However, we have to consider commissions (even though they're tiny these days) and potential slippage. Really, $0.18 doesn't make sense here.

So now we have to consider whether we like the opportunity enough to stretch the parameters to something that works better.

Amended Entry, Initial Stop Loss, and Amended P1 First Profit Target
I'm going to suggest we raise the level of the short entry to $10.37 from $10.27. This is much tighter to the channel support of $10.41 than before, but it is still lower than the support level, and I still like the opportunity (see Figure 4.53).

The initial stop can remain at $10.67, which means we're taking less risk on the trade—0.30 points now (as opposed to 0.40 points).

I'm also going to suggest that we extend our P1 profit target downward to $10.01, from $10.09. The $10.00 round number provides a natural support level, so let's stay on the cautious side of that.

This now gives us a P1 profit margin of $0.36 for the trade, which is still rather small, but our hope anyway is for a big move on the second half

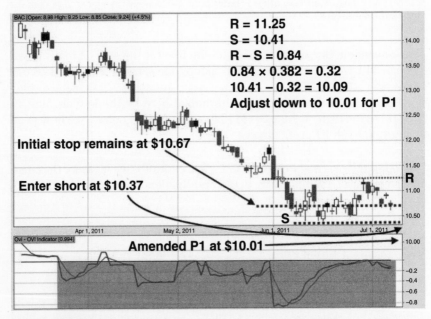

FIGURE 4.53 BAC Amended Entry, Initial Stop and Amended P1
Source: OVI Charts. Courtesy of FlagTrader.com. Go to www.theinsideredge.com for more information.

of the trade (P2), while absorbing very low risk with the first half of the trade (P1).

In order to facilitate an anticipated big P2 move, we're going to have to give the stock some slack to make its move down and allow for volatile retracements. Provided my P1 and overall position are protected, I'm going to be satisfied.

Notice I've used some discretion here while not disobeying my essential rules. We can make this trade work with very low risk, but we'll have to accept a rather low P1 first profit target. We're also going to give the stock plenty of room to move down for our hoped-for P2 windfall profit.

We can justify this because BAC does look so bearish, with many factors in place for a serious downturn. The entire financial sector at this time was in the doldrums and we're using our skills and discretion to capitalize on one of the weakest stocks in the sector at that time.

Although I'd like a slightly bigger P1 profit potential, this now makes much more sense as a trade.

In Figure 4.54, you can see how our P1 is reached just five days after the breakout. Once again, this occurs with no drawdown.

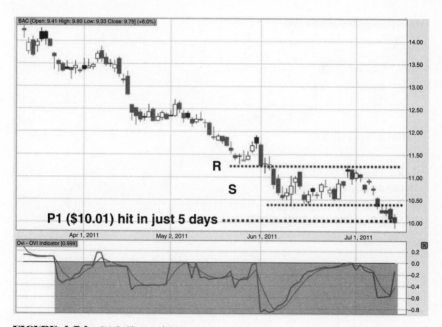

FIGURE 4.54 BAC Channel P1
Source: OVI Charts. Courtesy of FlagTrader.com. Go to www.theinsideredge.com for more information.

As per our rules, we close half of our position for a profit of $0.36 at P1 ($10.01), and now we have to manage the remaining stake for P2. Worth noting is that 0.36 points represents a profit of almost 3.5 percent in just five days. Compound that weekly to an annual return, and it's almost 500 percent! That's just a nibble at this stage.

Adjust the Initial Stop and Manage Trade for P2 Profit   We now adjust the initial stop by lowering it to near our entry level. This means that if the stock retraces above this point, the second half of our trade may yield nothing or even a very slight loss, but overall we still make profit on the trade.

Remember that with this particular trade we want to give BAC a really good chance to keep falling, so we're not going to be aggressive in the way we manage the P2 descending trendline.

Our short entry level here was $10.37 so, having reached P1 at $10.01, we can now lower the stop from its original level of $10.67 to just above the bottom of the channel—say at $10.43. This means that if the stock rises and tests the channel low we can still be in the trade if it bounces straight back down from the channel low level (see Figure 4.55).

FIGURE 4.55   BAC Channel—Adjusting the Initial Stop
Source: OVI Charts. Courtesy of FlagTrader.com. Go to www.theinsideredge.com for more information.

So BAC has reached our rather modest P1 target and now we have to be patient for a hopeful P2 windfall. The OVI remains negative and we want to give this maximum slack without jeopardizing our P1 profit.

To achieve this we can lower our trailing stop at $10.43, which is just above our original entry level ($10.37) and two little points above the channel low of $10.41, which may now form a resistance. This means if the stock retraces significantly, even touching our initial entry point, we're still active in the second half of our trade. It's quite common for stocks to break out and subsequently retrace to test the breakout, and our trailing stop here is prepared for just that.

In Figure 4.56, you can see how BAC continues its journey south and then retraces sharply for two bars. The key to this retracement is that it only reaches a high of $10.28 and doesn't breach our trailing stop at $10.43.

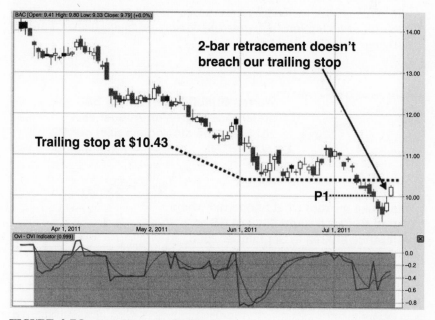

FIGURE 4.56 BAC Channel—Trailing Stop
Source: OVI Charts. Courtesy of FlagTrader.com. Go to www.theinsideredge.com for more information.

From here it's downhill all the way for BAC until August 25 (see Figure 4.57).

The big news was that Warren Buffett was buying $5 billion of preference shares in BAC, and the market responded wildly to it.

You'll see later, however, that the OVI only reacted positively for about five days before returning back to negative territory. Why was this, and why was I still publicly bearish about BAC despite the great man's investment?

The answer comes in two parts.

1. First, Buffett's investment was in *preference* shares. These are not equities. Rather, they are fixed coupon debt—with these being paid at 6 percent per annum. As part of the deal, he also received around $700 million in warrants (similar to long-dated call options). Preference shares are effectively a loan, but here they provided much-needed liquidity and confidence to Bank of America investors, while giving Mr. Buffett a fantastic return of 6 percent per annum, and that's before a redemption that would inevitably be much higher than the original $5 billion.

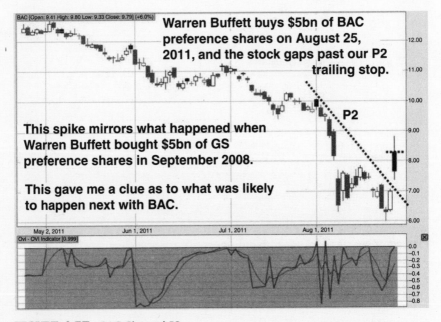

FIGURE 4.57   BAC Channel P2
Source: OVI Charts. Courtesy of FlagTrader.com. Go to www.theinsideredge.com for more information.

Remember: He did *not* buy equity shares in BAC, so the euphoria that followed this transaction lasted only a couple of days before the shares hit the skids again.

2. Secondly, Warren Buffett had done a very similar deal in September 2008 with Goldman Sachs (GS). In that case he earned a 10-percent coupon on the deal, with GS eventually buying him out for a hefty premium—and massive profit to him.

In the Goldman Sachs situation, the Buffett deal was announced around September 18, 2008 whereupon the GS stock price leapt up from a low of $85.88 to a high of $144.98 in just two days! However, the euphoria was short-lived, and the stock never reached those heights again until the end of May 2009 (see Figure 4.58).

You can see how GS's price action set the scene for BAC three years later, and why I remained bearish on it.

BAC shares surged from a low of $6.01 on August 23 to a high of $8.80 on August 25. That's a rise of 46 percent in two days, but it was back where it started within one month.

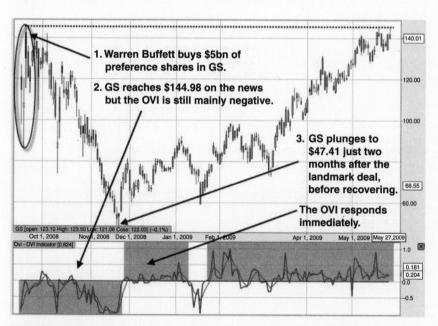

FIGURE 4.58   Warren Buffett—Goldman Sachs Preference Share Deal
Source: OVI Charts. Courtesy of FlagTrader.com. Go to www.theinsideredge.com for more information.

Alas, we were closed out at $8.29 (still a tidy profit) after the stock gapped up on the Buffett news, past our trailing stop of around $7.25, only then for the stock price to drift back down to a low of $5.13 in the following few weeks (see Figure 4.59).

Let's now wrap up this BAC trade and see how we were stopped out with a decent profit—though, as we know, it could have been so much better!

In Figure 4.60, you can see how our trailing stop line is gapped over, meaning that instead of being stopped out at $7.25, we're stopped out at the open on August 25 at $8.29.

Let's now summarize our BAC trade with all its peculiarities. Remember that while we saw big potential in BAC falling, we didn't like our original parameters for the trade, so we amended our entry level and our P1 first profit target.

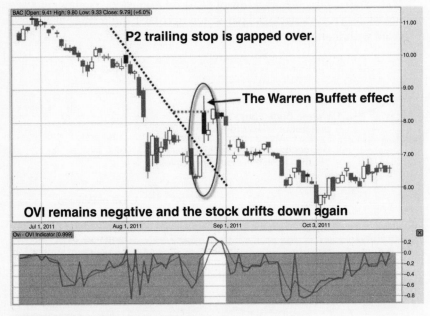

FIGURE 4.59 BAC Channel Post-Trade Action
Source: OVI Charts. Courtesy of FlagTrader.com. Go to www.theinsideredge.com for more information.

BAC [Open: 9.41 High: 9.80 Low 9.33 Close: 9.79] (+6.0%)

Initial short entry level

P2 stopped out at $8.29 after the stock gaps above our trailing stop line.

FIGURE 4.60 BAC Channel—P2 Stopped Out
Source: OVI Charts. Courtesy of FlagTrader.com. Go to www.theinsideredge.com for more information.

Summary of BAC Trade

Action	Price	Comment
Entry	$10.37	Channel low at $10.41.
		Sell stop limit to open at $10.37 filled on July 11.
Initial stop loss	$10.67	Set at a level that would confirm a breakout failure ($0.30 or 2.9% risk on the trade).
First profit target (P1)	$10.01	0.382 downward extension of the channel range beyond the channel low, plus a few more points to make the P1 worth achieving.
		0.36 points profit.
Trailing stop		Wide steps and descending trendline as BAC continued to fall. Designed to give the stock plenty of room to retrace while still trending down.
P2 Level	$8.29	Falling trendline gapped over on August 25 when the Buffett deal is announced. The stock opens at $8.29, thereby taking out our trailing stop.
		2.08 points profit.
Profit		• 0.36 points (3.47%) for the first half of the stake in just five days.
		• 2.08 points (20.06%) on the second half.
		• 1.22 points average profit (11.76% in just seven weeks).
		• Annualized compounded profit: 128%.

Again we have an annualized return of over 100 percent. This is excellent, but what a shame we didn't get to close out nearer that $6.01 low that was reached only two days before we were stopped out at $8.29. At $6.01 you're looking at a 42-percent return, and even at $7.00 you'd have made a 32-percent return on the second half of the trade, in just seven weeks. Compounded weekly to annual percentages, those returns are 1,256 percent and 937 percent, respectively!

This is a great example to show because it demonstrates how we can use discretion within the parameters of our trading plan. It also shows how real-life events out of our control can adversely impact our trade, but with a robust trading plan we still made a healthy profit here.

LEARNING POINTS

In this chapter we've worked through four detailed trades where you can see our trading plan in action step by step. In these examples we've had to consider each trade on its merits, and in each case we've formed a robust and conservative trading plan.

It would be easy to only highlight the really stellar examples like Bear Stearns and others, but I want this book to be balanced. Yes, we do find phenomenal windfall examples; that's the whole point of our trading methodology.

Many of our trades are completed within a couple of weeks and we move on to the next opportunity. Remember: You do have discretion to adjust your P2 trendline if you want to give your stock more space with which to move, like we did initially with BAC.

You can also reenter a trade if the stock is forming another flag or channel pattern.

At the beginning of the chapter we reviewed our trading plan and also the types of orders that are most relevant to our breakout trading method. Remember the steps we need to take. Here's the summary:

(i) Find the trade according to our preferred criteria (consolidations, preferably with a corroborating OVI). Neat patterns with clear areas of support and resistance are the best ones to focus on. You can see more about finding your trades using the tools and bonus materials on www.theinsideredge.com.

(ii) Check the news to ensure an earnings announcement isn't about to happen with the stock we're looking to trade. For more details how to quickly find when a stock is going to make an earnings announcement, go to www.theinsideredge.com.

(iii) Decide the strategy (are you trading stocks or options). Learn more about how to trade simple deep in-the-money option strategies at www.theinsideredge.com.

(iv) Place the trade.

(v) Manage the trade.

In terms of points (iv) and (v), placing and managing the trade consists of the following steps:

1. Enter just above resistance (when we're going long) or just below support (when we're shorting).

2. Set the initial stop loss at the same time.

3. Take half profits at first profit target (P1). This means you exit half your stake at the P1 level and leave the remaining half on.

4. Adjust the initial stop to near your initial entry point for the remaining half of the stake. This will now become a trailing stop if the stock continues to trend. For the trailing stop we use an adjustable diagonal trendline.

   (For uptrends our trendline rises diagonally just under the lows of the price bars. For downtrends our trendline falls diagonally just above the highs of the price bars. When the prices retrace sufficiently, our trendline is hit and our trailing stop is activated, meaning the second half of our trade is exited.)

5. Monitor and adjust the trailing stop as the price trends until you're stopped out for the second profit (P2).

As you've seen from this chapter, you can use some discretion with your trendline to manage your P2 profit. This includes adjusting the trendline angle and even pausing it horizontally where the stock is retracing or forming new flags and channels.

Also remember the following outcomes:

- No breakout means no losses because our trade isn't triggered in the first place.
- The price breaks out, triggering our entry, but then reverses before hitting our P1 target. In this case we're stopped out at our initial stop loss.
- The price breaks out, triggering our entry, reaches P1 for the first profit on half our stake, and then reverses. In this scenario we make the P1 for half our stake. Depending on how vicious the reversal is, our P2 could turn out to be the same amount as P1, less than P1, or even

just a breakeven if the reversal goes all the way back to our initial entry point.

- The price breaks out, triggering our entry, reaches P1 for the first profit on half our stake, and then keeps continues the direction of the dominant trend. In this scenario our P2 will be greater than our P1, potentially significantly so. There may even be the opportunity to pyramid into a new trade if the stock keeps making flags and channel breakouts as it trends. Where a price keeps trending, this is where we make our windfall profits seemingly effortlessly.

You've now learned how to take two well-established chart patterns (flags and channel breakouts) and use them with a robust trading plan, combining them with an innovative indicator, the OVI.

In Chapter 5, I'll summarize everything and suggest your next steps, including my favorite filters using the OVI.

What happens next is your choice, depending on how committed you are. But at least from the website, www.theinsideredge.com, you'll be able to make a start for free.

CHAPTER 5

Putting It All Together

In Chapter 4 we completed the trading plans for the four most important setups: bull flags, bear flags, and channels breaking up and down. Our edge comes where we find these patterns alongside corresponding OVI readings. Anticipated bullish breakouts go with positive OVIs, and bearish breakouts go with negative OVI readings.

We also covered the order types most relevant to this type of breakout trading: stop-limit orders and conditional orders.

In this chapter I'll summarize the method one more time, show you some more examples, and then outline what my best students and I do as routine.

As part of this book I'm giving away some great tools on the www .theinsideredge.com web site for free. These tools will put you on the path to consistent profitable gains in the market.

Part of what you'll receive when you register for free at www .theinsideredge.com is what I call the **OVI Express12**. This is a list of 12 big stocks that consistently display responsive OVI readings. Many of the stocks we've covered as examples in the book are members of the OVI Express12. On the web site you can view the OVI charts for these stocks every day.

This process will take you literally two or three minutes to determine if there's a tradeable setup among those dozen stocks, in accordance with what you've just learned. In addition to this, you'll receive tutorials and links to short videos in sequence to help consolidate the practical knowledge you've gained from this book.

There is of course a balancing act here. You do need tools, which is why I've delivered them on the www.theinsideredge.com web site completely free.

If you want to go a little deeper and have a greater choice of stocks, then you can also join my subscription services on www.ovitradersclub .com, which are very favorably priced indeed.

I wish I could provide everything for free, and there are of course some folks who expect everything in life to be that way. However, I hope you'll appreciate that running a software enterprise is rather expensive and must be run on commercial lines. Otherwise it dies, and everyone loses out.

Creativity can only blossom if the software business is run this way. Otherwise big talent would be lost to competitors, technology would stagnate, and students would become unhappy with lack of forward progress.

In fact, without the business there might not be an OVI in the first place, since it was thanks to a conversation with one of my students that the OVI was born.

The forerunner to the OVI was me making pictures in my mind of a line going up and down, and me making good judgment calls on the markets. This line was inspired from me looking at options chains every day, recalling the figures and mapping them mentally from day to day. Without having to consider my students, I may never have thought about making that task easier for myself and other people.

It was only when I articulated my mental processes to a student that the penny dropped and I wondered about making that line in my mind a physical reality. This would speed up the process give a wider choice of stocks to consider in this unique way, and, best of all, anyone could benefit from it immediately.

Books are sometimes accused of providing selective, limited information in order to facilitate a big back-end sale. I hope I've overcome that objection with the free tools available on www.theinsideredge.com.

As I mentioned, the web site contains OVI charts for 12 of the most responsive OVI stocks, plus a focused series of education via articles, blogs, and video content.

I'm giving away as much as I can along with this book, without committing economic suicide, and it's certainly enough to make this book tangibly repay you many times over.

For seriously committed folks, you may want to join my OVI Traders Club and possibly FlagTrader as well. Once you register on www .theinsideredge.com I'll provide details so you can choose how to proceed. (More about this later.)

SUMMARY OF THE OVI TRADING METHOD

At the very beginning of this book I mentioned that the stock market had produced more successful investors than any other financial instrument. I also mentioned that consolidation/breakout patterns were the most lucrative patterns, and that following the smart money was the smartest thing to do.

It's a question of stacking the odds in your favor by following a robust trading plan that enables you to take quick partial profits, while also allowing for a potential windfall profit if the stock goes on a roll.

I've also mentioned that with this method our profits manifest in bursts rather than plods. Some weeks will be busy and some will have very little to do. Don't expect any week to be the same.

As you're aware by now, our trading plan for flags and channel breakouts is very simple and worth repeating just one more time!

The outline of the process is as follows:

(i) Find the trade according to our preferred criteria (consolidations, preferably with a corroborating OVI). Tidy patterns with clear areas of support and resistance are the best ones to focus on.

Go through the dozen stocks in the OVI Express12 on the www .theinsideredge.com web site for free; if you want a greater selection of stocks, you can subscribe to the OVI Traders Club.

(ii) Check the news to ensure an earnings announcement isn't about to happen with the stock you're looking to trade.

You can do this by viewing and clicking on the earnings date itself or the earnings bell icon within the OVI Express results table.

(iii) Decide your strategy (are you trading stocks or options?).

You can learn more about how to trade simple deep in-the-money option strategies at www.theinsideredge.com.

(iv) Place the trade.

(v) Manage the trade.

Placing and Managing the Trade

1. Enter just above resistance (when you're going long) or just below support (when you're shorting). Use stop-limit or conditional orders to open your trades in order to avoid gapping.[1]

---

[1]Spreadbetting firms (mainly in the UK) still don't have stop-limit or conditional order capability at the time of writing. If you're using a spreadbetting account, you may have to place your stop or limit opening order during trading hours. Those with a traditional brokerage account can use stop-limit or conditional orders at any time.

2. Set the initial stop loss at the same time as your entry.

3. Take half profits at first profit target (P1). This means you exit half your stake at the P1 level, and leave the remaining half.

4. Adjust the initial stop to near your initial entry point for the remaining half of the stake. This will now become a trailing stop if the stock continues to trend. For the trailing stop we use an adjustable diagonal trendline. (For uptrends our trendline rises diagonally just under the lows of the price bars. For downtrends our trendline falls diagonally just above the highs of the price bars. When the prices retrace sufficiently, our trendline is hit and our trailing stop is activated, meaning the second half of our trade is exited.)

5. Monitor and adjust the trailing stop as the price trends until you're stopped out for the second profit (P2).

As you saw in Chapter 4, you can use some discretion with your trendline to manage your P2 profit. This includes adjusting the trendline angle, and even pausing it horizontally where the stock is retracing or forming new flags and channels.

Outcomes

- No breakout means no losses because our trade isn't triggered in the first place.
- The price does break out, triggering our entry, but then reverses before hitting our P1 target. In this case we're stopped out at our initial stop loss.
- The price breaks out, triggering our entry, reaches P1 for the first profit on half our stake, and then reverses. In this scenario we make the P1 for half our stake. Depending on how vicious the reversal is, our P2 could turn out to be the same amount as P1, less than P1, or even just a breakeven if the reversal retraces all the way back to our initial entry point.
- The price breaks out, triggering our entry, reaches P1 for the first profit on half our stake, and then continues in the direction of the dominant trend. In this scenario our P2 will be greater than our P1, potentially significantly so. There may even be the opportunity to pyramid into a new trade if the stock keeps making flag and channel breakouts as it trends. Where a price keeps trending, this is where we make our windfall profits seemingly effortlessly.

A FEW MORE EXAMPLES

Here are just a few more examples of high-profile stocks that have formed easily recognizable OVI trades.

Research in Motion (RIMM) was another stock that got badly beaten up in 2011, and the OVI made it clear from March onward (see Figure 5.1). It didn't take a genius to know that BlackBerry cell phones were light years behind the new generation of iPhones, Samsung, and HTC smartphone devices, so the portents were already bad for RIMM.

The only question was where and when to enter the short. The easiest opportunity came right at the beginning of June when the stock broke down around $42.61. By mid-August you could have exited with the stock around $25. This qualifies as a windfall profit for sure.

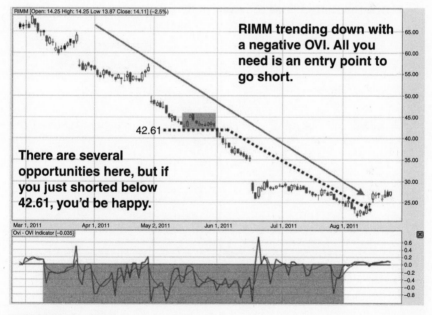

FIGURE 5.1 RIMM
Source: OVI Charts. Courtesy of FlagTrader.com. Go to www.theinsideredge.com for more information.

Here's Bank of America (BAC) again in Figure 5.2, this time at the beginning of 2012 where the OVI had flipped to positive.

Just look at the opportunities there are to enter long at the beginning of January above $6.00 and again a few days later—then at the beginning of February and again in early March.

Next up is Caterpillar (CAT), whose OVI turned nicely bullish well before it made a clean breakout past $100 in January 2012 (see Figure 5.3). Within days the stock had reached $110 and your profit was taken quickly before the stock drifted sideways.

Here's Goldman Sachs (GS) again in Figure 5.4. I highlighted this at the beginning of 2012 as a new bull flag type pattern formed when the OVI had decisively turned positive during the previous four days.

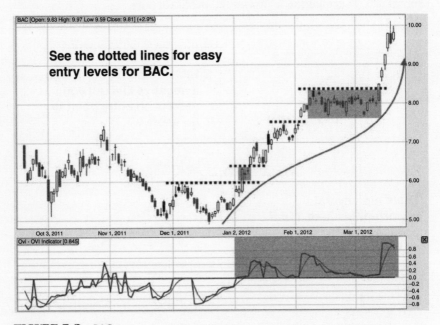

FIGURE 5.2 BAC

Source: OVI Charts. Courtesy of FlagTrader.com. Go to www.theinsideredge.com for more information.

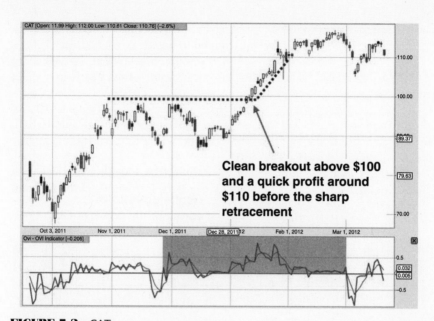

**Clean breakout above $100
and a quick profit around
$110 before the sharp
retracement**

FIGURE 5.3 CAT
Source: OVI Charts. Courtesy of FlagTrader.com. Go to www.theinsideredge.com for
more information.

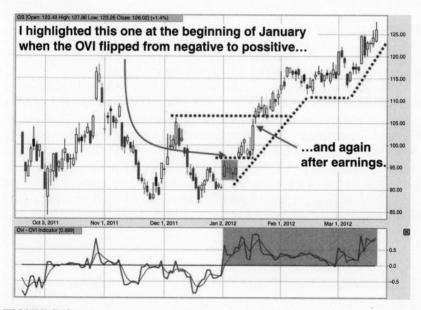

**I highlighted this one at the beginning of January
when the OVI flipped from negative to possitive...**

**...and again
after earnings.**

FIGURE 5.4 GS
Source: OVI Charts. Courtesy of FlagTrader.com. Go to www.theinsideredge.com for
more information.

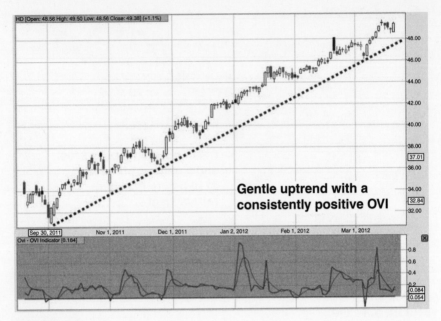

FIGURE 5.5 HD

Source: OVI Charts. Courtesy of FlagTrader.com. Go to www.theinsideredge.com for more information.

With Home Depot, Inc. (HD), see how we have a gentle uptrend accompanied by a consistently positive OVI (see Figure 5.5).

IBM's OVI turns positive in late November 2011 and pretty much stays there for several months (see Figure 5.6). During February the stock forms a cup and handle pattern, where the handle lasts for about a month before the stock breaks out from $195 for a decent, low-risk profit into mid-March.

I highlighted Netflix, Inc. (NFLX) in September 2011 and it broke down almost immediately (see Figure 5.7). On the first day it reached the P1 profit target and within two months the stock had halved in value. Although the OVI didn't produce the most beautiful signals, it was still negative nearly all the way and certainly wasn't suggesting anything bullish.

IBM breaks $195 and keeps going.

FIGURE 5.6 IBM

Source: OVI Charts. Courtesy of FlagTrader.com. Go to www.theinsideredge.com for more information.

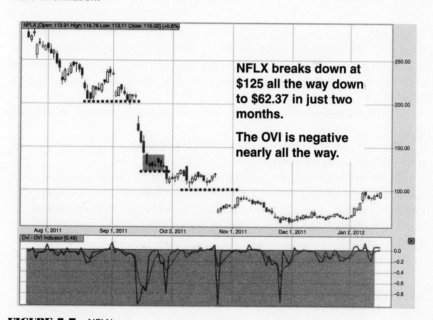

NFLX breaks down at $125 all the way down to $62.37 in just two months.

The OVI is negative nearly all the way.

FIGURE 5.7 NFLX

Source: OVI Charts. Courtesy of FlagTrader.com. Go to www.theinsideredge.com for more information.

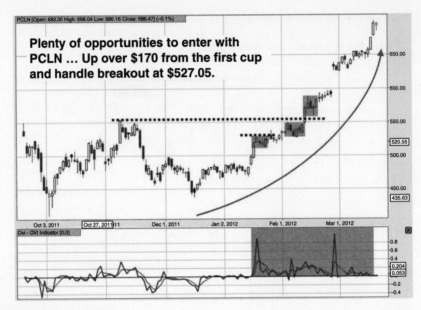

PCLN [Open: 693.30 High: 698.04 Low: 686.16 Close: 696.47] (–0.1%)

Plenty of opportunities to enter with PCLN ... Up over $170 from the first cup and handle breakout at $527.05.

FIGURE 5.8   PCLN
Source: OVI Charts. Courtesy of FlagTrader.com. Go to www.theinsideredge.com for more information.

Priceline.com Inc. (PCLN) gave so many opportunities to enter long from mid-January 2012 (see Figure 5.8). Three flags in a row with corroborating positive OVI signals. This stock gained over $170 in two months from the first bull flag at $527.25. This bull flag was also a cup and handle pattern.

I hope these examples give you a flavor for the opportunities that will present themselves.

Some trades will develop trends that run and run. These are the ones that will bring you windfall profits.

There are times where, having banked your P1 profit, you'll use your discretion and be very conservative with your initial P2 trailing stop. Provided you've banked and protected your P1, I'm happy with that. As you've seen, sometimes that can pay off big time; AAPL, NFLX, and PCLN are cases in point.

You're now ready to proceed to the next step—which is taking action!

ACTION STEPS

To start using this method immediately you need to register on this book's web site and start using the tools on it for free.

Action 1—Register for FREE on www.theinsideredge.com

When you register on the site, over the next few weeks, I'll e-mail you regularly to watch some video tutorials and review what you've just learned.

As part of your complimentary package you can review the OVI charts for the 12 stocks listed in the OVI Express12 every day.

Action 2—Get the OVI Dashboard App for FREE on your Desktop and on your Smartphone

When you register on this book's web site I'll also tell you about the OVI Dashboard app, which you can use on your desktop (no download required) and also on your smartphone for free.

The OVI Dashboard gives a market summary according to my way of looking at the market. It also provides more education in the form of articles and video content.

1. Specifically the OVI Dashboard summarizes the numbers of stocks that have shown up in six preset filters:
   - Standard bull flags
     vs.
     Standard bear flags.
   - Tight bull flags
     vs.
     Tight bear flags.
   - Standard bull flags with at least five consecutive days positive OVI
     vs.
     Standard bear flags with at least five consecutive days negative OVI.
   - Tight bull flags with at least five consecutive days positive OVI
     vs.
     Tight bear flags with at least five consecutive days negative OVI.
   - S&P 500 stocks that are forming bull flags, with at least five consecutive days positive OVI
     vs.
     S&P 500 stocks that are forming bear flags, with at least five consecutive days negative OVI.
   - S&P 500 stocks with five consecutive days positive OVI
     vs.
     S&P 500 stocks with five consecutive days negative OVI.

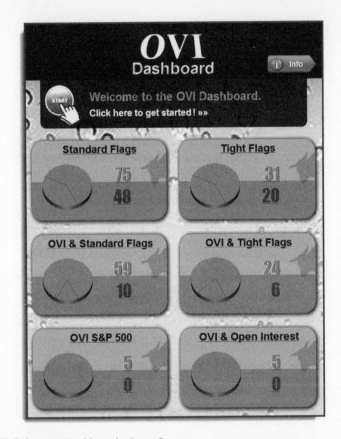

FIGURE 5.9   OVI Dashboard—Front Screen
Source: OVI Charts. Courtesy of FlagTrader.com. Go to www.theinsideredge.com for
more information.

I've summarized that into six pie charts that are all clickable for
further details. Figure 5.9 shows what it looks like.

This is the front screen of the Dashboard. Click on any of the
buttons (or pies) for more details of the count.

Alas, the black and white doesn't do the Dashboard justice, but
you can appreciate the market summaries according to our way of
doing things.

You'll find that the summaries are often very well correlated to
what's with the main indexes.

2. Once you click on a pie, it takes you to a more detailed view of that
   particular count of bulls versus bears, plus a list of five liquid bull and
   bear stocks that are part of the count (see Figure 5.10).

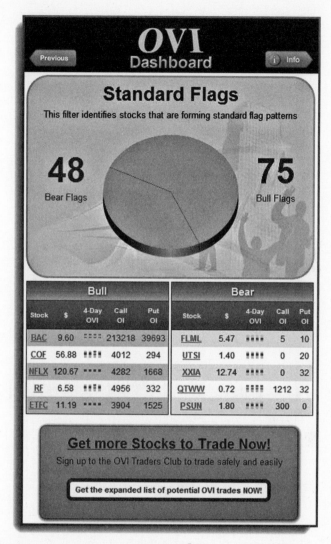

FIGURE 5.10 OVI Dashboard—Screen Count
Source: OVI Charts. Courtesy of FlagTrader.com. Go to www.theinsideredge.com for more information.

The second screen displays a larger pie chart, plus a list of five liquid bull and bear stocks that have been identified by the filter in question.

From here you can click on any of the stocks listed and see its OVI chart and further details for that stock.

FIGURE 5.11 OVI Dashboard—Stock Details
Source: OVI Charts. Courtesy of FlagTrader.com. Go to www.theinsideredge.com for more information.

3. Click on a stock for a more detailed view plus an OVI chart for it (see Figure 5.11).

The next screen displays the stock you've just selected from the previous screen, with various details, like its four-day OVI history, whether it's trending, and, of course, the OVI chart itself. You can pop the OVI chart out of this window on the desktop version.

FIGURE 5.12   OVI Dashboard—Education
Source: OVI Charts. Courtesy of FlagTrader.com. Go to www.theinsideredge.com for more information.

The OVI Dashboard also contains education in the form of articles and videos focused on this way of trading (see Figure 5.12).

From this screen you can link to articles about the Dashboard itself, the OVI, flags, and videos about our trading style.

Action Steps 1 and 2 are compulsory. After all, they're free, and they'll help you deepen the knowledge you've just accumulated.

Here are further Action Steps you can take to putting the principles of this book into practice.

Action Step 3 is also partly compulsory in terms of you using the OVI Express12 stocks.

Action 3—Review My Favorite OVI Charts

Review the 12 stocks listed in the OVI Express12 on the www
.theinsideredge.com web site. If you choose to upgrade to the OVI Traders
Club, then you'll be reviewing the OVI Express40 (see Action Step 4).

On any given day, I typically start by clicking through the OVI Express
stocks on my OVI Traders Club web site. This takes literally about 10 minutes. If you're using the www.theinsideredge.com web site, going through
the OVI Express12 stocks will take you just a couple of minutes.

All I'm looking for is a combination of a consolidation pattern and corroborating OVI reading. If I can't see something easily, then I move on.
If something does look interesting, then I see if there's any earnings announcement around the corner, and then, if all is clear, I'll consider a trade,
conditional on a breakout.

The www.theinsideredge.com web site contains the OVI Express12
stocks, which gives you fewer stocks but is still a very good start, and it's
completely free. It also contains focused education in the form of videos
and reports for you to develop your expertise in this method.

When you see the OVI chart, it'll be embedded within the window of
the web site page. Simply click on the icon at the very top left of the chart
to pop out the chart into its own window. (I like to see the chart in its own
window with dimensions of 1024 × 768. There's just something aesthet-
ically pleasing about this size. It may already be defaulted to this size by
the time you're reading this, but in any case you can do it by downloading
the free software application called "Sizer" from www.theinsideredge.com/
page/sizer.aspx.)

What you'll see is a chart like in Figure 5.13, where the OVI Express12
stocks will be preloaded on the left-hand side. Just click on a stock to see
its OVI chart. You can customize the chart settings, or scroll back and forth
using icons at the top.

Just to repeat for clarity, the www.theinsideredge.com web site contains the OVI Express12 stocks, and my OVI Traders Club web site contains the OVI Express40 stocks. I'd love to provide everything for free, but
as you may appreciate by now, the OVI is a very expensive piece of software to maintain, but justifiably so.

I click on a stock symbol to view its OVI chart. It takes me literally a
few seconds to see if there's an interesting setup for me. On the web page,
below the chart area, you can see a summary of the OVI Express stocks in
a table with clickable icons that you can mouse over for more information
(see Figure 5.14).

From left to right the columns display:

Stock symbol ‖ price ‖ volume ‖ next earnings date ‖ call open interest ‖ put open interest ‖ 4-day OVI summary ‖ Trend 1–2–6 months

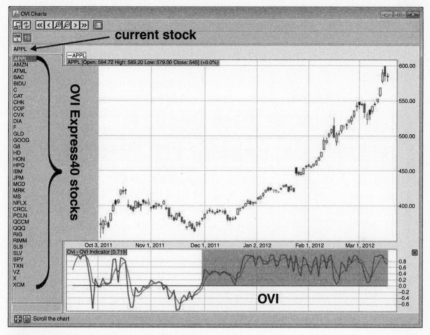

FIGURE 5.13 Pre-loaded OVI Express Stocks Chart[2]
Source: OVI Charts. Courtesy of FlagTrader.com. Go to www.theinsideredge.com for more information.

To the right of these columns is another column with various filter icons, which are all clickable.

It's important to note that sometimes you'll eyeball a flag pattern that somehow hasn't been picked up by my algorithms, and therefore the flag icon may not show up in the results table. The reason for this is typically when a flagpole hasn't thrusted sufficiently to be identified by the formula.

This actually happened in the case of our AAPL trade in this book. It was a bull flag, no question about that, but the thrust didn't quite reach the parameters I had set as a minimum for a flagpole. Fortunately AAPL is one of the OVI Express12 stocks, so it's a stock that you can watch every day.

Similarly, sometimes you'll see a stock is denoted as forming a flag, but on closer eyeballing you see it doesn't have the neat quality that we're looking for. That's fine, too. An algorithm can do so much, but we do need to quality-check with our eyes.

---

[2]Note: The www.theinsideredge.com web site contains 12 preloaded stocks, named the OVI Express12.

Neatness in a chart pattern suggests technical trading. Technical trading conditions are more predictable and easier to trade. So it pays to focus on neat patterns.

When you see the results table on the web site, it's in full color, which is easier on the eyes (Figure 5.14).

Stock Symbol	Stock Price	Volume	Earnings Date	Call OI	Put OI	4-day OVI	Trend Months 1 2 6	Filters
AAPL	544.47	21,523,112	-	0	0			
AIG	29.45	6,138,733	-	0	0			
AMZN	180.04	6,337,085	-	0	0			
BA	75.08	4,151,126	-	0	0			
BAC	8.12	287,036,704	-	0	0			
BIDU	138.87	6,622,488	-	0	0			
C	34.13	41,630,728	-	0	0			
CAT	113.39	5,913,621	-	0	0			
CVX	109.76	6,352,463	-	0	0			
DIA	129.57	6,418,168	-					
EQR	57.41	1,608,575	-	83	93			
F	12.66	44,101,452	-					
FCX	42.91	16,680,725	-	0	0			
FRT	96.08	447,780	-	75	356			
FXI	40.32	14,588,425	-	0	0			
GLD	166.61	13,492,457	-	0	0			
GOOG	622.40	2,326,114	-	0	0			
GS	121.13	5,535,215	-	0	0			
HD	47.46	9,235,665	-	0	0			
HIG	20.66	10,710,402	-	8,078	9,694			
HOV	2.80	3,457,766	7-Mar-2012	3,867	850			
HPO	25.25	21,206,286	-	0	0			
JLL	48.08	386,155	-	121	5			
MCD	99.25	4,262,820	-	0	0			
MET	38.97	7,508,237	-	3,470	1,430			
MMM	87.49	2,766,277	-	0	0			
MRK	37.79	11,742,603	-	7,903	5,972			
PRU	62.01	2,996,202	-	2,274	110			
PSA	134.15	771,875	-	423	342			
QQQ	64.92	49,093,936	-	0	0			
SLG	76.50	746,563	-	182	56			

FIGURE 5.14 OVI Express Results Table[3]
Source: OVI Charts. Courtesy of FlagTrader.com. Go to www.theinsideredge.com for more information.

---

[3]Note: The www.theinsideredge.com web site contains 12 preloaded stocks, named the OVI Express12.

TABLE 5.1 Ideal OVI and Chart Pattern Combinations for OVI Express Stocks

Chart Pattern	Corroborating OVI
Bull Flag	Positive OVI (preferably for the last 5 consecutive days)
Bullish Channel*	Positive OVI (preferably for the last 5 consecutive days)
Bear Flag	Negative OVI (preferably for the last 5 consecutive days)
Bearish Channel*	Negative OVI (preferably for the last 5 consecutive days)

*Note that you eyeball a channel rather than filter for them.

Ideally, we look for the OVI to have been positive for the last five-plus consecutive days in the case of bull flags and upward channel breakouts, and negative for the last five-plus consecutive days in the case of bear flags and downward channel breakouts (see Table 5.1).

If the OVI Express stocks show no tradeable patterns, you either wait for a new day, or, if you want more choice, you can subscribe to my OVI Traders Club web site, where you have more stocks to choose from. I would mention at this point that the OVI Express12 stocks contain the most consistent performers for this type of trading. These stocks include AAPL, GS, XOM, and others, including the SPY and QQQ, which are the ETFs for the S&P 500 and Nasdaq respectively.[4]

If you choose to join my OVI Traders Club, then you have more selection and can also enjoy other filters.

Action 4—For OVI Traders Club Members: Review the OVI Express40 Stocks

This is exactly the same process as Action Step 3 but will take around 10 minutes. That's still a very small amount of time.

---

[4]Note: I may from time to time replace stocks that are not displaying responsive OVI readings with stocks that are conforming.

Action 5—For OVI Traders Club Members: Review the CANSLIM Filtered Stocks

Within the OVI Traders Club I also include my own version of the William O'Neill CANSLIM filter. I provide this particular filter via the TeleChart charting program, which is only about $30 per month for the end-of-day version.

When you become a member of my OVI Traders Club, you'll be given the link to a free trial for TeleChart and my two versions of William O'Neill's famous formula for the highest-quality stocks. One version is a replica and the other is a "Lite" version, where I've relaxed some of his stringent criteria in order to get more choice.

The idea is to dovetail these high-quality stocks with our favored OVI and chart patterns combinations. In this way we're filtering for stocks with great fundamentals that are also forming our favored technical analysis parameters.

This is also part of my 10-minute routine. Being a bullish market technique, the CANSLIM method is a good bellwether for the market. Where the market is bullish, we find plenty of stocks fitting the criteria, and when the market is bearish, we find very few.

All the information for this is on the OVI Traders Club web site. I'll send you information about it over the next few weeks even if you're just a free member of the www.theinsideredge.com web site.

Action 6—For FlagTrader Members: Use the Filters on FlagTrader.com

For those who want to go all the way, you can filter without any limitations for stocks with my FlagTrader application, which you can get as an add-on within the OVI Traders Club.

FlagTrader gives you customizable filters as well as my own Quick Presets, which mirror those on the Dashboard but with no restrictions on how many stocks are listed in the results (see Figure 5.15). This is a premium application and a fantastic tool for finding flags with or without the OVI.

The filters I look for first are as follows:

If I'm looking for bullish setups:

- Tight bull flags
- OVI positive for five consecutive days
- Open interest greater than 500
- Open interest calls greater than puts by 50 percent or more

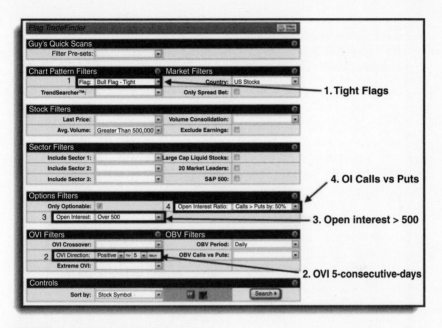

FIGURE 5.15 FlagTrader Filters
Source: OVI Charts. Courtesy of FlagTrader.com. Go to www.theinsideredge.com for more information.

If I'm looking for bearish setups:

- Tight bear flags
- OVI negative for five consecutive days
- Open interest greater than 500
- Open interest puts greater than calls by 50 percent or more

If there aren't enough tight flags, I discard the open interest put/call comparison filter or relax the flag setting to standard. If there are too many, I may restrict my selection to the S&P 500 stocks.

FlagTrader gives a lot of flexibility without being overwhelming to use.

Flag Results	10												?

Stock Symbol	Stock Price	Volume	Earnings Date	Call OI	Put OI	4-day OVI	Call OBV	Put OBV	Trend Months 1 2 6			Filters	
BPZ	4.17	2,390,929	-	2,898	63	▮▮▮▮	0	0		▶ ○ ⌐		♣ ⊘	
CBG	20.86	3,555,829	-	722	2	▮▮▮▮	0	0		▶ ○ ⌐ ⌐ ◈		♣ ⊘	
DHI	15.93	7,764,233	-	9,287	1,297	▮▮▮▮	96	203	◢	▶ ○ ⌐ ⌐ ◈		♣ ⊘	
JAH	39.57	1,381,736	-	1,417	86	▮▮▮▮	0	1	◢	▶ ○ ⌐ ⌐ ◈		♣ ⊘	
MCP	29.46	5,091,185	-	2,209	1,234	▮▮▮▮	1,595	62		▶ ○ ⌐ ⌐		♣ ⊘	
QSFT	24.07	1,385,197	-	1,789	32	▮▮▮▮	0	0		▶ ○ ⌐ ⌐ ◈		♣ ⊘	
SPF	4.70	3,270,306	-	530	0	▮▮▮▮	10	0		▶ ○ ⌐	◈	♣ ⊘	
SWHC	6.80	1,233,290	-	954	449	▮▮▮▮	0	17	◢ ◢	▶ ○ ⌐ ⌐ ◈		♣ ⊘	
THLD	7.08	5,801,338	-	2,266	1,173	▮▮▮▮	213	10	◢	▶ ○	⌐	♣ ⊘	
TSO	29.91	3,347,889	-	3,130	60	▮▮▮▮	0	135		▶ ○ ⌐ ⌐ ◈		♣ ⊘	

Flag TradeFinder Key			
SYMB	Bull flag stock symbol. Click this to view the headlines for the stock.	SYMB	Bear flag stock symbol. Click this to view the headlines for the stock.
▶	Bull Flag.	▶	Bear Flag.
▶	Bull Flag Tight.	▶	Bear Flag Tight.
◢	Stock which is trending up. Hover your mouse over to see the trend period.	◣	Stock which is trending down. Hover your mouse over to see the trend period.
◣	Volume falling in the last 3 days.	⌐	Volume rising prior to the last 3 days.
⊡	US stock.	▦	UK stock.
♣	Earnings announcement coming soon.	◈	Spread-bet stock.
⊘	Open Interest Link where calls are greater than puts. Click this to view the option chains for the stock.	⊘	Open Interest Link where puts are greater than calls. Click this to view the option chains for the stock.
○	Optionable stock.	✦	Signifies a Market Leader Stock.
◢	Signifies a Large Cap Liquid Stock.		

FIGURE 5.16 FlagTrader Results Table

Source: OVI Charts. Courtesy of FlagTrader.com. Go to www.theinsideredge.com for more information.

The results are presented in a user-friendly format with all icons being clickable for more information (see Figure 5.16). (Again, black and white doesn't do the image justice but it gives you an idea.)

Finally, here's an extra Action Step relating to another method not contained here. Obviously this book is all about trading with the trend, using breakouts from flags and rangebound channels.

However, when the markets aren't trending, we may wish to consider trading reversal patterns, which can also be lucrative if it's done correctly. Some of my students swear by this method, so if you're going to join my OVI Traders Club you might want to learn this method.

Action 7—For OVI Traders Club Members: Use the Reversal TradeFinder

Trading reversals is obviously a different technique from what we've been discussing in this book.

However, I've had some astonishing testimonials from students using this technique and software application I created for them, so I've made it part of the OVI Traders Club membership.

I won't elaborate on it here, but if you choose to become a member of the OVI Traders Club you can find it by clicking on the "OTC TradeFinders" tab, where you can use the filters and watch the videos that detail the reversal trading technique.

SUMMARY OF TOOLS FOR YOU TO USE

As you can appreciate by now, I have created a number of tools to make our lives easier especially for finding flags and OVI stocks. You can get started immediately by registering for free on www.theinsideredge.com and using the OVI charts there.

Table 5.2 is a summary of the tools that I've mentioned in the Action Steps above.

TABLE 5.2 Tools Summary

Tools	Insider Edge Web Site	OVI Traders Club Web Site
OVI Charts	✓ FREE • OVI Express12 charts and filter summary of the 12 most responsive OVI stocks. • www.theinsideredge.com	✓ Subscription only • OVI Express40 charts and filter summary of the 40 most responsive OVI stocks. • Unlimited chart lookups.
CANSLIM Filters	✗	✓
FlagTrader Filters	✗ • Tutorial videos available, but not the TradeFinder itself.	✓ Add-on subscription only • The FlagTrader TradeFinder is available as an add-on for OVI Traders Club members, or separately via www.flagtrader.com.
Reversal TradeFinder	✗	✓
OVI Alert E-mails and Blogs	✓	✓
OVI Dashboard	Available for free when you register on any of my web sites.	

The OVI Traders Club has many more features, but the main thing to remember is that this book's web site will get you started with the method we've focused on.

TAKE THE NEXT STEP NOW!

Register for free at www.theinsideredge.com and you'll soon be looking at the OVI Express12 stocks every day for possible breakouts and OVI combinations. I'll also send you a link for the OVI Dashboard App for your desktop and your smartphone device.

That's it! If you want to do more, you'll be most welcome. As a member of my OVI Traders Club, you can attend regular webinars with me, so I may see you there, too, or even at one of my live workshops perhaps.

You now have a phenomenal method with which to trade and not be stuck to your screens. If you're fussy with your trade selections you'll be right a lot more than you're wrong. And the amount by which you're right will be more than the amount by which you're wrong. Therefore, the odds are already drifting in your favor.

All the best, good luck, and thank you for reading!

About the Author

An innovator in financial trading, Guy Cohen is the creator and originator of the unique OVI Indicator, FlagTrader, and OptionEasy platforms, among others. Guy is also an established best-selling author, commentator, and entertaining speaker on trading and the financial markets.

His published work is complemented by pioneering breakthroughs in the areas of trading and technical indicators, especially the OVI.

Guy specializes in trading stock and options, with his hallmark being his user-friendly approach and liberal use of illustrations. With Guy, you will find proven techniques to succeed, complemented by industry-leading customer service.

An entertaining speaker, Guy has an MBA in finance from City University (Cass) Business School, London.

Index

AAPL. *See* Apple, Inc.

Action steps:
  get OVI Dashboard app, 227–231
  register on book website, 227
  review CANSLIM filtered stocks, 236
  review OVI charts, 232–235
  review OVI Express40 stocks, 235
  use filters on FlagTrader, 236–238
  use reversal TradeFinder, 238–239

Amazon.com, Inc. (AMZN), 10

Apple, Inc. (AAPL):
  breakout, xii
  bull flag, 112
  bull flag breakout, 113
  bull flag trading plan example,
      161–172
  downtrend, 32
  Hammer bar, 22
  Hammer reversal, 23
  post earnings bull flag, 149
  post earnings bull flag setup, 148
  resistance and support, 21
  rounded bottom, 125, 126
  sideways trend, 31
  uptrend, 31
  volatility in nine-month chart, 33

April 2010, OVI for, 7

BAC:
  breakouts to downside, xii–xiii
  channel breakout trading plan
      (down) example, 202–214
  overview of, 202–204
  OVI chart, 222

Baidu (BIDU), 89–92

Bear flags:
  applying first profit target with,
      140–143
  avoiding descending wedges with,
      123–124
  avoiding market manipulation with,
      121–122
  ideal, 118–121
  overview of, 37–38, 126–127
  rounded bottoms, 124–126
  SFLY, 120, 121
  SFLY P1, 142
  SFLY P1 setup, 141
  volume with, 122–123

Bear flag trading plan:
  adjusting initial stop, 176, 183–184
  entry, 172, 178, 180
  first profit target, 173–175, 181–183
  initial stop loss, 172–173, 178–181
  managing trade for P2 profit,
      184–186
  SFLY example, 178–186
  trailing stop, 177–178

Bear Stearns (BSC):
  indicator and share price, ix–x
  in March 2008, 5, 84–86

Book, web site for, 11, 69, 216,
      217–218, 227

Break of resistance, 95, 96

Break of support, 93, 94

Breakout trading. *See also* Channel
      breakout patterns
  overview of, 13–14
  SLB, 100

BSC. *See* Bear Stearns

Buffett, Warren, 210–211
Bull flags. *See also* Bull flag trading
plan
AAPL, 112, 113
AAPL P1, 140
AAPL P1 setup, 139
AAPL post earnings, 149
AAPL post earnings setup, 148
applying first profit target with,
138–140
avoiding market manipulation with,
112–113
avoiding rising wedges with, 115
BIDU, 89, 90, 91, 92
GLD, 74, 75
ideal, 110–112
IRM, 87
overview of, 34–36, 116, 118
rounded tops, 116
SLV, 76, 77
volume with, 114–115
Bull flag trading plan:
AAPL example, 161–172
adjusting initial stop, 159–160,
164–165
entry, 156, 161–163
first profit target, 157–159, 163–164
initial stop loss, 156–157, 161–163
managing trade for P2 profit,
165–170
overview of, 155–156
trailing stop, 160–161
Buying:
options, 59–60
stop-limit order, 154

Calls, 60, 63, 64
Candlestick charts, price bars in, 16–20
CANSLIM filtered stocks, reviewing,
236
Caterpillar (CAT):
breakout, 222, 223
cup and handle, 96–98, 99
Channel breakout patterns. *See also*
Channel breakout trading plan
(down); Channel breakout
trading plan (up)

applying first profit target with,
143–146
avoiding market manipulation with,
133
as favorite, 109–110
GS, 132–133
ideal, 128–133
overview of, 133–134
XOM, 131
Channel breakout trading plan (down):
adjusting initial stop, 200–201, 208
BAC example, 202–214
entry, 198–199, 204–205
first profit target, 199–200, 205–208
initial stop loss, 199, 204–205
managing trade for P2 profit,
208–213
overview of, 198
trailing stop, 201–202, 209
Channel breakout trading plan (up):
adjusting initial stop, 189–190, 195
entry, 187, 192–193
first profit target, 188–189, 193–194
initial stop loss, 187–188, 192–193
managing trade for P2 profit,
194–197
overview of, 186
trailing stop, 190–191
XOM example, 191–197
Chart patterns, tradeable. *See also*
specific patterns
flag patterns and consolidations,
33–43
focus on, 2
forms of, 20
head and shoulders, 43–48
ideal OVI combinations for, 235
importance of, 15–16
individual price bars in, 16–20
overview of, 51–52
OVI and, xii
support and resistance, 20–30
trends, 30–33
Chevron (CVX), 95–96
Chipotle Mexican Group, Inc. (CMG),
116, 117
Closing price on price bars, 17, 18

CNBC, 5
Comparative Relative Strength tool, 51
Consolidations:
    bear flags and, 38, 118
    bull flags and, 35
    ideal bull flags and, 110–111
    overview of, 34
Continuation patterns, 20
Cup and handle patterns:
    reverse cup and handle, 38–39
        CAT, 97, 98
        CMG, 117
        overview of, 36
        PEIX, 150
        PEIX setup, 149
CVX (Chevron), 95–96

Dark pools of volume, 13
Descending wedges, avoiding with
        bear flags, 123–124
Divergence and OVI, 72–74
Doji bars, 19, 203
Double bottoms, 37
Downtrend. *See also* Channel breakout
        trading plan (down)
    bear flags, 37–38
    definition of, 30
    example of, 32

Earnings, as sensitive area, 48
Elliott Wave technique, 24, 27–28
Entry:
    bear flag trading plan, 172, 178, 180
    bull flag trading plan, 156, 161–163
    channel breakout trading plan
        (down), 198–199, 204–205
    channel breakout trading plan (up),
        187, 192–193
Equal drive pattern, 134–135
ETFs (exchange-traded funds) and
        OVI. *See also* SPY
    divergence and, 72–74
    overview of, 68–71
Events and OVI:
    Bear Stearns, 84–86
    Iron Mountain Inc., 86–88
    overview of, 83–84

Expiration dates of options, 60–61
Extreme candlesticks, 19–20
Exxon Mobil (XOM):
    channel breakout, 131
    channel breakout trading plan (up)
        example, 191–197
    channel P1, 145
    channel P1 setup, 144
    obvious trades, 102–105
    OVI and, 65–66
    sideways channel, 130

Fibonacci technique:
    Elliott Wave and, 27
    expansion example, 26–27
    overview of, 24–25
    retracement example, 26
Filters on FlagTrader.com, 236–238
First profit target (P1):
    applying with bear flags, 140–143
    applying with bull flags, 138–140
    applying with channels, 143–146
    bear flag trading plan, 173–175,
        181–183
    bull flag trading plan, 157–159,
        163–164
    calculating, 137–138
    channel breakout trading plan
        (down), 199–200, 205–208
    channel breakout trading plan (up),
        188–189, 193–194
    head and shoulders pattern and,
        93
    modifying one to one theory,
        136–137
    need for target, 135–136
    one to one theory, 134–135
Flag patterns. *See also* Bear flags; Bull
        flags
    bear flag overview, 37–38, 118–127
    bull flag overview, 34–36, 110–118
    channel breakouts compared to,
        188
    cup and handle, 36
    as favorite, 109–110
    megaphone, 42–43
    overview of, 33–34

Flag patterns (*Continued*)
  rounded tops, rounded bottoms, and
    flag failures, 39–41
  with strong OVI signal, 127–128
FlagTrader.com, 218, 236–238
Flash crash, 42, 43, 73, 74
Flat OVI, 66–67
Forecasting markets, 21, 49
Forex and OVI, 76–78
Fortunes created from stock market,
  1–2
FXE and OVI, 77–78

Gann, W. D., 28
Gann technique, 24, 28–29
Gapping stocks, 22–23
GLD and OVI, 74–75
Golden Ratio, 25
Goldman Sachs (GS):
  Buffett preference share deal, 211
  bull flag, 222, 223
  channel breakdown, 132–133
  channel P1, 146
  channel P1 setup, 145
  head and shoulders, 44
  head and shoulders breakout, 45, 80
  head and shoulders setup, 79
  sideways channel, 131–132
Google (GOOG):
  reverse head and shoulders, 46, 47
  reverse head and shoulders
    breakout, 47, 82–83
  reverse head and shoulders setup,
    80–82
GS. *See* Goldman Sachs

Hammer bars, 19–20, 22
Head and shoulders patterns. *See also*
    Reverse head and shoulders
    patterns
  GOOG, 79, 80
  reverse, 44–48
  standard, 43–44
Hidden trading activities, 13
High price on price bars, 17
Historical volatility, 64

Home Depot, Inc. (HD), 224
Honeywell (HON), 92–95
Horizontal OVI, 67

IBM, 224, 225
Implied volatility in OVI, 63–64
Indicators:
  MACD, 50
  moving averages, 49–50
  overview of, 48–49
  relative strength index, 51
  stochastics, 50
Indices and OVI. *See also* SPY
  Forex, 76–78
  GLD and SLV, 74–76, 77
  overview of, 68–71
Individual price bars, 16–20
Informed trading:
  definition of, 1
  options market and, 61
  OVI and, 11–12
Initial stop, adjusting:
  bear flag trading plan, 176, 183–184
  bull flag trading plan, 159–160,
    164–165
  channel breakout trading plan
    (down), 200–201, 208
  channel breakout trading plan (up),
    189–190, 195
Insider's rationale, 12–13, 61
In-the-money for puts and calls, 64
Intrinsic value of puts and calls, 60, 63
Iron Mountain Inc. (IRM):
  events and, 86–88
  flat OVI, 66

Japanese candlesticks, reading, 18

Kramer, Jim, 5

Lagging indicators, 48, 109
Large cap stocks, focus on, 88
Leading indicators, 48–49. *See also* OVI
Less-is-more approach, 2
Limit order, 154
Low price on price bars, 17

MACD (moving average
    convergence-divergence), 50
Madoff, Bernie, 147
Managing trades, 152
March 2008, OVI in, 3–5
March 2009, OVI in, 6
March 2011, OVI in, 8
Market. *See also* Psychology of market
  forecasting, 21, 49
  fortunes created from, 1–2
Market manipulation, avoiding:
  with bear flags, 121–122
  with bull flags, 112–113
  with channels, 133
Megaphone pattern, 42–43
Moving average
    convergence-divergence
    (MACD), 50
Moving averages, 49–50

Netflix, Inc. (NFLX), 224, 225
Noise and moving averages, 49
Non-qualifying OVI, 66

Obvious charts, trading:
  Baidu, 89–92
  Caterpillar, 96–98, 99
  Chevron, 95–96
  Exxon Mobil, 102–105
  Honeywell, 92–95
  overview of, 89
  Schlumberger Ltd., 98, 100–102
O'Neill, William, 13, 236
One to one (1:1) theory, 134–135
Opening price on price bars, 17, 18
Open interest in OVI, 62–63
Option chain for stocks, 54, 55
Options:
  basics of, 59–61
  definition of, 59
  factors affecting premium, 63–64
  smart money and, xii
  symbols, 54–55
Order types, 153–155
Out-of-the-money for puts and calls, 64
Overbought/oversold analysis, 50–51

OVI (Options Volatility Indicator):
  April 2010, 7
  Bear Stearns and, 5
  components of, 61
  divergence and, 72–74
  ease of use of, 56–58
  effectiveness of, 61
  events and, 83–88
  implied volatility, 63–64
  with indices and ETFs, 68–78
  March 2008, 4
  March 2009, 6
  March 2011, 8
  open interest, 62–63
  options relevant for, 64
  option volume, 61–62
  origins of, 54–55, 218
  overview of, xi–xii, 53, 59, 106–107
  predictive ability of, xii–xiii
  price charts and, xii, 58–59
  qualifying stocks, 65–66
  reversals and, 105
  September 2011, 10
  as simple line, 56
  simplicity of, xiii
  stocks and, 78–83
  Summer 2011, 9, 11–12
  unreadable, 66–67
  uses of, 64–65
OVI Dashboard:
  education, 231
  front screen, 228
  overview of, 227–228
  screen count, 229
  stock details, 230
OVI Express12, 217, 232
OVI Express40:
  overview of, 232
  results table, 234
  reviewing, 235
  stocks chart, 233
OVI Traders Club:
  Express40 stocks, 232
  reversal TradeFinder, 238–239
  reviewing CANSLIM filtered stocks,
    236

OVI Traders Club (*Continued*)
  as subscription service, 218
  webinars, 240

Pacific Ethanol, Inc. (PEIX):
  cup and handle, 148, 150
  cup and handle setup, 149
Parabolic, stocks going, 89
Placing trades, 152
P1. *See* Profit target, first
Preference shares, 210
Price bars, 16–20
Price charts and OVI, xii, 58–59
Priceline.com Inc. (PCLN), 226
Privileged information, use of,
  1–2
Profit-taking strategies, 89
Profit target, first (P1):
  applying with bear flags, 140–143
  applying with bull flags, 138–140
  applying with channels, 143–146
  bear flag trading plan, 173–175,
    181–183
  bull flag trading plan, 157–159,
    163–164
  calculating, 137–138
  channel breakout trading plan
    (down), 199–200, 205–208
  channel breakout trading plan (up),
    188–189, 193–194
  head and shoulders, 93
  modifying one to one theory,
    136–137
  need for target, 135–136
  one to one theory, 134–135
Profit target, second (P2):
  bear flag trading plan, 184–186
  bull flag trading plan, 160–161,
    165–170
  channel breakout trading plan
    (down), 208–213
  channel breakout trading plan (up),
    190–191, 194–197
  discretion managing, 152–153
Psychology of market:
  being right and, 25
  leading indicators, 48–49

need for first profit target, 135–136
  support and resistance, 20–21, 29
P2. *See* Profit target, second
Puts, 60, 63, 64

QQQ and divergence, 72–74
Qualifying OVI, 65
Qualifying stocks, 65–66

Relative strength index (RSI), 51
Research in Motion (RIMM), OVI chart
    for, 8, 221
Resistance:
  mathematically derived levels of,
    24–29
  overview of, 20–23, 29–30
Reversal patterns:
  Hammer bar and, 20
  OVI and, 105
  trading, 238–239
Reverse cup and handle, 38–39
Reverse head and shoulders patterns.
    See also Head and shoulders
    patterns
  GOOG, 81, 82, 83
  overview of, 44–48
Reviewing:
  CANSLIM filtered stocks, 236
  OVI charts, 232–235
  OVI Express40 stocks, 235
RIMM (Research in Motion), OVI chart
    for, 8, 221
Rising wedges, avoiding with bull
    flags, 115
Rounded bottoms:
  AAPL, 125, 126
  bear flags, 124–126
  with flag patterns, 41
Rounded tops:
  with bull flags, 116
  CMG, 117
  with flag patterns, 40
RSI (relative strength index), 51

Schlumberger Ltd. (SLB), 98, 100–102
Second profit target (P2):
  bear flag trading plan, 184–186

bull flag trading plan, 160–161, 165–170

channel breakout trading plan (down), 208–213

channel breakout trading plan (up), 190–191, 194–197

discretion in management of, 152–153

Selling:

naked, 59–60

stop-limit order, 155

September 2011, OVI in, 10

Shutterfly, Inc. (SFLY):

bear flag, 120, 121

bear flag P1, 142

bear flag P1 setup, 141

bear flag trading plan example, 178–186

Sideways channel breakouts. *See also* Channel breakout trading plan (up)

GS, 131–132

ideal, 198

overview of, 128–133

XOM, 130, 192

Sideways trend, 30, 31

SLB (Schlumberger Ltd.), 98, 100–102

SLV and OVI, 74, 76, 77

S&P chart:

in April 2010, 7

in March 2009, 6

in 2008, 4

SPY (S&P 500 Exchange Traded Fund):

blank chart with OVI, 57

chart with OVI, 58

July 2011, 70–71

July 2011 breakout, 70, 71

June 2011, 69

June 2011 breakout, 70

Summer 2011, 9, 11–12

Stochastics, 50

Stock market. *See also* Psychology of market

forecasting, 21, 49

fortunes created from, 1–2

Stocks:

gapping, 22–23

large cap, focus on, 88

option chain for, 54, 55

OVI with, 78–83

parabolic, 89

qualifying, 65–66

Stop-limit orders in trading plans, 22–23

Stop loss, initial:

bear flag trading plan, 172–173, 178–181

bull flag trading plan, 156–157, 161–163

channel breakout trading plan (down), 199, 204–205

channel breakout trading plan (up), 187–188, 192–193

Stop orders, 153–154

Strike price, 60

Strong OVI signal, flags with, 127–128

Success, equation for, xi

Summer 2011, OVI in, 9, 11–12

Support:

mathematically derived levels of, 24–29

overview of, 20–23, 29–30

QQQ, 73

Technical analysis. *See also* Chart patterns, tradeable

forms of, 15–16

indicators, 48–51

Time frames for trading trends, 32

Time value of puts and calls, 63

Tools summary, 239

Trading. *See also* Informed trading; Obvious charts, trading; Options; Trading plan

breakout, 13–14

overview of, 24–25

Trading plan. *See also* Bear flag trading plan; Bull flag trading plan; Channel breakout trading plan (down)

chart patterns and, 16, 21, 127

creating and sticking to, 2

Trading plan (*Continued*)
  entry point and, 115
  examples, 221–226
  outcomes, 220
  overview of, 13–14, 151–153, 155, 219
  placing and managing trades,
        219–220
  stop-limit orders and, 22–23
Trailing stops:
  bear flag trading plan, 177–178
  bull flag trading plan, 160–161
  channel breakout trading plan
        (down), 201–202, 209
  channel breakout trading plan (up),
        190–191
  trend lines and, 152
Trend lines, 32–33, 152
Trends. *See also* Downtrend; Uptrend
  defining, 30–32
  moving averages and, 50
  opportunities and, 58
Tutorials, 69

Unreadable OVI, 66–67
Uptrend. *See also* Channel breakout
        trading plan (up)
  bull flags, 34–36
  CAT, 99

  definition of, 30
  example of, 31
  megaphone pattern, 42–43
  SLB, 101
  XOM, 102, 103, 104

Video tutorials, 69
Volatility:
  historical, 64
  implied, in OVI, 63–64
  megaphone pattern, 42–43
  observing, 32
Volume:
  with bear flags, 122–123
  with bull flags, 114–115
  dark pools of, 13
  option volume in OVI, 61–62
  overview of, 51

Web site for book, 11, 69, 216, 217–218,
        227
Windfall profits, 104. *See also* Second
        profit target

XOM. *See* Exxon Mobil

Zanger, Dan, 13